INTEGRATING TECHNOLOGY

A Practical Guide

JAMES G. LENGEL

Education and Technology Consultant

KATHLEEN M. LENGEL

Massachusetts Elementary School Principals' Association

PEARSON

Boston   New York   San Francisco

Mexico City   Montreal   Toronto   London   Madrid   Munich   Paris

Hong Kong   Singapore   Tokyo   Cape Town   Sydney

Senior Editor: *Arnis E. Burvikovs*
Editorial Assistant: *Kelly Hopkins*
Marketing Manager: *Tara Kelly*
Editorial Production Service: *Omegatype Typography, Inc.*
Composition and Manufacturing Buyer: *Andrew Turso*
Electronic Composition: *Omegatype Typography, Inc.*
Cover Administrator: *Joel Gendron*

For related titles and support materials, visit our online catalog at www.ablongman.com.

Between the time web site information is gathered and then published, it is not unusual for some sites to have closed. Also, the transcription of URLs can result in typographical errors. The publisher would appreciate notification where these errors occur so that they may be corrected in subsequent editions.

Many of the designations used by manufacturers and sellers to distinguish their products are claimed as trademarks. Where those designations appear in this book, and Allyn and Bacon was aware of a trademark claim, the designations have been printed in initial or all caps.

CIP data not available at the time of publication.
ISBN: 0-205-45939-0

Printed in the United States of America

10   9   8   7   6   5   4   3   2   1   10   09   08   07   06   05

Credits: Screen shots appearing on pp. 81, 111, 161, 169, 170, 171, 172, and 173 reprinted by permission from Microsoft Corporation. The Adobe product screen shot appearing on p. 185 reprinted with permission from Adobe Systems Incorporated. Screen shots appearing on pp. 81, 192, 193, 200, 201, 202, and 203 reprinted courtesy of Apple Computer, Inc.

CONTENTS

CHAPTER TWELVE
Video   196

CHAPTER THIRTEEN
Media in the Classroom   216

CHAPTER FOURTEEN
Presenting Ideas   227

CHAPTER FIFTEEN

Online Learning   239

PREFACE

This book grows out of our combined forty years of experience in helping teachers from kindergarten through college to integrate technology into their teaching. It is a practical, hands-on, how-to guide that places computer and internet technology into a context based on the nature of our students and the demands of the subjects we teach. It's designed for beginners who are just getting started and need ideas and support to move them along, as well as for experienced users who need a handbook of concrete strategies and instructions for taking the next step. We hope that it can serve as well as a resource for teachers-in-training.

This is not a book about computers, though you may learn a bit about how computers work as you read the chapters. Nor is it a guide to the best software in each subject area, though you will encounter many interesting application programs along the way. Instead, the book focuses on the craft of teaching and how technology can make it more effective and more fun.

We have assembled a book that shows teachers exactly how to do the things they want to do with computers and the Internet. While the first part of the book explains briefly *why* you might want to use technology, the bulk of the writing shows you *how*. The chapters are based on the materials we have used in our classes and workshops, and so have been tried and tested on thousands of teachers, from primary school through graduate school.

Part One of *Integrating Technology* looks at the nature of today's students and teachers and classrooms in an attempt to answer the question of *why* we should integrate technology into our work. It also considers the changes that have taken place in homes and workplaces, brought on by the new communication technologies, and with serious implications for the way we teach.

Part Two shows you how to get started setting up your technology, and how to begin rethinking the way you do things so as to take full advantage of the computers, the networks, and the communication skills of our students. It includes a detailed description of a new process for student research, thinking, and publishing called the *paperless paper.*

Part Three takes you for a ride on the information highway, starting with the basics of browsing and driving, then on to using the Internet in the curriculum and publishing on the Web. You'll find here much practical advice on how you and your students can become online authors, and how to use the Internet as an educational medium.

Part Four considers the basic media types we use for teaching—text, images, numbers, audio, and video—and how the new technologies enable us and our students to employ them in new and creative ways. Full chapters on presentation methods and on distance learning underscore the importance of these new possibilities.

Each chapter takes a particular topic, puts it into an educational context, and then provides step-by-step instructions for making it happen. Chapters begin with a familiar anecdote or example taken from school experience, and then go on to explain the technologies that are involved. Frequent *How to . . .* sections show you exactly how to apply this idea to your own work. And at the end of each chapter, we provide online references where you can further your knowledge of the topic we introduced.

Some technology books for teachers, designed for schools of education, provide the research and theory behind the use of technology in schools, but very little practical advice. Other specific how-to books on particular software programs contain many technical details but very little educational context. This book falls somewhere in between, a practical guide in a solid educational context designed for the active teacher.

The best way to use this book is to read the text, reflect on the ideas, and then carry out each of the practical *How to . . .* applications. No matter what subject you teach, or at what level, you will find something to make you think or to suggest a new approach to teaching. You may also use this as a reference book, looking up the topics and technologies you need as you confront them in your work, in a just-in-time fashion.

The book does not end with these pages. The Integrating Technology web site complements the printed work with online versions of most of the *How to . . .* sections and with a wide variety of references and extensions, as well as a discussion forum for readers. And we would enjoy continuing the conversation started with you in these pages—**you can find us online at www.ablongman.com/lengel1e.**

ACKNOWLEDGMENTS

We would like to thank the following reviewers for their helpful comments on this manuscript: John H. Curry, Brigham Young University–Idaho; Adam Friedman, University of North Carolina at Charlotte; Richard Hartshorne, University of North Carolina at Charlotte; Craid Kaml, Western Michigan University; Eugene Provenzo, University of Miami; Lynne Schrum, University of Utah; Barbara Stebbins, University of Southern Maine; and Sandra Sutherland, Carlsbad Unified School District. Lastly, we would like to thank our daughters, Annie and Molly, for supporting our work.

Kathleen M. Lengel is a seasoned elementary school principal now working as a technology educator at the Massachusetts Elementary School Principals' Association. She is called upon all over the world to help teachers and schools to make the best use of technology in the classroom. She is currently researching the use of wireless laptop computing in European elementary and secondary schools. She can be reached at kathi@lengel.net.

James G. Lengel is a former Dean of Faculty at the Benjamin Franklin Institute of Technology. He has written four recent books in Addison-Wesley's Web Wizard series, as well *Kids, Computers, and Homework* for Random House. An experienced college teacher and educational technology consultant, he is currently engaged in a number of national and international projects, including helping four French universities to develop their first online degree program. Contact him at jim@lengel.net.

PART I

WHY SHOULD WE INTEGRATE TECHNOLOGY?

This part looks at the nature of today's students and teachers and classrooms. It considers the changes that have taken place in homes and classrooms, brought about by new communication technologies.

CHAPTER ONE

KIDS

IN THIS CHAPTER

- **Why Can't They Be Like We Were?**
- **The Digital Divide**
- **Attendance**
- **Learn More . . .**

We begin this book not with technology or curriculum or teaching, but with students. Whether they are in kindergarten or college, artistic or athletic, musical or mathematical, they form the focus of our educational endeavor. By starting from the characteristics and capabilities of our students, we can better set the context for integrating technology into our work.

The first part of this chapter looks at how the current generation of students is growing up in a social and technological context that makes them very different from their predecessors. Then we look at two issues that affect our students' ability to integrate technology into their work: the digital divide and the problem of school attendance. This chapter sets a general human and social context for the practical suggestions that follow in the rest of the book.

WHY CAN'T THEY BE LIKE WE WERE?

. . . Perfect in Every Way?

Each generation contributes in its own way to making the world a better place. Tom Brokaw's book *The Greatest Generation* describes how the World War II generation paved the way for the prosperity enjoyed by the generations born in the forties, fifties, and sixties. And the upcoming generation, the future pillars of our communities, contributors to our Social Security, the first to come to maturity in the new millennium—what are they like?

Take, for example, the class of '06. They were born in 1984, six years after the first Apple computers appeared in classrooms, three years after the advent of the IBM PC, the year that the Macintosh computer was introduced. This cohort is not at all like those before them. They grew up in a very different world from most of their teachers, shaped by a very different series of events and by a very different set of technologies.

They grew up in a time that was, as no other, full and free. It was full of prosperity—the longest period of uninterrupted economic growth on record, of unprecedented abundance, and of consumer excess. Not all of the members of this generation enjoyed the fruits of this prosperity, but all of them watched it happen and saw the results flaunted around them. While full of prosperity, this time was relatively free of major war with large numbers of American casualties. No generation for more than a century had grown up without a major war. Our current young people have lived most or all of their lives after the fall of the Soviet Union, at a time when the United States was the unchallenged and only world superpower.

During the upbringing of the current school-aged generation, our culture has adopted more new personal technologies at a faster pace than ever before—the computer, the Internet, the cell phone, the PDA (personal digital assistant), the MP3, the CD, satellite TV, wireless. These are *their* technologies. Instead of demonstrating in the streets, they were watching television. And listening to music. And to the radio. And going to the movies. They grew up with hundreds of TV channels all their life. Radios appeared in every room, car, and pocket. They frequented huge cinema complexes with dozens of screens to choose from. Their choices of entertainment grew exponentially as they grew up. And it seems they chose them all.

A New Culture

Out of this unique upbringing, they have created for themselves a new culture, a culture that for the most part they alone understand.

Theirs is a connected culture. They seek out friends, correspondents, and ideas, and exchange thoughts with them. They use any and all means available to them to make and maintain these connections—telephone, email, instant messaging (IM), PalmPilot, web sites, discussion boards, chat rooms, street corners, sports events, the Internet, shouting down the corridor and watching web cams. Some of them maintain more regular correspondents than most of their parents and teachers. And they carry on the connection no matter where they are or what time it is. And they can keep several parallel connections open simultaneously.

Choices

In their culture they suffer a cacophony of choices. Hundreds of channels on the cable, scores of movies at the theater, hundreds of names on the buddy list, 50 stations on the radio, 500 MP3s on the iPod, dozens of numbers in the cell phone speed dial, scores of email addresses, racks full of DVDs and CDs and magazines, millions of web sites. They face more choices for information and ideas than any time in human history. How do they decide what to do at any given moment? Who's guiding those choices?

Multitasking

This younger generation can talk on the phone, sip a drink, drive the car, and carry on a face-to-face conversation, all at once. Perhaps they learn to multitask so as not to have to make a clear choice. In the classroom they can listen to my lecture, and still have enough brain power to watch the news on cnn.com, carry on three instant messenger conversations, and compose an email—all at the same time. And do just as well on the test. They have discovered that the human brain is fully capable, with a little practice, of conducting several mental activities in parallel, with little detriment to any one task. They do it all the time, and they are good at it.

Why do they do all this? Because they want to communicate ideas with other people. They want to listen, to talk, to watch, to create, to investigate, to discover, to initiate, to share. These are natural human tendencies. They do more of it because they have more channels for communication. Theirs is a culture of rampant communication.

HOW TO . . . GAUGE YOUR TECHNOLOGY QUOTIENT

You need: The following checklist; a person of a different generation to interview.

You get: A sense of the contrast between the technology use of your generation and that of the one you have chosen to compare.

Find yourself a person of a different generation to interview. If you were not born between 1980 and 1994, compare yourself with someone who was. Enter their responses into the third column. Enter your own responses into the second column. Approximations are OK.

	YOU	OTHER PERSON
Number of working computers in your home		
Number of names on your instant messenger buddy list		
Number of names in your email address book		
Number of appointments and names in your PDA (Palm)		
Number of MP3 songs you have downloaded this week		
Number of emails you sent this week		
Number of names in your cell phone directory		
Number of hours spent online this week		
Number of CDs or DVDs created this week		
Number of text messages sent this week		
Total		

Compute the total for each column. How does your total compare with that of the other generation?

■ ■ ■ ■ ■ ■ ■ ■ ■ ■

SCHOOLS AND SOCIETY

The Changing Workplace

Along with the communication capabilities of young people, the workplace has changed enormously over the past ten years. Business and industry have been quick to adopt those same millennium technologies that do things more efficiently or less expensively. The office doesn't consist of an individual at a desk with a telephone and a typewriter, working mostly alone from the seat of his pants with the information in his head. Today's office looks more like a small group of people, connected to information of all kinds and to other people through a computer, solving a problem by gathering facts and applying the intelligence of the group.

The laboratory does not consist of materials stored in jars on the shelf with sturdy work tables for carrying out experiments. It's more likely to look like a work room full of information and communication technologies, electronics, and devices that communicate to each other through wires and networks.

Nor does the doctor look like the *Father Knows Best* figure, consulting a book from his medical school days for information that will help his patient. Today's physician is more likely to view body scans over the network on her computer screen, and consult the latest research online. Even the family doctor (now called the PCP, or primary care physician) works this way.

Neither is the life of a news reporter like it used to be. Newsprint, shoe leather, and the reporter's notebook have less and less value to the journalism business these days. The workplace of the journalist—or the researcher or the novelist or the librarian—is with his computer, wherever it is.

Synchrony

School, students, and society, while never exactly in synch, have been over the years for the most part a tightly-knit threesome. It's easier to run a school, or be a student, or succeed in society when they are close.

But the distance between schools and society seems to be increasing. Some observers see today's students and workplaces moving rapidly down the road toward rampant information, continuous communication, and complex multitasking, while the school remains tied to pencil and paper and books and tests. This can be frustrating when you are trying to run a good school.

U.S. educators have been running pretty good schools. For most of the past 200 years, we have each year expanded the number of students who complete high school, from almost none 200 years ago to 80 percent in 1995. And the proportion who enter college has increased every year during that period. But in the past few years, this trend of steady progress has leveled off and, in many states, has begun to drop—a smaller proportion of their students complete high school today than five years ago. Why?

We face a tough job as we design and operate our schools, made tougher by the demands of the new technologies. But they're not the only things making demands on us. The parents of this millennium generation, like the parents before these, want the best for their kids. And parents aren't the only ones. The politicians want us to deliver as well. Higher scores, statewide tests, curriculum frameworks, clear standards, fewer dropouts, schools that promote economic growth and require fewer taxes. They demand schools that are responsive to parents, schools for everybody—where no child is left behind. (Except, of course, those who score below average on the graduation test.) And they want proof that all this is happening. Mission impossible.

What To Do?

So, in the face of all this, what can we do?

We need to look for actions that will keep students in school, that will reverse the direction of the school completion trend and establish a school that in students' minds is more relevant to the world of work and college study. At the same time, whatever we do must result in a better mastery of the basics—reading, writing, math, science, history, and the other subjects on the test. Whatever we do must prepare students for the workplace and college, not of today, but as those might be a decade from now.

To accomplish this successfully, we must somehow capitalize on this generation's competence with the new information technologies, their need to communicate with each other, and on their ability to do many things at once. Today's kids harbor mental powers and technologies that we are not taking advantage of in our schools. What can we do in our schools that accomplishes all of these goals? How do we integrate technology so that our schools can better serve the needs of today's students and tomorrow's society?

We should work on four As: Access, Assimilation, Accommodation, and Activity.

- We should expand students' and teachers' *access* to the new communication technologies and the information that's on the network, so that access in school is easy and natural, from all over the school. We know from careful study and common sense that students with more access learn more.
- We should look for ways to *assimilate* these new technologies and skills—the ones the students are already so familiar with—into the existing curriculum. We know that this is possible, even for teachers who grew up before the computer or the Internet existed.
- We must also move beyond assimilation, and look for ways that curriculum can change to *accommodate* itself to children's new competencies and to the realities of the workplace and higher education. Without accommodation there can be no progress.
- We should get the students *actively* working with the technology, with the subject at hand, with their teachers, and with each other. The more interactive the education, the better it works.

What Works?

We know better today what works when it comes to technology and teaching. The National Science Foundation (NSF) and other respectable organizations have funded considerable research on which approaches produce the desired results. The folks at Apple computer, who collaborated with the NSF on some of this research with its Apple Classrooms of Tomorrow project, have gathered much of the findings together for your perusal on their web site (www.apple.com/acot).

In summary, the research suggests that if you provide the four As, you can count on better attendance, better scores on the tests, more extensive and better writing, and a more positive attitude toward school. The chapters that follow provide practical examples of how to integrate the four As into your classroom and your school.

- Consider the one-to-one computing concept that educators are implementing in the state of Maine—that's a laptop for each student. But it's more than that—it's also teacher development, curriculum changes, alterations to the buildings, and a new way of think-ing about how students should work during the school day. You'll learn more about this in Chapter 3.

■ Consider the Internet. This grass-roots technology changed forever, in less than a generation, the possibilities and realities of how we store and communicate with information and ideas. Chapters 6 and 7 show you how to take advantage of this online phenomenon to improve your teaching.

■ Consider multimedia. It's been hyped for a decade as the next big thing by all the media conglomerates, but does it work in school? If so, how does it help students understand science or math or literature? The old wisdom says we remember 15% of what we read, 40% of what we hear and see, and 80% of what we hear, see, and do. For true understanding, students need not simply to watch, but to make their own multimedia. Chapters 9–14 look at how students are creating their own books, pre-sentations, movies, and simulations as part of their study of all these subjects.

How can all this technology be integrated into the school day, by the stable of experi-enced, tenured, and technology-fearing teachers and professors that staff our schools? Is it possible? When do we do it? Where? How do we learn it? These are the key questions that this book seeks to answer.

THE DIGITAL DIVIDE

In the old days, if you grew up in a home full of books and learned to love them at an early age, you did better in school than students with little exposure or access to printed infor-mation. In the current days, if you grow up with your own computer connected at high speed to the Internet, we might expect you to do better in school than students who are not as blessed with digital resources. Today about half the homes with school-aged children in the United States enjoy this access, while half do not. And the results of the "digital divide" are being felt in classrooms at all levels. In some places, such as the state of Maine, author-ities have passed legislation supplying computers and connections to all students in order to erase the advantage of the wealthier computer owners, in the same spirit as the builders of public libraries of a century ago. The basic tools of learning and information, they reason, should be available equally to all.

This section looks at the nature of the digital divide in a different way. Simply own-ing a computer and subscribing to the Internet does not bring you the advantage of con-nectedness. It's what you *do* with the computer that counts.

Most of the students at today's leading universities arrive at school equipped for com-puting. Ninety-eight percent of the freshmen at Boston University, for example, come to school with a computer in their hands, and most have been using it daily for a decade. But on the first day of class, when we query them closely on what they actually know how to do with a computer, their answers sound like this:

I do instant messenger with my friends, we email, and I surf the web. For what?
Oh, movies, news, sports, that kind of stuff.

> All my music is on the computer, I have over 2,000 MP3s that I have down-loaded, and I make my own CDs and give them to my friends. And I do the reg-ular stuff: email, IM, and I write my school papers on it.

> We keep up with the latest multi-player games, all the cool ones. Have you seen Raiders of the Lost Wooly Mammoth? The graphics will scare you senseless . . .

> My new laptop can play an entire DVD on a single battery. I can watch in my room, on the bus, even in class if I use headphones . . .

Will any of these students do better in school than their non computer-owning peers? Not if that's all they do with their digital resources. These kinds of activities will not make them better writers, historians, scientists, or mathematicians. Using email and instant messenger may make them faster at the keyboard, and the games may develop their mousing skills, but these do not translate to a big advantage in the curriculum.

And these students' experiences are not far from the mainstream. Broad surveys of high school and college students' use of computers find that their top activities are email and entertainment. Even if every student were issued a free computer upon entry into kindergarten, if they continued in this pattern of usage, the effects on their learning would be slim.

The digital divide we should fear most is the split between the educational and enter-tainment uses of the new technologies. If these new and powerful tools in the hands of our young people end up focused on trivial pursuits, if they become defined by the society as grown-up Gameboys, and if we find ourselves as educators on the wrong side of the divide, we will have lost a major battle with the forces of ignorance.

The folks in Maine who are implementing the computer-in-every-knapsack cam-paign are finding that, in order to take full advantage of the digital equity they have bestowed, the schools and teachers and parents must ensure that the computers and net-works are occupied by educational forces. Teachers are learning to give homework assign-ments that force students to use the technology for serious writing, deep historical research, sophisticated science, and new ways of looking at math. They are making sure that the students' time with the technology is taken up, for the most part, in worthwhile pursuits. Of course these students use instant messengers and listen to music on their com-puters, but that's not the chief usage. In fact, today in many poor Maine communities we can find more accomplished young masters of technology than in the wealthy computer-owning suburbs on the other side of the digital divide. What the Mainers do with their computers is far more valuable to them than the trivial usages of their wealthier peers. They will, as a result, know how to use a computer to find worthwhile facts and interest-ing opinions, to use a variety of digital tools for analysis and thinking, and be able to pre-sent their ideas in the most appropriate electronic form. This will make them better students, more competitive in college courses, and more fitted to the world of work than their well-to-do counterparts.

The digital divide is real, but it goes far deeper than who has a computer and who does not. It's a divide stretched by the forces of entertainment pulling in one direction, and of education in the other. As educators, we have a responsibility to do as much as we can to provide the assignments and expectations that attract the computers to our side of the moun-tain. The chapters that follow provide a practical guide to making this happen.

HOW TO . . . DETERMINE THE DIGITAL DIVIDE

You need: The following table; a group of young people.

You get: An analysis of the divide between the educational and entertainment uses of the new technologies.

Most of the new technologies can be used to entertain as well as to educate. Discuss how people used the following technologies over the past week. Into each column enter an example or two.

TECHNOLOGY	ENTERTAINMENT	EDUCATION
Web browser		
MP3 player		
DVD player		
PDA (e.g., Palm)		
Email		
Instant messenging		
Discussion board or chat room		
Digital video camera		

Which column was easier to find examples for? How many of these technologies did people use for educational purposes this week?

■ ■ ■ ■ ■ ■ ■ ■ ■ ■

ATTENDANCE

It's not often that schools, violence, and technology are mentioned in the same sentence in the *New York Times,* except perhaps when someone newsworthy complains about the effects of video games on the crime rate. In an op-ed piece entitled *The Blackboard Jungle: Tamer Than You Think,* by John M. Beam of Fordham University, published on January 20, 2004, and based on a recent study of rates of attendance and crime in New York City public schools, Beam concludes that:

> Schools with higher attendance rates tend to have lower rates of suspensions, major crimes and police incidents. Schools with fully functioning libraries and modern computers average better attendance.

School attendance rate is becoming more and more of a problem. Fewer students are completing high school these days, and more students are developing negative attitudes toward the value of school. (See "To Cut Failure Rate, Schools Shed Students" from the *New York Times* of July 31, 2003, and the National Center for Educational Statistics report on student attitude toward high school from 2002.) So when we see a correlation between computers and dropouts—especially a negative one—we read further.

The full report from Fordham University explains the finding in detail:

> At elementary and middle schools with computers equipped with CD-ROM drives or internet access, average daily attendance was 92.3 percent, compared to 89.9 percent at schools without such capacity. This difference translates roughly to an extra week of school per year.

School Reform

A key indicator of success in the school reform movement is an increase in attendance rates. Can technology actually have such an effect? In the case studies of education reform published on the web site of the U.S. Department of Education, we find Northbrook Middle School, where "65% receive free or reduced lunch; 25% are classified as LEP [limited English proficiency] or NEP [no English proficiency]; and 11% receive special education services. The majority of the student population is Hispanic (59%), followed by 29% Caucasian, Non-Hispanic; 6% African American; and 6% Asian/Pacific Islander. Only about 5% of the students have computers at home." (Northbrook's reform efforts focused on technology, including the provision of 400 computers for its 640 students, almost a 1-to-1 ratio. What do they do with all this technology? According to the USDE,

> Students' higher-level thinking is promoted by multifaceted activities that teachers plan using technology. For example, in a seventh-grade math project on the use of spreadsheets, students estimated and collected measurements of body dimensions, entered data on spreadsheets, explored ways of representing the data graphically, and wrote a brief narrative at the word processor describing their approach and results.
>
>   In industrial technology classes, students worked in collaborative groups to design and produce a variety of products. Projects as long as a semester are interdisciplinary, involving reading (e.g., reviewing manuals, conducting market research), writing (e.g., technical reports and project descriptions), math (e.g., drafting and scaling product designs, calculating costs of materials), science (e.g., studying physics as it relates to the performance of materials), and design (e.g., computer-assisted drafting and design). Students formed companies and produced products for sale. They are encouraged to access outside information via the state education network or from CD-ROM.

Clearly, this kind of activity grows from careful and creative teacher development and a strong support system for the computers. The results of this reform are clear.

- An attendance rate of 97%, high by local as well as national averages
- A second-place score in the district math test, despite the school's 6th (out of 7) ranking in socioeconomic status
- Above-average scores on the state assessment test

Technology Experiments

According to a report published by the Council of Great City Schools, a group looking to stem the dropout rate, technology has proven itself to be a positive force. At West High

School in Columbus, Ohio, 120 students and nine teachers were selected randomly to work in a set of classrooms designed to provide students and teachers access to technology tools that support group work, with a Macintosh computer on each student's desk for more individualized work. These four classrooms were also equipped with scanners, cartridge drives, MIDI equipment, laser printers, videotape players, modems, and selected software programs.

After several years of working in this technology-intensive environment, these experimental students were compared with their peers in normal classrooms. Significant differences emerged:

> Compared to the general student population at West High School, which has a 33% dropout rate, these students have a 0% dropout rate.

> While 15% of West High School students are college bound, 90% of the experimental students are college bound.

> Compared to non-technology students, these students not only wrote more, but they also wrote more effectively.

What's the Attraction?

The technology in these schools and cities seems somehow to have kept the students in school and increased their skills and attitudes. It could be because so few of them enjoyed the technology at home, and school was the only place it was available. It might stem from the creative and practical ways that the teachers and students used the computers, more like the ways they are used in business and industry. Or perhaps the technology provided a spark and a focus that lit up an otherwise dull academic environment.

Technology can be more than a tool to increase our productivity and make our research more efficient. It can also improve the overall learning environment of our schools and enhance the engagement of our students so that they feel more connected to the school and stay there longer. Used creatively, and fully integrated into the classroom and the curriculum, technology attracts.

LEARN MORE . . .

About Kids and Technology

www.pewinternet.org
> The Digital Disconnect: The Widening Gap between Internet-Savvy Students and Their Schools. Prepared by Douglas Levin and Sousan Arafeh, American Institutes for Research, for the Pew Internet & American Life Project, Washington, DC 20036.

www.nces.ed.gov
> National Center for Education Statistics. The Condition of Education 2002. U.S. Department of Education, Washington, DC, 2002.

www.apple.com/education/research/pdf/EduResearchFSv2.pdf
> The Impact of Technology on Student Achievement: A Summary of Research Findings on Technology's Impact in the Classroom. Apple Computer, Inc., 2003.

www.state.me.us/mlti
> Maine Learning Technology Initiative web site with information about the project, research results, and links to involved schools.

About School Attendance

www.nytimes.com/2004/01/20/opinion/20BEAM.html
> This link gets you to the article in the *New York Times* about increased attendance in schools equipt with adequate, well-used technology.

www.ncscatfordham.org
> The full Fordham University report on the impact of technology on school attendance.

■ ■ ■ ■ ■

CHAPTER TWO

TEACHERS

IN THIS CHAPTER

■ **Getting a Move On: Teachers As Learners**

■ **What Teachers Need: AEIOU**

■ **Designing Technology-Rich Lesson Plans**

■ **An Example: Notecards**

■ **Techy-Talk A to Z**

■ **Learn More . . .**

This chapter speaks to how teachers come to use technology as a tool in their classrooms, describes the stages they go through as they get started, and presents some tips for helping the teachers in your school get moving on technology integration. Then, you'll read an example of the "disconnect" students feel when a teacher has not yet proceeded through the stages to a point where he accepts student use of technology in day-to-day situations. An alphabet of technology terms will familiarize you with some of the acronyms you've heard floating around you. What do teachers need in order to take full advantage of technology for teaching? AEIOU—and, sometimes, Y! Lastly, you are introduced to two models for designing technology-rich lessons. This chapter is for you if you are a teacher or someone helping teachers get started in using technology in the classroom.

GETTING A MOVE ON: TEACHERS AS LEARNERS

Walk through the halls of your school after 4:00 any afternoon and look for evidence that technology is being used by teachers. What do you see?

A classroom with a bunch of computers, a scanner or two, a couple of digital cameras, bulletin boards covered with printed copies of digitally produced work, and the teacher still hard at work, eager to show you a student's latest

HyperStudio project: Jupiter is flying around the outside of the screen while a rock song plays in the background.

Next door, the lights are off and you have to look pretty hard to locate the classroom's one computer—there it is, over in the corner, with a dustcover on it, covered with . . . dust (or a stack of papers, a plant, or some books). It's not even plugged in.

Down the hall, there's a classroom with neatly printed poems—you know, the ones where the students take the letters of their names and write a word describing themselves: **J***oyful* **I***ntelligent* **M***ighty. You recall that this is an activity that this particular teacher always does in February for friendship month, but now it's March.*

On the second floor, you see a classroom festooned with computer-generated banners and student certificates. The one computer you see is on the teacher's desk, safe from the students.

Finally, you see a classroom that seems to have several computers and peripherals such as cameras and scanners, but the focus is clearly on the curriculum—maps, globes, books, essential questions posted on the bulletin board to inspire student investigations, and a timeline for an upcoming project listing milestones, are all in evidence.

If you are like most educators in the United States, you can identify several classrooms in your school that match each of these descriptions. Why aren't all classrooms like that last one? With the investment that school districts across the country have made on technology over the past several years, what is going on here? How is it that there are computers gathering dust? How is it that some teachers have so much, while others have so little? Didn't the school buy enough computers? Didn't they run enough professional development programs? Shouldn't the school leaders *do* something?

The Five Stages of Technology Adoption

Back in the 1980s, Apple Computer commissioned a study of classroom teachers to discover how they come to technology. The Apple Classrooms of Tomorrow (ACOT) study continues to serve as a source for educators wishing to integrate technology into their school curricula and striving to provide effective professional development for their teachers.

Briefly, the project involved putting computers into the hands of teachers and students, and then watching to see what changes occurred in classrooms as a result. Typically, participants volunteered to be an ACOT site, then were given state-of-the-art Apple computers. The teachers were given minimal training, and then asked to integrate the computers and reflect on their experience, using a journal. There were several variations to this model. The first involved each student and the teacher receiving a classroom computer; the second was more expansive and included additional computers for the home of each student and teacher; a third involved what was then a brand-new concept: a laptop computer for each student and one for the teacher.

ACOT projects were located all over the country, included large and small schools (Cabot, VT, participated in the laptop research—it had 250 students, K–12!), and were diverse in their populations as well. In some schools, a whole team joined the project. In others, a single teacher participated. So, the project represented a range of opportunities and challenges for integrating technology. You can see a more extensive description of ACOT by visiting the *Apple Classrooms of Tomorrow* site (www.apple.com/education/k12/leadership/acot).

Over time, the teachers submitted journals to Apple that were passed along to various universities for analysis. The study went on for about ten years and spawned many follow-up reports and reflections that may be of interest to you (www.apple.com/education/k12/leadership/acot/library.html). This chapter focuses on one narrow part of the findings: how teachers come to adopt technology tools that enhance instruction. In my role of technology integration specialist and professional development trainer in over twenty-seven states and six European countries since 1996, these stages have provided a framework that allows teachers to honor their own learning. And they have helped me understand better the challenges facing my teachers when I was an elementary school principal for eleven years prior to entering the field of technology integration training. The issues surrounding how to get teachers going with appropriate technologies are worldwide. So are the stages.

The ACOT research showed that teachers go through a sequence of five stages once technology arrives in their classrooms. As you read the following, think about what you know of Piagetian learning theory. Think about teachers you know who are at each stage. Think about your own evolution in the use of technology tools. Think about yourself as an adult learner.

■ **Entry.** The teacher is aware of the technology but chooses not to get involved in it. Teachers at Entry level may be fine teachers otherwise. They simply do not buy into a connection between technology and their core mission of teaching kids the curriculum. They would love to leave the technology to the technology teacher. Even if they have to go with their kids to the lab, they will not touch the mouse. Entry level teachers also distrust new technologies, imagining threats to curriculum, classroom management, and security. If they are assigned to attend a technology workshop, they will avoid it, if possible. If they are forced, they will attend, but will avoid having to actually use the tools.

■ **Adoption.** The teacher adopts one or two technology tools that make sense to her/him. These are usually personal productivity tools that make work easier for the teacher. The tools involved rarely have anything to do with teaching and learning. You might see a teacher very excited about Bannermania or email, word processing of class assignments, or PrintShop Deluxe. These are all tools that allow the teacher to accomplish a productivity task that is more difficult to accomplish without technology. Adoption level teachers still think of technology as something taught by someone else as a separate subject. They are reluctant to have students use the computer in their classroom, largely because they have difficulty troubleshooting themselves and worry that the students will run into a problem that the teacher can't solve. So, the computer sits safely on the teacher's desk.

■ **Adaptation.** This is where the rubber hits the road! The teacher finally begins to try to use some technology with the students. Often, the first attempts are using word processing and having every student in the class create the same kind of document. However, it's a huge challenge, largely because the teacher is still not really sure how to manage a whole-class project. Without changing anything else in the curriculum, the teacher puts the computer on as an additional layer to the lesson. Students write their assignment on paper, then bring the paper to the computer, then type onto the computer, then print on paper. There is no value added by using the technology. And, it's slow work. Often, in frustration, the teacher goes back to the Adoption stage where life was simpler. Adaptation is a tentative stage, one that teachers return to several times as their confidence builds.

■ **Appropriation.** This is a stage of excess, where the teacher, now filled with confidence and mission, embeds technology in every possible curriculum activity. This is the teacher who manages to appropriate all the technologies in the building, try them out, and make them central to his or her daily classroom life. This is the teacher who waltzes into the library, stakes out the new digital camera, waits a few days, then pounces. "I notice we have a new camera." "Yes," says the innocent library-media specialist, "It's for the whole school." "Of, course, I understand, but no one is using it. It's been on the shelf all week. How about I sign it out and you'll let me know when someone asks for it." Score! When the librarian comes calling a month later, the camera is being used for a project on a daily basis and can't be spared. Eventually, the Appropriation teacher will tap some little-used fund in the school to buy several digital cameras that can be used just in his or her classroom. The challenge for the Appropriation teacher is to get to all the curriculum requirements while using as many technology tools as possible.

■ **Innovation.** The Innovation teacher is more selective in the use of technology and has returned to the curriculum focus that is central to good teaching. Technology is just one of the tools in the classroom, not the only tool. Students have a choice of presentation methods: digital slide shows, skits, dioramas, and so on. The important thing is the curriculum: has the student demonstrated an understanding of the topic at hand? A student can no longer dazzle this teacher with a slide show of digital images and music devoid of content. Rubrics for assessing curriculum content, standards met, and appropriate media are used to grade the student's achievement.

Innovation is the ideal but it's a moving target. The research showed, and experience proves, that you can reach the Innovation stage with one set of technology tools, but when a new tool appears on the horizon, you are likely to react from an Entry standpoint.

Case Study #1

Here's an example: I was a school principal in a small suburban district outside Boston. The first on the administrative team to own my own laptop (bought with my own money), I was quick to use it in administrative team meetings to take my notes. And, I began to use the laptop to document teacher observations—a move that changed my administrative life! After a while, I could be finished with my observation report by the end of a class period. I felt very strong in my computer skills, very confident that I had truly integrated this new tool. Then, my husband, much geekier than I, brought the Internet into our home. He was instantly smitten. I was instantly resistant. His Internet activity lasted well into the night, with frequent (and loud) restarts of the computer. It was 1991, the Internet was still relatively new, and browsers were prone to crashing spontaneously. In the morning, he would tell me all about the cool sites he'd visited. I figured this was a passing phase, like CB radio on a computer

screen. I saw no connection between this newfangled thing and my life, personal or professional. I was in the Entry stage with the Internet. I stayed there for months, while happily
using my laptop for my administrative tasks, expanding my expertise to include spreadsheets
and data analysis. Then, something happened to push me into the Adoption stage overnight.

Our eldest daughter went to college. What was the first thing Annie did after plugging
in her new computer? She sent her dad an email. At first, I was able to ignore it. Then, I began
to receive daily emails on my breakfast plate . . . this was not fair! Finally, I had to overcome
my reluctance and get an email account so I could stay connected with my daughter asynchronously (no college student is in communication during normal, parent time). I found that
basic email was not difficult, and the Internet was a small step away. But, did I immediately
go to professional sites? I'm afraid not. My first visits were to commercial sites that interested me: www.llbean.com, www.boston.com, www.airfrance.com, and so on. I'd get to
school and regale my colleagues with tales of designing a new car on the Subaru site, entering my zip code and seeing a list of cars matching my description on the local dealer's lot. I
carried on like this for some time before finding a need to use the Internet professionally.

The need to incorporate Internet resources into my professional life presented itself
when my teachers and I decided to take a look at homogeneous versus heterogeneous
grouping of students. "Aha," says I, "I'll bet I can find some research that supports my con-
tention that ability grouping does more harm than good to elementary students." Sure
enough, time spent searching the ERIC files online (www.eric.ed.gov) gave me more than
enough. But I wasn't happy with just using ERIC. I did a quick search on www.yahoo.com
using the keywords *heterogeneous grouping,* and got over 50,000 hits! Here was plenty of
ammunition but I had few skills to sift through all the material—back to Adoption for me!
I had several more opportunities to learn how to search and sift before feeling confident.
Did I go through an Appropriation stage with email and the Internet? Absolutely!

Not long after beginning to use online resources for my work, I got the bright idea that
I needed to be connected all day, every day. Remember, this was 1991, when very few schools
were wired for the Internet. But, once an email junky, it's hard to turn back. So, I appropri-
ated the usually idle phone line that was attached to the school's fax machine in the outer
office, ran a wire across the ceiling, through a new hole above my office door, across another
ceiling and down the wall to my desk. It was excessive, but I was happy and could check my
email every 5 minutes instead of waiting until I got home. Soon, my use of the online environment moderated and I was safely in the Innovation stage, getting online as needed.

For classroom teachers, the path from Entry to Innovation can take some time. The
ACOT research found that, if teachers only have access in their classrooms, the journey can
take up to five years. However, if the teacher has a computer at home, or a laptop that goes
back and forth, eighteen months was the norm. The first, and biggest leap, from Entry to
Adoption, only happens when the teacher has a real, and personal, reason to jump. If the
school goal is to have an entire faculty using appropriate technologies with students, this
first step may need to be facilitated. A couple of stories illustrate this point.

Case Study #2

In the mid-1990s, long before I had ever heard of these stages, I made the mistake of trying
to haul a reluctant teacher into using technology with her students. It wasn't pretty. My
motives were not bad: I had six third-grade classrooms, five of which were led by teachers

who were making great use of the available technologies. Ms. Strong's kids visited technology once a week in the computer lab where they played some games and Ms. Strong kept order. When her kids went on to fourth grade, they were at a disadvantage among groups of kids who were used to creating presentation and books, going online to educational sites, and using technology as part of the classroom toolset. Ms. Strong was a good teacher, loved by her kids and their parents. In fact, she was the school's expert on children's literature, a great resource for authors and new books. As the educational leader in the building, I had no qualms about sitting her down one fall and laying out the goals: Internet by January, student-produced books and presentations by April. I'd even created a master schedule that allowed her access to the technology teacher during her planning periods. That should have done it, right? The end result was not as successful as I'd have wished, but she did begin using the tools with her students. She, however, was pretty uncomfortable and I felt like a bully. I wish now that I'd understood the stages. It would have been so easy to pull her into the Adoption stage by showing her web sites of either children's authors (her school passion) or geneology (her outside-of-school passion). She would have found technology she liked and moved more comfortably through the stages. Hindsight has 20–20 vision.

Case Study #3

Fast-forward a few years to a time when I had a good grasp of the stages. I was presenting the first of two two-technology integration workshops in a school district on Long Island. In the first workshop, I'd be helping them get started with some basic tools, including Apple-Works slide shows, scanners, digital cameras, and music. Six weeks later, I'd be returning to add more skills in multimedia, working with video and HyperStudio. In both workshops, the participants would be introduced to the tools, get a chance to use them in a sample classroom project, then adapt an existing classroom lesson or unit to incorporate the new tools. The group in front of me was a mixture of Adoption and Adaptation level teachers. One teacher stood out, though. Becky didn't touch the mouse for the entire two days. She had come with her fellow second-grade teachers, participated in their group conversation, had lunch with them, but did not get her hands dirty with the technology. I figured her for an Entry teacher and predicted that she was unlikely to come back for the next, more intense, workshop. I was wrong. When I arrived six weeks later to begin the second workshop, she was just arriving, clutching a dozen Polaroid pictures of the first grandchild to grace this earth. Justin had been born the day before and Becky couldn't wait to show her buddies. "Aha," I said to myself, "I've got her now!" Once the others had started on their HyperStudio tour of the planets, I drew Becky aside. "Would you like to make a little slide show presentation about Justin for your students?" "Do you think I could? I've never used the scanner or any of that. I'm no techie." To make a long story short, Becky did learn to scan that morning, and she made a six-slide presentation to her class before they left that day. They cheered. As we were cleaning up from the workshop, I offered her my Sony Mavica camera and a box of floppy disks to take to the hospital that night. She came to the workshop the next morning with at least forty pictures of the new baby. So, on Day Two, she learned how to import and edit digital photos, put them into her slide show, and add a soundtrack (the song, "Baby Beluga"), and then presented her slide show to her colleagues. More cheers! Becky was on her way, had crept tentatively out of Entry and, by the end of the day, was investigating the prices and features of digital cameras. And, she'd had fun using technology—something she absolutely did not expect. She was not yet ready to use technology within her curriculum, but she was invested in using technology to present her grandson to her peers and her students. I checked in with the superintendent a few years later and learned that Becky was very comfortable using technology to support her curriculum.

Piaget and Stages of Learning

Earlier in this chapter, you were asked to keep Piaget in mind as you learned about teachers and stages of technology integration. While Piaget devoted his research to child development (see www.piaget.org/biography/biog.html for a short biographical review), some of his findings apply to adult learning as well. Put simply, he found that children's understanding of their world progresses through a series of stages, each building upon understandings from the prior stage. Stages are not skipped. Children move naturally from one stage to the next if given opportunities to play and explore at each stage, and if they are exposed to others at the next highest stage. Those of us who spent time in primary classrooms do not need to be reminded of the necessity of play and exploration in the classroom. Imagine what would happen if you dropped a pile of Unifix Cubes (small, colorful, plastic cubes that snap together, often used to teach number theory in the primary grades) on the table in front of a group of 7-year-olds and you immediately asked them to show you an addition equation using the cubes. You would be thwarted instantly because the kids would ignore you and begin building with the cubes, sorting them into like colors, snapping long chains of cubes together, and so on. The smart primary teacher introduces math manipulatives as toys long before the children are scheduled to use them as tools for number theory.

Piaget's stage theory in combination with the ACOT stages offers huge implications for schools wishing to get teachers engaged in using technology for learning. Remember Ms. Strong? I had not provided any opportunity to play with technology before asking her to jump into adapting lessons to incorporate it. I was asking, okay, *demanding,* that she skip the Adoption stage. I did not give her the opportunity to work with the tools in her own way, on a project that interested her. By the time I got to Becky, I understood the stages better and was ready to hand her the appropriate technology, once she handed me the topic that most interested her at the moment: baby Justin. Much later, I realized that I needn't have bumped heads with Ms. Strong. Her passion, you may remember, was children's literature. Had I been more aware, I would have mentioned in passing, that I'd come across Jan Brett's web site (www.janbrett.com), a treasure trove of information, illustrations, classroom activities, and stories from Ms. Strong's favorite author. I'd have begun to leave printed web pages in Ms. Strong's mailbox at school. Ms. Strong had a second, more personal, passion: historic graveyards. She belongs to an association that investigates the origins and stories of old gravestones and markers. I could also have pointed her to a site where there are many links to resources on cemetery history and preservation (www.potifos.com/cemeteries.html). My work would have been done. As it happens, I saw Ms. Strong a couple of years ago and she told me all about her Internet discoveries. She did go back to the Adoption stage and learned all about the Internet—searching and sifting, exploring, downloading, and so on. She did move through the stages, on her own terms, and in spite of my intervention, not because of it.

HOW TO . . . HELP TEACHERS MOVE
TO A NEW LEVEL

Whatever your role in education, your newfound awareness can help other teachers (or you) be more successful if you keep the following tips in mind:

- With an Entry level teacher, it's all about the hook. You sometimes have to be creative in figuring out what will bring an Entry teacher into Adoption. The hook may come from a fellow teacher who is happily in the Adoption stage. Remember that the hook may have nothing to do with classroom integration but is likely to make the teacher's personal or professional life easier.

- Provide exposure to folks at the next stage. For every stage, this is critical. Exposure may take the form of short celebrations at staff meetings of teachers' latest projects. Make sure you ask teachers at different stages to share. Exposure may take place by asking two teachers to work on developing a curriculum project together, with one member of the pair at a higher stage than the other.

- You need to walk the walk. If you've a mind to bring other teachers along the stages of technology integration, consider your own use of technology and your own path through the stages. Teachers notice right away if their leader or peer is a comfortable learner, especially in the area of technology. If you model the use of appropriate tools for your job (word processing, spreadsheets, presentations, Internet research, and so on) and make sure you are working on new skills and talking about your challenges, you create a safe environment for teachers to be learners as well.

- Recognize your own Entry behavior and find your own hook. When you are introduced to a new technology, it's fine to be cautious, but if you suspect it may be useful for your work, consider how you might use the technology for your own personal interest. The research tells us that playing with a new tool for yourself allows you to learn it more easily. So, take that digital camera on a family trip, build yourself a small web page, or use iMovie to produce a video of a family party.

- Work to create a climate where everyone is a learner. If you are public about your own learning, this comes more easily. Encourage other teachers to try incorporating appropriate technology into a lesson you will observe. Then, applaud their risks, understand their challenges, and don't get too critical if some part of the technology doesn't work. Work with your technology teacher or your Innovation teachers to set up open lab time for teachers to get coaching on whatever technologies they are trying to master. These can occur before or after school, on a release day, or online as an email or discussion board.

Enjoy your passage through the stages and welcome other teachers as fellow travelers!

■ ■ ■ ■ ■ ■ ■ ■ ■ ■

HOW TO . . . ANALYZE A TEACHER'S
DEVELOPMENTAL STAGE

You need: The description of stages in this chapter; a sample of fellow teachers; the following table.

You get: An analysis of the stages of development of your colleagues.

In the second column in the table below enter the names of teachers that you think are at each of the stages of development in integrating technology. Enter your name as well. You will find a description of each stage above in this chapter.

STAGE	TEACHERS
Entry	
Adoption	
Adaptation	
Appropriation	
Innovation	

■ ■ ■ ■ ■ ■ ■ ■ ■ ■

WHAT TEACHERS NEED: AEIOU

We've all heard the discussion many times: The schools are falling behind in their use of the new information technologies for learning. Unlike other professions, teachers are not as adept at adopting the use of computers in the classroom. But last week the discussion took place at Rey Fernando VI high school in Spain, with a group of teachers and a representative of the Spanish Ministry of Education. And this time the question came down to, What do teachers need in order to take full advantage of technology for teaching? This section looks at some possible answers to this seemingly universal question.

What do teachers need? Six things: **A**ccess, **E**ncouragement, **I**nspiration, **O**rganization, **U**nderpinnings, and (sometimes) **Y**outh. Here's what I mean.

A: Access

Without constant access to computers and networks, teachers cannot be expected to learn and practice the new skills necessary to exploit the educational possibilities of the new technologies. This means access at any time, whether during the school day or at home in the evening and on weekends; from any place, including the classroom, the library, the study hall, the office (at home or school), and the living room. If we look at professions that have successfully adopted the new technologies, we see this kind of universal access.

Access means that a teacher can turn to her desk, to her briefcase, wherever she is working, and get to the information she needs and the communication she desires. Access does not mean availability down the hall or in the lab at certain hours; the last decade has proven that this kind of limited access separated from the daily flow of the teacher's work results in little growth.

Without access for a teacher, it's a waste of time to go any further—the rest of this list is fruitless unless access is established first.

It's more than access to a computer that a teacher needs. It's a computer with the tools that the teacher needs, connected to a free and open network. It's a personal access, so he can deal with his own email, conduct his own research, and save his own documents. How much access do you enjoy?

- How far do you have to go at school to work on a computer with the tools and connections you need? At home?
- What tools do you have available? How up-to-date, reliable, and efficient are they?
- During what proportion of the day do you enjoy this access?

E: Encouragement

Few teachers grew up with computers and high-speed internet access. Most need considerable encouragement to learn the new skills and practice the novel educational techniques that information technology makes possible. They need encouragement from many sources: their department chairs, their principals, state and local education leaders, their students, the local school board, and their fellows in the profession. This encouragement can take the form of an expectation by a supervisor that the teacher add a technology-using lesson plan this semester; it can appear as a laptop with wireless connection provided by school officials; it can arise from a technology workshop conducted by the local or state teacher's association.

Encouragement can also mean fostering a spirit of experimentation, permission to try new ways of teaching, patience to be satisfied with small steps forward, and willingness to let people learn from their mistakes. Rewarding and recognizing those who incorporate technology, the very beginners as well as the pioneers, goes a long way to encourage others to try new things.

And school leaders who model the effective use of technology in their own personal work—from the department chair to the principal to the curriculum supervisor to the dean to the superintendent—can serve as beacons to guide the rest of the team through the waters of the new media.

- How much encouragement do you receive for integrating technology into your teaching?
- Is technology use part of your professional development plan or evaluation goals?
- How many times this year have you seen a teacher recognized or rewarded for making good use of technology?
- How many of your school, district, and state leaders use technology personally and visibly in their work?

I: Inspiration

Access and encouragement, while necessary conditions for growth, are seldom sufficient to get people moving. Teachers need to be inspired to try something new. They need to see examples of other teachers in their subject or grade teaching better through technology. They enjoy watching demonstrations of new tools and techniques that are directly relevant to what they teach. And they enjoy even more a chance to try these things out for themselves, hands-on and with friendly support. There are many ways to get new ideas flowing through teachers' minds.

- A district technology showcase that features fellow teachers demonstrating (and not simply talking about) ways they have applied new technologies to their classrooms
- A visit to the Apple Learning Interchange, or the WebQuest page, or the Math Forum to suggest methods and show practical examples in a variety of levels and topics
- Participation in state and regional conferences that include technology workshops
- A weekly visit to the Power to Learn web site

Consider how much inspiration you are getting these days.

- When is the last time that a department or school faculty meeting included an interesting demonstration of technology for teaching?
- How often do you actively search the Web (or other sources of information) to get new ideas for teaching?
- How did you learn about the most recent innovation you've made in your teaching?

O: Organization

Many teachers spend most of their day out of contact with their colleagues. But research proves that technology implementation works better when teachers form groups that support each other through the process of inspiration, experimentation, and adaptation. Fellow faculty are often the best source of new ideas, of help in getting started, and of assistance in times of trouble. It's a lot easier to ask a close colleague—who perhaps has just been through it himself—for help getting through that little glitch that is driving you crazy. An organization of peers, whether formally appointed or loosely assembled, is almost essential to making good use of new technology in teaching.

The group—we might call it a community of practice—and the help it offers, need not be in the same building, or even the same state. The Web offers an opportunity for teachers to form self-help groups among geographically diverse but job-alike folks. Through chat and instant messenger, email and discussion forums, teachers can help each other discover new ideas and escape from sticky situations. And when the professional colleague groups are coupled with competent technical support help, it's much more likely that people find the courage to experiment and the support to carry through even the tough issues that arise.

Analyze the people that you may call on for guidance and assistance.

- Who in your school or district is available and interested to provide you with ideas for using technology?
- Who would you call on right now if something went wrong with your computer, that you could not fix yourself?
- When is the last time you discussed with fellow teachers your successes and failures in using technology?

U: Underpinnings

Behind each of the wonderful examples of technology innovation in school sits a collection of cables, connections, computers, and competence that was carefully planned and diligently managed; as well as servers, systems, and support that are reliable and efficient. These are the necessary underpinnings of a teacher's successful use of technology in the classroom. They are the infrastructure that, although seldom seen and understood, nevertheless makes possible the new educational capabilities.

How many of these capabilities underpin the technology in your school?

- A connection to the Internet that is fast, reliable, always available, and freely open for the teacher's use
- Email for all teachers, students, and staff in the school, with a directory service, and access from outside the school
- File servers with plenty of room to store student and teacher projects, and with easy but protected access from school and home
- Wireless network access throughout the school
- Hard-wired Ethernet connections as necessary throughout the school
- Enough printers, conveniently located, for teachers and students
- A staff that keeps these hardware and software infrastructures running smoothly
- Web servers available for student and teacher web site publishing, including HTML, mail, and video
- Access to appropriate administrative and logistical information, from home and school
- Effective and quick systems for repair and replacement of hardware and software
- Standard, up-to-date productivity software available at all stations
- Specialized production software for video, audio, graphics, web, and multimedia projects
- Digital resources for teaching available through the network (maps, references, image collections)

And Sometimes . . . Youth (Y)

Learning a new skill or subject calls for a youthful spirit, one that is not afraid of the discomfort of ignorance but curious about new discoveries. An attitude of wonder and willingness to be surprised helps the teacher to be open to inspiration from unknown sources, and leads her to make those experiments with technology that can lead to new ways of teaching and learning. A childlike sense of play helps a teacher to take advantage of the access, encouragement, inspiration, organization, and underpinnings that are provided for him. Just as it's tough to make a word in English (or Spanish) without a vowel, it's tough for teachers to advance in their use of technology in the absence of these six conditions.

HOW TO . . . ANALYZE THE CONDITIONS FOR GROWTH

You need: The following table.

You get: An analysis of the conditions for growth in integrating technology in your school.

Indicate on this table how your school rates on each condition for growth.

1 = Hardly at all
2 = Just a little
3 = Somewhat
4 = Quite a bit
5 = Extensively

CONDITION			RATING		
Access					
A computer with the connections I need is at my fingertips.	1	2	3	4	5
It has the software tools I need, up-to-date, reliable, and efficient.	1	2	3	4	5
It's available to me throughout the school day.	1	2	3	4	5
Encouragement					
I am encouraged to integrate technology into my teaching.	1	2	3	4	5
Technology use is part of my professional development or evaluation plan.	1	2	3	4	5
I have seen teachers recognized for making good use of technology.	1	2	3	4	5
My school and district leaders use technology personally and visibly.	1	2	3	4	5
Inspiration					
Faculty meetings include interesting demonstrations of technology.	1	2	3	4	5
I actively search the web to get new ideas for teaching.	1	2	3	4	5
I have recently made an innovation in my teaching.	1	2	3	4	5
Organization					
Staff are available to provide me with ideas for using technology.	1	2	3	4	5
I know who to call on for help fixing my computer.	1	2	3	4	5
I discuss with fellow teachers my successes and failures in using technology.	1	2	3	4	5
Underpinnings					
Our connection to the internet is fast, reliable, and open for the teacher's use.	1	2	3	4	5
Email is provided for each teacher, student, and staff in the school.	1	2	3	4	5
File servers with plenty of room to store student and teacher projects.	1	2	3	4	5
Wireless network access throughout the school.	1	2	3	4	5
Hard-wired Ethernet connections as necessary throughout the school.	1	2	3	4	5
Enough printers, conveniently located, for teachers and students.	1	2	3	4	5

A staff that keeps this infrastructure running smoothly.	1	2	3	4	5
Web servers available for student and teacher web site publishing.	1	2	3	4	5
Online access to appropriate administrative and logistical information.	1	2	3	4	5
Effective systems for repair and replacement of hardware and software.	1	2	3	4	5
Standard, up-to-date productivity software available at all stations.	1	2	3	4	5
Software for video, audio, graphics, web, and multimedia projects.	1	2	3	4	5
Digital resources for teaching available through the network.	1	2	3	4	5

Youth

I have a youthful spirit that is not afraid of the discomfort of ignorance.	1	2	3	4	5
I am curious about new discoveries.	1	2	3	4	5
I have an attitude of wonder and willingness to be surprised.	1	2	3	4	5
I am open to inspiration from unknown sources.	1	2	3	4	5
I have a childlike sense of play.	1	2	3	4	5

■ ■ ■ ■ ■ ■ ■ ■ ■

DESIGNING TECHNOLOGY-RICH LESSON PLANS

*"We've got computers now. We don't need textbooks or lesson plans anymore,"
pronounced the new teacher in her first faculty meeting. "Anything you want to
learn can be found on the Internet. We just provide the infrastructure of the
information highway in the school and classroom, and away they go, constructing their own knowledge. Our job is to serve as the Guide on the Side,
answering their questions as they arise and fixing things when they go wrong,
right?"*

Teachers have been designing lessons at least as long as architects have been designing
buildings. Socrates in the first century BCE was famous for his challenging lessons that
involved direct dialog between student and teacher. The onset of the printed book after the
sixteenth century widened the possibilities for teaching and demanded a new kind of lesson
plan with more independent work by the student. Later we developed lesson plans for incorporating film, newspapers, radio, and television into the curriculum and into the classroom.
The arrival of the computer simply adds a new dimension to the important task of planning
the act of teaching and learning. This section looks at two of many approaches to planning
a lesson that uses technology. They provide food for thought as we integrate technology
into our profession.

Unit of Practice

This approach to lesson design was developed in the 1990s by Apple Computer as part of
its Classrooms of Tomorrow research project. With funds from the National Science Foun-

dation, Apple worked with a wide variety of teachers and schools throughout the country to develop a common vocabulary and process for designing an effective lesson. The Unit of Practice (UOP) approach proposes eight parts of a good lesson plan:

1. *Invitation.* Here you briefly and provocatively describe the project in an inviting way. How will this lesson improve student learning?
2. *Tasks.* What exactly will the student do? What is the nature of the work to be accomplished?
3. *Interactions.* What happens? Who talks and works with whom? Who initiates interactions? Are students in groups, teams, or do they work individually while working on the task?
4. *Situations.* What's the setting? Where will the learning take place? What's the nature of the environment?
5. *Time Frame:* How long does this lesson last? What is your time frame for the lesson or unit?
6. *Tools.* What technologies and materials are provided to present the ideas and enable student work?
7. *Standards.* What objectives are set for the students? Which of the local, district, state, or national standards are addressed by this lesson?
8. *Assessment.* How will you evaluate the students' work? The Unit of Practice approach encourages the use of authentic assessments.

A good place to learn more about this approach is at Apple's own web site (www.ali.apple.com/ali_help/help_units.shtml), where you will find a database of lesson plans as well as instructions for designing your own lesson. Next, take a look at their rubric for evaluating a Unit of Practice (www.newbraunfels.txed.net/TechDept/CyberConn/PhaseIIIdocs/uoprubric.pdf).

The Unit of Practice approach has been widely adopted, as the collection of lesson plans at The Eighth Floor will prove. Connect to their web site (www.eighthfloor.org/resources/units/units.htm). You will be able to read a wide variety of lesson plans. Another source for sample lessons based on the Unit of Practice approach can be found at Tennille's Technology Tips (http://coe.west.asu.edu/students/stennille/ST3/unitofpractice.htm).

Many school districts use the Unit of Practice as their own lesson planning rubric, as you may see at the site of *Learning Environments for the New Century* from the Carteret County Schools (www.carteretcountyschools.org/lenc/uop/uop.htm). Here you will find a description of the approach, a template for writing a lesson plan, and examples of lessons created by Carteret County teachers.

Webquest

This lesson design strategy, very popular these days among teachers, is focused on planning lessons that use resources from the Internet in a structured way that's tied to traditional curriculum goals. You will find a good definition of the WebQuest approach at http://edweb.sdsu.edu/courses/edtec596/about_webquests.html, and you'll find more general info on the concept at http://webquest.sdsu.edu.

Webquests have these parts:

- An *introduction* that sets the stage and provides some background information
- A *task* that is doable and interesting
- A set of *information sources* needed to complete the task
- A description of the *process* the learners should go through in accomplishing the task
- Some *guidance on how to organize* the information acquired
- A *conclusion* that brings closure to the quest, reminds the learners about what they've learned, and perhaps encourages them to extend the experience into other domains

The most valuable information on this approach is found in the hundreds of lesson examples that teachers have created and posted on the Web. A good place to start your examination of the best of these is at the Webquest Portal (http://webquest.org); click on Top in the left-side menu. These are the lesson plans that have been judged best by a panel of experts. A good way to begin is to browse through those in your field. It may not be obvious at first, but all of these share a common set of elements.

To see how this approach is applied by educators, take a look at a lesson design page from the Natrona County, Wyoming school district (http://ncsdweb.ncsd.k12.wy.us/dherman/lesley/week2/lesson_design.html).

Next time someone tells you that computers and the Internet have made all of the old methods obsolete, send them off to see how some very creative teachers have melded tradition and technology. Here's an example of someone who needs to rethink a traditional assignment, note cards.

AN EXAMPLE: NOTECARDS

"No, that's not acceptable," insisted Mr. Ludd as Jamal turned in his history homework. "They're supposed to be on note cards."

"These are note cards," replied Jamal. "Look, here are all the notes I took on Lewis and Clark's trip up the Missouri River." Jamal had more notes than anyone else in the class. They were clearly printed, came from many original sources in the library and online, and evidenced a wide array of information on the early explorations of the American West.

"No, I mean regular note cards. You know, four by six inches with blue lines on them. And a red line at the top. Look at Molly's note cards. That's what I mean."

Molly's six note cards, though smudged and bent and hard to read, were indeed of the style that Mr. Ludd expected. "See how nicely she's written her notes."

Molly smiled as she wiped the ink of her left index finger. "It was hard work," she said, "copying all those words from the textbook and the encyclopedia."

"And I am sure you learned all about Meriwether Lewis as you carefully took your notes," beamed Mr. Ludd.

"Meriwether who?" questioned Molly.

This exchange took place in a classroom near you last week. It's a true story. Jamal's work was unacceptable because it was done on a computer. In fact, both Jamal and Molly spent about the same amount of time on this assignment. But most of Molly's was spent in the low-level task of copying by hand sentences from a textbook. Most of Jamal's time was spent learning about Lewis and Clark. His notes were a combination of copy-and-paste quotations from his sources, and his own typed summaries of what he had learned. Jamal, who has spent several hours each day at the keyboard since he was six, can type faster than Molly and Mr. Ludd and his parents put together.

But somehow, to Mr. Ludd and to many other educators, Jamal's work does not seem as valuable as Molly's. Somehow, the computer makes it seem all too easy. If gathering knowledge is not a struggle, they fear, then it will not be properly appreciated.

But in today's world, the finding of information is not the struggle it used to be. Nor is the recording and saving of information very difficult or time consuming. Jamal and many of his counterparts who grew up with computers have found much more efficient and effective ways to find what they need to know and to record it on their own digital version of note cards.

What they lack are the intellectual tools to make sense out of all the data they have collected. The struggle that should ensue in Mr. Ludd's classroom is the wrestling with ideas, not the bending of note cards. Both Jamal and Molly need to move beyond the easily observable facts about the expedition and into the realm of comparison, contrast, and meaning. Back in the old days, these realms were open only to the few with rich home libraries, lots of time to gather the facts through reading, and the discipline to record them on note cards. But today we have the opportunity, through networked digital information, to accomplish the fact-gathering more quickly and more interestingly, with more time left for analysis and evaluation.

The New Basic Skills

To take advantage of this opportunity, we need to change the rules and the expectations in our classrooms and in our assignments. And we need to teach some new skills. For Mr. Ludd's U.S. History research assignment, for instance, the new basic skills might include:

Finding information from a wide variety of sources. In the old days, we could only expect students to access the books in the classroom and in the library. So our expectations on breadth and depth and point-of-view of sources were necessarily limited. And the use of original sources was almost impossible. Today, the range available to a typical high school student, from school or from home, is enormous. In fact, the student's problem is one of making intelligent choices from an overabundance of sources.

Locating five different perspectives on the same event. This, too, would have been difficult or impossible in the old days—the books in the library might provide at most two different perspectives on the passage past Great Falls, and these were both secondary sources. But Jerika today will find dozens of perspectives on this event, many in their original voices, some with images to make them clearer and more understandable.

Judging the quality of a source. Would a web site from the American Indian Movement, or a book written by Thomas Jefferson, be a more reliable source on the events covered by this research project? Or would a diary written by one of the members of the expedition? Or Stephen Ambrose's writings 200 years after the fact? When the sources were few, the students seldom faced this problem of evaluation. But today this type of judgment-making is a basic skill.

Knowing what's worth reading. And saving. Molly could be expected to read all there was in the school library about the expedition—there wasn't much, and so she was not forced to decide what to choose or what to copy. Jamal, on the other hand (or on the keyboard), was faced immediately with a decision on which of the thousands of sources was appropriate to his task and worth his while. And once studied, which parts to be noted or saved.

Rather than rant and rave over note cards, Mr. Ludd should be considering how to work these new basic skills into his curriculum. These are not easy skills to teach, nor are they simple to evaluate. But they are more fun and more valuable and rewarding for both teacher and student.

TECHY-TALK A TO Z

When talking with students, computer coordinators, or anyone technical, we often confront a language barrier. They use terms that we don't fully understand, especially acronyms that have arisen recently and may not appear in the dictionary on your desk. This section provides an acronym alphabet of some of the acronyms most likely to appear in the life of a technology-using teacher.

AAC: Advanced Audio Codec. A new technology for compressing music files that's used in the Apple iPod and iTunes. Many people say it will replace MP3. See www.vialicensing.com/products/mpeg4aac/standard.html

BBEdit: BBEdit. A program used by HTML programmers to create web pages. The rest of us use WYSIWYG programs such as Dreamweaver.

CD-ROM: Compact Disc Read-Only Memory. An optical storage medium for computer data that your computer can read from, but not write to. Most software today that is not downloaded from the Web is delivered on CD-ROM. (They are round and silver.)

DHTML: Dynamic HTML. Language used to program Web pages that change based on what the user does, using style sheets and scripts. Not for the faint of heart.

EXE: Executable. Filename extension used for application programs in the Windows operating system. Many viruses often arrive unwanted with this moniker. Never open an .exe file whose provenance you doubt.

FTP: File Transfer Protocol. A system for transferring files over the Internet, used most often to move files between your computer and a server.

GIF: Graphics Interchange Format. Pronounced with a hard G. Not peanut butter. A filename extension for graphics files compressed in this standard format.

HTML: Hyper Text Markup Language. Coding used in web pages. Geeks write HTML code directly; the rest of us use web page editors that write the HTML code for us.

IP: Internet Protocol. Without it there'd be no Internet, no World Wide Web. It's the standard syntax used to assemble and manage the packets of data that send information back and forth across the net.

JPEG: Joint Photographer Expert Group. A system for compressing image data, especially photographs. As a filename extension, it appears as .jpg. Digital cameras commonly use JPEG compression.

K: Kilo. Greek for thousand. A kilobit is a thousand bits of data. A Kilobyte is a thousand bytes, bytes consisting of eight to ten bits, depending on who's counting.

LAN: Local Area Network (pronounced as a word that rhymes with "ran"). The network that connects the computers together in your office or school, or maybe even at home. Can be wireless or cabled, most commonly using Ethernet.

MP3: MPEG audio layer 3. A scheme for compressing music files. MPEG stands for Motion Picture Expert Group, which designed this method originally for use in compressing digital video.

NAT: Network Address Translating. Since every computer on the Internet needs its own unique IP address and there are not enough addresses to go around, NAT is used in many LANs to allow more computers to be online, by translating the LAN's address through to the individual computers.

OS X: Operating System X (Ten). The software that performs the basic operations on the new Apple Macintosh computers. Based on the Unix operating system, OS X and Linux are the leading (and growing and relatively virus-free) competitors to the Windows operating system from Microsoft.

PNG: Portable Network Graphics. A scheme for compressing image files, most often seen as a filename extension. Though all the new browsers can handle .png files, they are not as common as .gif and .jpg images.

QWERTY: Not really an acronym, it's how American keyboards are described. Look on your keyboard and you will see why. French keyboards are called AZERTY. An alternative method of laying out the keys, Dvorak, puts the commonly used characters AOEUI on the middle row.

RTSP: Real Time Streaming Protocol. A syntax for arranging the data in packets and managing their passage over the Internet, used for video and audio streaming such as QuickTime and RealVideo. Since RTSP uses UDP packets, some types of network security software block it.

SMTP: Simple Mail Transfer Protocol. The system of arranging and tracking packets of data in email messages that travel across the Internet. Emails are sent, and received, by an SMTP server.

T1: Telecommunications 1 megabit. A way of describing the bandwidth of a communications connection. If your school is connected to the Internet with a T1 line, you can pass more data more quickly than a school with a cable modem or ISDN line, but not as quickly as a university or lab with a T100 line.

UDP: User-Defined Protocol. Yet another method for arranging and managing data packets that flow across the Internet, this one open to a variety of syntaxes. UDP packets are often used for streaming audio and video, such as RTSP, but they can also be used for compromising a network's security.

VR: Virtual Reality. Not what a philosopher might think, VR refers to a wide range of technologies that attempt to produce the perception of the real world through representations of digital data. Often used to describe three-dimensional applications such as QuickTime VR.

WYSIWYG: What You See Is What You Get (pronounced *wizzywig*). Often used to describe page-layout or web page editing programs that display on the editing screen a facsimile of what the user will see. Dreamweaver is a WYSIWYG program.

XML: eXtensible Markup Language. Like HTML, a coding system for designing web pages. In XML, you define your own tags and can adjust them to display differently depending on the way the data is used.

Y2K: Year 2 Kilo. Shorthand to refer to the year 2000, when we all feared our computers would crash because we now needed four instead of two digits to represent the year. You will still find software labeled *Y2K compliant.* Did your computer survive?

ZIP: Zipped file, or Zip disk. The first is a filename extension used to denote files that have been compressed using the Zip method. The second is a type of disk storage, commonly called a Zip disk.

These twenty-six terms are just a start at learning the jargon of technology. You can learn hundreds more at the high-tech dictionary (www.computeruser.com/resources/dictionary), or the FOLDOC (Free Online Dictionary of Computing) (http://wombat.doc.ic.ac.uk/foldoc).

LEARN MORE . . .

About the Stages Teachers Go Through

www.apple.com/education/k12/leadership/acot
   This is the site where you'll find the research behind Apple Classrooms of Tomorrow (ACOT).

www.apple.com/education/k12/leadership/acot/library.html
   Here are a number of reports and reflections on the ACOT research.

www.janbrett.com
   This is an example of an author's page—a good place to start using the Internet in a primary classroom!

About Inspiring Teachers To Use Technology

Some places to start getting new ideas flowing through teachers' minds.

www.ali.apple.com
> A rich resource for teachers to see media-rich curriculum lessons. These are submitted by teachers K–12 and show both the results of the lessons and the planning behind them.

http://webquest.sdsu.edu
> The webquest page at San Diego State University gives excellent examples of K–12 webquests across the curriculum. It also gives the format for great webquests and guidance for their development.

www.powertolearn.com
> The Power to Learn site contains many resources for K–12 teachers who use the Internet for curriculum purposes.

About Lesson Planning Tools

The Unit of Practice (UOP) is a format that was developed by Apple as part of the ACOT project.

http://ali.apple.com/ali_help/help_units.shtml
> This section of the Apple site explains the UOP format and its foundations.

http://coe.west.asu.edu/students/stennille/ST3/unitofpractice.htm
> Tennille's Technology Tips page gives examples of UOPs K–8.

www.newbraunfels.txed.net/TechDept/CyberConn/PhaseIIIdocs/uoprubric.pdf
> This is a downloadable rubric for assessing lessons designed using the Unit of Practice format.

CHAPTER THREE

CLASSROOMS

IN THIS CHAPTER

- **Classrooms Yesterday and Today**
- **Computers for Communication**
- **One-to-One Computing**
- **Learning and Working Environments**
- **Looking Ahead: Transition to College**
- **Learn More . . .**

Students spend the bulk of their day in classrooms. And the classroom is the one environment over which the individual teacher maintains a large measure of control. This chapter examines the state of the classroom today, and then offers some practical ways to make your classroom more amenable to the integration of technology.

The first part of the chapter compares the classroom with the home and the workplace, and provides you with a checklist for analyzing the integration of technology into your own classroom. The second part of the chapter provides concrete examples of how schools and teachers are ensuring that computers and networks are fully integrated into the lives of students.

CLASSROOMS YESTERDAY AND TODAY

In Boston these days, the world's largest public works project is burying six lanes of Interstate 93 right through the heart of downtown. Bostonians call it the Big Dig. They've uncovered lots of historical artifacts in this work, including parts of a school from the seventeenth century. This finding forms the basis of this chapter.

Imagine a moment in the future, a very long time from now. Our culture is buried deep beneath the ruins of time. An archaeologist many eons advanced uncovers a perfectly preserved home of the early twenty-first century. The first room he dusts off is an adolescent's bedroom. What does he find?

There's a computer. Next to it, an Ethernet connector that leads to the Internet—at 500 kilobytes per second. On top of it a mobile phone, with worldwide coverage, nights and weekends free. There is a radio, AM and FM, with CD player. Next to that an MP3 player with 500 songs (but not much Mozart). On the desk a connector for the digital camcorder. Just around the corner is a television, cable-ready with 120 channels.

Is this a typical find? Will he find more rooms like this in the neighborhood? What conclusions will he draw from his collection of artifacts?

Now imagine the same archaeologist digs down the road a few miles, and uncovers a school. Its cornerstone indicates it was built in 2004. He unearths a classroom, perhaps one that housed the occupant of the bedroom mentioned in Chapter 1. What communication technologies does he find there? A chalkboard. A whiteboard. A lectern. Chairs. Perhaps he finds an Ethernet drop, but nothing's connected to it. What conclusions will the archeologist draw from this collection of artifacts? What will he conclude when he compares them with the list from the bedroom?

Glance into a school classroom now. Or look carefully through your own. What information technologies are in evidence? How are the classroom, and the people in it, connected with the world of facts and people and ideas outside? In many classrooms, students are asked to check their laptops and palm pilots—their information technologies—at the door.

Today's Classrooms

No matter what the age, our classrooms are not unfriendly places. For the most part they are orderly and clean, which is more than you can say for the student's bedroom. Yet, it's the rare classroom in the United States where each student can, from her desk, turn to the Internet and find out the size of the middle class in Iraq or read Act II of *Hamlet* or call up a map of central Asia. Nor can the teacher. But most of those students, at home, could do that in an instant.

Think back to the classroom of twenty years ago, shortly before the current generation of high school students was born. How does it compare with today's classroom? What went on there back then? How different is it from what happens in the classroom today? How much have our classrooms changed as a result of the information revolution? Would a teacher from 1986, if transported into your classroom today, be able to get the students through the morning curriculum and down to the lunchroom?

Look at Winslow Homer's painting *The Country School* of 1871 (http://govschl.ndsu .nodak.edu/~rausch/homer.htm). Would the teacher pictured there know what to do in a modern classroom? How long would she survive with today's second grade? And Homer's kids—what would they think of that twenty-first-century bedroom? Would they know what to do?

In the world outside of school, there's been a revolution in how we collect, store, work with, and access information. Information of all kinds, from bare facts to fully embellished works of art, from personal calendars to institutional stock trades, from scholarly research to *The Simpsons*—it's done online now.

Our students, growing up in the midst of this revolution, are among its most ardent participants, using the new media extensively for interpersonal communication. Not only do they communicate, they also research, download, store, listen, and watch with these technologies, often all at the same time. Their access to information, their extensive level of communication with each other, and their ability to multitask, set them apart from previous generations. And from their teachers.

The Digital Disconnect

What happens when kids of this generation go to school? When they walk into your class-room? Is the information technology revolution reflected in the educational environment? A research study published recently by the Pew Foundation suggests that these students experience a *digital disconnect* when they enter the classroom door. So it should come to us as no surprise that in a 2002 survey by the National Center For Educational Statistics, students found school less useful and less relevant that the students who came before them. Fewer of them saw their schoolwork as meaningful, interesting, or relevant to their futures as students had done five or ten years before.

The Teacher's Role

What's a teacher to do in this situation? The digital disconnect can certainly make our work more difficult. But we can also take advantage of what's happening in the world outside of school to enhance our teaching. We can:

End the disconnect—get plugged in. Learn to use the new communication technologies as our students and businesses do. Invest in a cell phone, a PalmPilot, a laptop, and high-speed Internet access at home. Prepare lessons online. Get an instant messenger account and use it with your friends and students. Learn to use the digital resources and tools in your subject area.

Capitalize on our kids' competencies. Design lessons that challenge students to use the Internet for academic purposes. Channel their searching skills into productive endeavors in the classroom and library and at home. Use instant messenger in the classroom to develop writing and keyboarding skills. Post assignments and resources on the Web.

Advocate for information access. Don't let your school's information resources fall behind. Press for Internet access in every classroom, wireless networks, and the encouragement to use laptops throughout the school. Form a faculty technology committee to influence the school's technology investments.

None of us will be alive when the archeologists of the future dig up our bedrooms and schools. But we can all work today to ensure that our schools and classrooms reflect the best aspects of the digital era.

HOW TO . . . ASSESS YOUR CLASSROOM TECHNOLOGY QUOTIENT

You need: The following rating scale, and a close inspection of your classroom.

You get: An analysis of how well your classroom is prepared for the integration of technology.

Indicate on this table how your classroom rates on each criterion.

    1 = Hardly at all
    2 = Just a little
    3 = Somewhat
    4 = Quite a bit
    5 = Extensively

CONDITION	RATING				
These information technologies are found in my classroom:					
Multimedia computer with full and open access to the internet	1	2	3	4	5
Instant messaging (used in the curriculum)	1	2	3	4	5
CD player	1	2	3	4	5
DVD player	1	2	3	4	5
Television	1	2	3	4	5
Radio	1	2	3	4	5
Telephone with outside line	1	2	3	4	5
Computer projector	1	2	3	4	5
MP3 player	1	2	3	4	5
A computer for each student	1	2	3	4	5
Wireless network connection	1	2	3	4	5
Internet research used in teaching	1	2	3	4	5
Computer display used in place of chalkboard	1	2	3	4	5
Portable storage devices (USB memory, pocket FireWire drive, etc.)	1	2	3	4	5
Digital still camera, photo editing software	1	2	3	4	5
Digital video camera, video editing software	1	2	3	4	5

Calculate the classroom technology quotient:

    0–20   Technology-poor
  21–40   Technology-minimal
  41–60   Technology-adequate
  61–80   Technology-rich

■ ■ ■ ■ ■ ■ ■ ■ ■ ■

COMPUTERS FOR COMMUNICATION

Computers spend very little time computing. Most of us—and most of our students—use computers not for adding and subtracting and finding square roots, but for email, word processing, instant messaging, and web surfing. These four are tasks of communication, not of computing. To many people, it's not a PC (personal computer) but an IC (interpersonal communicator). The growth in computer use by the general public is not in solving math problems, but in communicating with each other. Computers (ICs) enable us to communicate with more people, in more different ways, at more times and places, and much more efficiently, than the other forms of communication that we have invented over the last 10,000 years.

Therefore, professions and places that are built on the act of communication, such as teaching in classrooms, need to consider how best to take advantage of these new communication capabilities. Teachers communicate ideas. A central task of education is to gather information effectively from a variety of sources, process that information, and then distribute it to the people who need it to do their work. This can be any kind of information—from attendance records to student opinions, from the text of an historic speech to the basketball schedule, from the science curriculum plan to the fourth-grade math test. Communication is at the center of what schools and teachers do. Those who communicate well succeed.

Thus we see a growing interest in instant messaging, webcasting, email, radio, blogs, discussion boards, and the other things that characterize today's IC users. These tools, and technologies like them, have changed the ways other professions communicate—banking, political fundraising, journalism, retail sales, and so forth—and we are now confronted with how they will change the profession of education.

Here's a brief summary of each of these tools of communication, and how they might apply to what we do in school.

Instant Messaging (IM)

> Good morning, Dottie, *types Mrs. Brooks into the IM box,* do you have a copy of Hemingway's *The Old Man and the Sea* down there? We need it for our eighth-grade literature class this morning. *Dottie, the librarian, types back,* Just a minute . . . *A few moments later she enters,* Yes, I found it and it's here on my desk.

> Why, do you think, did your survey find such resistance to no-smoking laws? *typed the eleventh-grade social studies group into the IM box. After a few moments of heated discussion, their counterparts at the French lycée (high school) typed back,* Because French people believe more strongly in the rights of the individual than you do in America. *(A cordial but heated exchange of views among the corresponding groups followed this simple beginning.)*

Instant messaging, known as IM, or AIM for AOL Instant Messenger, or MSN, or ICQ, lets me type a message into a box on my computer that it displayed instantly on the computer of my correspondent. It's like a telephone call in text. Instead of talking, we type back and forth. More and more of the Internet's traffic consists of instant messages like the ones described above, reflecting a rapid growth in the use of this technology by the public. With IM I can communicate with one person at a time, or set up a conference call and work with several at once. This multiparty messaging is sometimes called an *online chat*. It's interactive, immediately responsive, but uses writing rather than voice.

If as an administrator or teacher you have used the telephone to accomplish your goals, consider how you might substitute an IM session or a chat for the phone call. IM is less intrusive—it does not ring and interrupt what you were doing, you need not answer if you don't want to, you can do other things while you IM (yes, I used the acronym as a verb, reflecting current usage among my students), and you have a written record of the conversation. And people tend to think more before writing than they do before talking. So the quality of an IM is often higher than a spoken conversation.

Webcasting

> *"Welcome to the new academic year at Dismal Seepage School District," said Superintendent Smith. "Rather than bring you all together in the high school auditorium, we are webcasting this year's opening day inservice to all of you in your various schools." Mrs. Brooks looked closely at the video image on the computer display, and then leaned over to whisper to her neighbor, "I think she's coloring her hair."*

> *The night-vision camera connected to the webcasting station picked up the turtles coming ashore to lay their eggs. "Watch how they each stake out their own nesting spot," said Susan to Miguel as they observed on the laptop in the back of the sixth-grade classroom. It's 2 A.M. in Malaysia, according to the clock in the corner of the webcast.*

In this form of communication I broadcast my message to a large audience, using the World Wide Web for distribution. A webcast can be like radio, with voice and music; or like television, with video and sound. Like radio and TV it can be live or pre-recorded. Anyone with a computer connected to the Internet can see and hear the webcast (if I want to let them; I can protect it with a password, if desired). Instead of traveling over the airwaves or through the cable, the webcast is carried over the Internet. CNN, ABC, and Sports Illustrated, among others, carry frequent webcasts. Companies use them to communicate with their stockholders, and scientists use them to conduct research symposia.

You can webcast to a single person, a small group, or the whole world. You need neither an FCC license nor a powerful transmitter—you can do it from your own computer. (To serve thousands of listeners, you need a server with a solid connection to the net.) This democratization of the mass media of radio and TV holds interesting promise for the profession of education.

Discussion Boards and Blogs

> Our group's survey found that most people support the smoking ban, *read Ricardo from the discussion board for the twelfth-grade government class.*

Immediately he clicked the Reply button and typed, Our team found just the opposite. How did you word your survey question? *He posted his response, and reminded himself to come back later that day to see the reactions.*

The problem with moving American literature to the tenth grade, *wrote Mrs. Brooks on March 25,* is that it would no longer link with the U.S. History course we teach in the eleventh grade. *Two days later we see that Mr. Rivers posts to the school's curriculum blog,* The books we read in this class are more appropriate to the tenth graders, while the world literature selections are better for the older students.

Consider the democracy wall in Beijing in the early 1980s, on which the Chinese citizens posted political messages for others to read. I post one message, you read it and then post your own response next to it. It's similar to Letters to the Editor in a newspaper, except that there's no editor to control what gets posted. The online discussion board works in the same way. I type my ideas, and they are posted on the board for others to see. And to respond to with their own postings. *Blog* is short for weblog, a discussion board that looks like a web site—it's actually a web site made up of the postings of its contributors. Some discussion boards and blogs are open to anyone who connects; others are only available to registered users. Some are censored by an editor; others let all postings remain, no matter how irrelevant or obscene.

Blogs are similar in function to the Internet newsgroups of the late 1980s and early 1990s, a way for people with a common interest to share information and ideas. I communicate daily with the Pearson 27 discussion forum, a group of about a hundred people around the country who own the same model of sailboat. Anyone with access to a web server or Internet service provider (ISP) can set up a discussion board or blog, using commonly available software. See Blogwise (www.blogwise.com) for some examples. These are simply new ways to communicate information; nothing in the technology guarantees the worth or quality of the content. (As I have been writing this section of the chapter, I received five emails, three instant messages, and checked in once with the Pearson 27 blog. But no one called me on the phone. I am lost!)

Do It Yourself

The question for educators is how to capitalize on these new capabilities of communication, and to incorporate them appropriately into the ways we teach and learn. And the best way to begin seeking the answer to that question is to use these new technologies yourself—try them out, see how they work, and reflect on how they might contribute to your work. You can download AOL or MSN Instant Messenger software free from aol.com or msn.com; iChat comes free on all new Apple computers. You can use your browser to find and connect to a variety of blogs and discussion boards in your areas of interest. And you can find audio and video webcasts throughout the Web. If you can't figure it out, ask one of your students to help you get started.

HOW TO . . . USE INSTANT MESSAGING
IN THE CLASSROOM

You need: A computer with Internet access; instant messaging software; instant messaging account.

You get: Many new possibilities for integrating technology into teaching and learning.

1. **Learn to use instant messaging.** Download IM software from the Internet (AOL Instant messenger at www.aim.com, MSN Messenger at messenger.msn.com, Yahoo Messenger at messenger.yahoo.com, or iChat at www.apple.com/ichat/download). While you are there, sign up for an account—in most cases an account is free. Find a friend or co-worker on the same IM system, and correspond with them. Set up a list of people you know, called on AOL a Buddy List, so that you will know when each one is connected and available. Use IM to replace email messages or telephone conversations with these people. If you need help figuring this out, it is likely that some of your students would be more than willing to get you online and conversing.
2. **Work IM into a curriculum assignment.** Find an opportunity to require students to use instant messaging in their work: a group project that requires out-of-class online collaboration; a pen-pal exchange with another group of students far away; a round-robin story carried out over IM.
3. **Invite your students to use IM to contact you.** Ask students to put you on their Buddy List. Encourage them to communicate their homework questions to you whenever they see that your are online and available on IM outside of school hours.

■ ■ ■ ■ ■ ■ ■ ■ ■ ■

HOW TO . . . USE DISCUSSION BOARDS
IN THE CLASSROOM

You need: A computer with Internet access; access to a discussion board, bulletin board, or blog.

You get: Many new possibilities for integrating technology into teaching and learning.

1. **Learn to use online discussion.** Locate a discussion board you can use, perhaps on the web site of a professional organization to which you belong, or on your school or district web site, or one of the blog sites mentioned in the chapter. Read some messages, respond to a few, and otherwise enter into the conversation. Take the time to observe the tone of the conversation before adding your ideas.
2. **Work online discussion into a curriculum assignment.** Find an opportunity to require students to use online discussion in their work: a homework assignment that requires the posting of student responses or findings; a discussion that begins in the

classroom and is extended online for several additional days; a small-group collaborative assignment to be carried out in the evenings and weekends.

3. **Locate discussion-board software you can use.** Talk with your school or district computer coordinator to see what systems might already be set up. If your system licenses Blackboard or Web CT or FirstClass, you may use these for your discussions. If not, you can set up your own discussion on Yahoo Groups at http://groups.yahoo .com, or on some of the blog sites mentioned in this chapter.

■ ■ ■ ■ ■ ■ ■ ■ ■ ■

ONE-TO-ONE COMPUTING

In Chapter 1, we discussed the growing trend toward laptop computers for teachers and students. We considered the reality of high school and college students bringing their computers to the classroom and lecture hall. This development among students is serving as a strong force to bring technology into the classroom. But not everyone sees this as a necessarily positive movement.

At the Institut für Wissenmedien* at the University of Tübingen in Germany, when this idea was broached among a group of teachers and researchers, most immediately praised this new trend. How wonderful to have immediate wireless information access from your seat in the lecture hall or from your desk in the classroom. But a few of the more reflective teachers wondered aloud about the educational value of this trend. What happens, they asked, to the ability of the teacher to capture students' attention in the lecture hall, or to control the nature of learning in the classroom? What happens to the authority of the teacher when students have access to information that might contradict the teacher's pronouncements? Are we sure we want this to happen? Are teachers ready for this? Should they be?

These are good questions. Picture your classroom with each student armed with a connected laptop, with which they can access the Internet, find answers, raise questions, watch movies, and IM with their friends, whenever they want. The implications of one-to-one computing for our profession are profound.

You may be aware of the initiative in the state of Maine, where every student in the seventh grade gets a laptop computer as a matter of course. And so do their teachers. To follow up on this report, I asked Larry Frazier, the director of technology in one of those Maine school districts, to summarize what difference it has made to his schools. Larry works in Yarmouth, a small town near the coast in southern Maine. Larry reports:

> Over the last 15 years, Yarmouth's vision of technology has grown from using technology as a tool to using technology to do things we've never been able to do before. Yarmouth has long had an extensive staff development program consisting of summer courses, before and after school workshops, release days, and "just in time" sessions. We created

---

*I didn't know what *Institut für Wissenmedien* meant, but at the time I was connected wirelessly from my laptop at the dining room table, and so I could call up the online translator that told me this was the Institute for Knowledge Media. I could also connect to their web site at www.iwm-kmrc.de and learn (from the English version of their site) that they call themselves the Knowledge Media Research Center.

computer labs in every school and established a 3:1 student-to-computer ratio. The results were dramatic, but not transformational. Teacher newsletters began to rival commercial ventures, and incredible slide shows were created for parents and school boards. Students learned to do their work using technology, but their work did not change much. Papers were written by high school students and, though they were very well researched using the Internet and they looked very professional, much of the student work remained simply word processing. More and more teachers began to use technology in new and exciting ways with their students, but learning and teaching didn't change as much as I had hoped it would.

Then, in the fall of 2002, the Maine Learning Technology Initiative provided Apple iBooks to all seventh grade students and teachers in Maine. In September 2003, the program was extended to cover eighth graders as well. All of a sudden, technology was available to students and staff 24 hours a day, seven days a week. Everything changed. With continuing staff development from the state and local districts, more and more teachers began to realize that technology could transform teaching and learning. Providing information to students who had the entire world of knowledge at their fingertips was no longer the role of a teacher in the 21st century. Instead of fighting the future, they embraced it. No matter where I go, no matter which classroom, I see teachers and students exploring new ways to use technology. A science class may be experimenting with recording data on Pasco probes, downloading the information into their iBooks, and evaluating the data graphs. A math class might be exploring interactive web sites to illustrate a concept. A language arts class may be taking digital photos to illustrate their poetry. A social studies class might be video taping commercials for their American colony in the 1770's to post on their classroom web site.

Having 1:1 technology available all the time and in the classroom learning environment has changed the integration of technology into instruction from incremental to transformational. We are seeing the beginning of a revolution in teaching and learning, and I'm pleased that Maine has been a leader in this movement.

So, we have two points of view from either side of the Atlantic as food for thought. Sooner or later, this laptop issue will raise its head (or its cover) in your classroom, whether through the natural trend of students bringing their own computers, or from a public policy initiative. Either way, one-to-one computing will change how our students learn, and how we teach.

HOW TO . . . PREPARE YOUR CLASSROOM FOR ONE-TO-ONE COMPUTING

You need: The potential for your students to bring laptops with them into your classroom.
You get: Ways to use this one-to-one capability to enhance learning.

1. **Set up wireless access.** Talk with your school's computer coordinator about putting a wireless access point into your classroom. This enables students with wireless laptops to connect to the school network and to the Internet. Such an access point

requires a single Ethernet connection and a small $150 device, but enables the entire class to access the Web simultaneously through their laptops.

2. **Prepare yourself for inattention.** A lesson delivered to a class full of laptop-armed students will not be the same as a standard lesson. Think through how you will react to faces that will move back and forth between looking and you and looking at the computer display.

3. **Put your outline online.** To keep students with you, and to discourage online wandering, put the outline of your lesson online as a word-processing document, and give students time to connect to it at the beginning of your work. They will find this very useful for taking notes and responding to the questions that arise in the lesson. You might even require students to submit these notes at the end of the lesson.

4. **Integrate online research into your lesson.** Think of how you can capitalize on the newfound ability for each student to compute and connect. Pose questions in the lesson that call for a quick bit of Internet research, or for some mathematical analysis with a spreadsheet.

■ ■ ■ ■ ■ ■ ■ ■ ■ ■

LEARNING AND WORKING ENVIRONMENTS

As the load increased, you could hear the strain on the six-horsepower electric motor. But its speed never varied—it adjusted itself automatically to acquire more power from the source. The variations in load, and the measurements of speed, temperature, voltage, amperage, and resistance all displayed themselves in real time, graphically and numerically, on the computer monitor. In this testing lab, not a scrap of paper could be seen—all of the recording of data, all of the instructions, were online. Not a pencil, not a pocket protector could be found on any of the technicians.

"Napoleon? I think he was King of Italy back in the 1600s. Let me find out . . ." said one sixth-grader to another as she entered some search terms into the online history index. "No, he was French," explained a classmate, "and we are supposed to compare him with Thomas Jefferson, who lived in the 1800s. Let me send you this picture of Jefferson over the instant messenger, so we can put it up next to your picture of Napoleon. . . . It says here he was born in Corsica, not in France . . ." Neither paper nor pencil nor boring lecture will prevent these students from learning their world history.

These two scenes, and many others like them that I have witnessed recently in schools and factories, portend a sea-change in the nature of the environments in which we work and learn. Field trips to labs, offices, assembly plants, schools, and colleges over the last few months show that the tools we use and the methods we apply to get our work done are far different from even five years ago. What is the nature of this environmental change? How will it change the nature of our classrooms? And what should we do to prepare our students for it?

From Paper and Pencil, to Screen and Mouse

The most evident change is in the nature of our reading and writing. We read much less form paper, and much more from the computer screen these days, both at work and at school. That's because paper documents are much more difficult and expensive to produce, store, index, distribute, and retrieve than computer documents. And they are not nearly as useful—engine speed data written on paper cannot talk to temperature data and graph itself in real time. Nor can paper pictures or proclamations of world leaders be found and sorted and shared and compared as efficiently as digital documents.

From the Classroom to the Laboratory

In my trips to leading-edge schools, I saw students at work in libraries, labs, and workrooms in small groups. I seldom saw large groups in classrooms at desks in their chairs lined up with the teacher at the front. In fact, the learning environment at these schools is growing more and more to resemble the working environment, which seldom organizes itself in class-sized groupings in large rooms.

From the Chalkboard to the Computer Display

Not once did I see, in either schoolroom or workplace, the use of a chalkboard to explain an idea or work out a problem. The math teacher instead used an equation editor on her laptop displayed on the wall of the classroom (on a screen that covered up the old chalkboard), while in the electric factory the data from the motors was displayed on a large monitor for all to see and use. The computer screen has the advantage of being dynamic, unlimited and adjustable in size, faster to write on, savable, and not nearly as dusty as a chalkboard.

From Books and Libraries to Online Documents and Search Engines

Perhaps somewhere in the school library the sixth-graders might have found a picture of Napoleon, and perhaps the text of one of his speeches. But this task would have taken them half the class period, and their findings would be difficult to compare and record. And the recent research on variable reluctance electric motors is not published on paper in the library—the workers have no choice but to consult the documents they need through the World Wide Web.

From the School to Anywhere

Did the small group of sixth-graders need to be at school to do their social studies assignment? Could they have been in the town library, at the coffee shop, or at home? Go back and read the scene above, and consider where it might have taken place, and whether or not they all need to be in the same room. (By the way, the electric motor experiment requires several days of continuous running. The temperature data is saved automatically to the hard disk of a computer that is connected to the Web and thus accessible to the factory worker from his computer at home, twenty-four hours a day.)

From Defined Hours to Anytime

History need not be learned exclusively between the hours of 1:17 and 2:05 P.M. Nor need the motor restrict its running to the nine to five schedule of the factory. New technologies allow more flexibility in when the work gets done. Because the assignments, the documents, the research, and the data are accessible from anywhere, they are also accessible at any time by the students or the workers. Even discussions with others can take place asynchronously. This flexibility changes the way we think about time and work and schedules, and how we manage our time.

From Professor to Tutor

In light of these other shifts, there is less reason or opportunity for a teacher to stand and profess, or for the foreman to address all the workers as a group. And so we search in vain in the leading-edge schools and factories to find a classic delivering-of-information session. Instead we find teachers and supervisors preparing materials, setting up workspaces and assignments, tutoring and advising in small groups, and measuring the results.

From Listeners to Actors

If most of what you need to know and the tools you need to do your work are available online, there is little reason to sit and listen. Students spend more time working, researching, reading, writing, building, investigating, and experimenting than they do listening to the teacher and taking notes. In fact, their daily life in school is more like the office or lab worker than the student of old.

From One-Way to Interactive

In the modern school, as in the modern workplace, we see an equivalence in the amount of communication that passes between teacher and student—the student provides as much information to the teacher as the teacher provides to the student. This two-way equal interactivity takes place in person, online, in writing, by talking, and through presentations. In effect it means just as much work for the teacher, but more for the students, and the net result is an overall increase in the amount of communication between them.

From Pyramid to Web

We may think of the shape of education in these cutting-edge schools, and the relationships among the parties, as being more like a spider web, with multiple connections among the teacher and students, in contrast to a pyramid with the teacher at the top and students at the bottom.

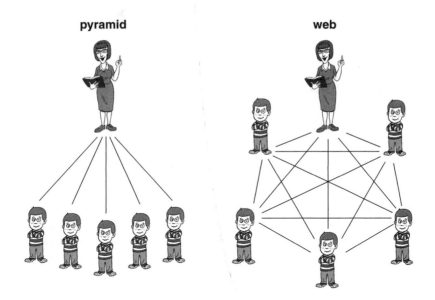

From Oral to Written

Much of the information in the traditional classroom has been delivered by word of mouth, as it has been for centuries. But with the invention of writing 3,000 years ago, the printing press 500 years ago, the word processor 25 years ago, and the World Wide Web 15 years ago, more and more of us are committing our ideas to written form. It is very easy today for a teacher, even in the elementary grades, to provide to students written, visual, and video versions of what was formerly spoken. These versions are savable, transmittable, searchable, and always available, as oral versions are not. We see the same trend in the business world: email (written) is rapidly displacing the telephone (oral) as the preferred means of communication.

From 90 to 30

In both schools and workplaces, the length of continuous time devoted to a single activity is decreasing. Where the typical lecture or lesson might have averaged in the old days 60 to 90 minutes, today's workers and students are more likely to devote shorter chunks of time, averaging 30 to 50 minutes, to the various aspects of the many projects they are working on.

From Final Exam to Multi Mini Projects

Workers in today's and tomorrow's schools and businesses produce many more small products, on which they are evaluated frequently, rather than waiting for the end of the year or the term for a single massive measurement of progress. This fits in with the increased level and frequency of communication between teacher and student that is engendered by digital technologies, and with the natural division of work and learning tasks into smaller chunks.

Research in both management and in education has shown that more frequent evaluation produces better results.

From Static to Dynamic

The book is, by its nature, a static medium: once printed, its text and images are fixed and cumbersome to modify and republish. Digital media, on which schools and factories depend more and more, can animate, move, change, and update themselves automatically. They can respond to the user's clicks and questions and adjustment of parameters. From the graphs produced in real time at the electric motor plant, to the interactive graphing calculator, to the juxtaposition of the faces of Napoleon and Jefferson, we expect our materials to be dynamic and interactive.

If the world of work and the world of learning are both moving in these directions, what are the implications for your classroom, or for your course? How might you change its content or methods or assignments or schedule to better fit the possibilities and prerequisites that your students will face in their lifetimes?

HOW TO . . . ANALYZE YOUR CLASSROOM AS A DIGITAL LEARNING ENVIRONMENT

You need: The text of this chapter, the rating scale shown below, and a chance to reflect on the way things are done in your classroom.

You get: An analysis of the extent of the digital learning environment in your classroom.

Indicate where your classroom stands today on the continuum for each element.

For written work, we use mostly . . .
        Pencil and paper ├───────────────┤ **Keyboard and mouse**

Furniture is arranged . . .
        Classroom-style ├───────────────┤ **Laboratory-style**

Demonstrations are conducted mostly . . .
        At the chalkboard ├───────────────┤ **On the computer display**

We find information mostly from . . .
        Books and libraries ├───────────────┤ **Online sources**

Students can do their assignments mostly . . .
        In school ├───────────────┤ **No matter where they are**

Students can do most of their learning . . .
        During school hours ├───────────────┤ **At any time**

The teacher spends most of his or her time . . .
        Professing ├───────────────┤ **Tutoring**

Students spend most of their classroom time . . .

Listening ├────────────────────────┤ **Working and investigating**

Communication is mostly . . .

**One-way teacher
to student** ├────────────────────────┤ **Fully interactive**

Interaction between teacher and students is more like . . .

A pyramid ├────────────────────────┤ **A web**

Verbal interaction is mostly . . .

Oral ├────────────────────────┤ **Written**

The average time of an activity is closer to . . .

90 minutes ├────────────────────────┤ **30 minutes**

Evaluation is based mostly on . . .

A final exam ├────────────────────────┤ **Several projects**

Most of the learning materials we use are . . .

Static ├────────────────────────┤ **Dynamic**

■ ■ ■ ■ ■ ■ ■ ■ ■

LOOKING AHEAD: TRANSITION TO COLLEGE

Another way to analyze your classroom is in terms of how well it prepares your students for their future. Not all of your students will go on to college, but most of them aspire to it and all of them would benefit from education beyond the twelfth grade. College is a great opportunity to learn new things, to develop independence, and to develop mature social and intellectual powers. If this section were truly aimed at preparing for college, I'd advise you to spend every ounce of your time and energy in the classroom getting your students to:

Read, listen, and observe. Take in the world around them in all its forms. Learn the languages of literature, music, painting, poetry, mathematics, and science, and use them all to absorb the best that our creator and our species have built.

Analyze, think, and reflect. Try to make sense out of what they observe. Learn to use the tools of measurement, comparison, evaluation. Don't be afraid to criticize, or to praise. Talk with others. In the end, always ask what it means, and what it's good for.

Play, experiment, and create. The best way to learn is to play with ideas, facts, objects, and other people. Develop unguided play into careful experimentation (but don't lose the playful spirit). Provide many opportunities for them to create their own contributions.

Students who do more of these things have a better chance of getting into the college of their choice, and of taking the most advantage of what they find in the academy. They are also more likely to be happy and fulfilled people. If your classroom and your students' lives focus on these tasks, they'll score better on the SAT, and school will be a good place.

But this book is not about happiness or college entrance. It's about how to use technology in teaching, which in colleges as well as K–12 schools is a quickly changing subject. This section looks at how students use technology in college, and from that observation develops some advice for using technology in the K–12 classroom.

What Students Do

When they get to college, most students spend more time with their computer than they did at home. And mostly they read, listen, and observe (see above). But only a small proportion of what they are looking at comes from their studies. The chief use of computers by students at college is email and instant messaging—they use their computer, and the fine, high-speed, always-and-everywhere accessible Internet provided by the college, to communicate with other people. In writing. Yes, they communicate with their teachers, but mostly they communicate with their classmates, friends, and family. And they do it all the time, from the laptops they bring to their dormitories, from the public access stations in the hallways and libraries, and even from the computers in my classroom (even while I am teaching). The college culture is one of constant communication. This is good. They are writing. They are sharing ideas with others. They are solving problems and asking questions. They are creating community.

Most students seem to need no special training to use email and instant messaging, but for those without computers at home you may need to make sure that this basic computing skill is developed in your classroom. Not just writing the messages, but also using email address books and understanding how email and IM work. If your school does not provide email for your students, get together with other teachers and request this service—it is not expensive, and can be controlled for internal use only, with software such as FirstClass. If your school blocks instant messaging, ask them to unblock it for the computers in your classroom.

Then develop some curriculum assignments that employ messaging between students to investigate issues and solve problems. This can be as simple as assigning a difficult math problem to a small group of students, and asking them to solve it online, by sharing their results over email and IM. Or it can be as complex as a webquest (see Chapter 7) that sends the group off to the Web in search of data on the disappearance of wolves in the northwest, which they share (in writing) online, then produce a group report. Such assignments mimic the ways they'll be using technology in college. Ask them to save all their emails from these assignments, and send them to you for evaluation. By making messaging a serious academic pursuit, you not only prepare them for college but enhance the subject matter.

The Tools They Use

Beyond messaging software, the college student's next most popular tool is the Web browser. They use this, as you might suspect, to read and observe the movie listings, sports scores, and daily news, and to listen to music. But they also use it to access the resources of the college library, to look up their assignments in their courses, sign up for seminars, and receive their grades. Most colleges have put most of their internal communication on the

Web, accessible by a Web browser. This includes academic as well as administrative functions. At many universities, there are no more paper forms—the only way now for a student to enroll in a course is to fill out a form on the Web. When they do, they are automatically linked to the syllabus and all the other information the professor has posted on the course web site. And the professor is automatically linked to all her students—one click of a button sends them all an email, or puts an assignment into their in-box, or returns comments on their writing.

As a K–12 teacher, consider ways to get your students using the Web browser for serious academic and administrative functions in the classroom. The webquest, as mentioned above and covered in more depth in Chapter 7, sets them off on a Web adventure that you guide with provocative questions and suitable sites. Encourage your school to do its attendance, lunch count, and other sign-ups on the Web. Post your worksheets, assignments, readings, calendars, and other class materials on the Web, on your own site or your school's site. Make students use the browser to get what they need, and you'll be helping them prepare for college.

Deeper Thoughts

College is supposed to get students beyond simple observation and into complex analysis and deep thinking. And more and more of this kind of work is accomplished with a computer at hand. As they study a poem in English 203, college students use special online indices to locate obscure but fascinating interpretations and criticisms. As they explore physics they create complex simulations of interplanetary events with the Interactive Physics software program. In advanced math they develop graphical analyses with MatLab. Or they use a spreadsheet in history to track population changes over time and see if the changes fit predictable patterns. The computer tools enable students to analyze in ways previously impossible, and their professors force them to think through and explain the meaning of their results.

Most of these same analytical tools, or junior versions of them, are available for K–12 students. Use them in your assignments. Try to have at least one assignment a week that causes students to apply an analytical software tool, such as an index, a spreadsheet, or a simulation. These can work well in just about every subject area, including art. (I have watched middle-school students who were using Photoshop to quantify the amount and distribution of color in the paintings of the old masters.) Using analytical tools for curriculum assignments makes sense now and for their future.

Telling Stories

In a good college, students will be asked to tell lots of stories, from a written explanation of the supernatural in *Macbeth,* to a visual presentation of a fungal growth experiment, to a 4-minute dramatic film, to an equation-laden annotated proof of a topological theorem. Even if they are not required to do so, virtually all of them will prepare these creative works on a computer. The computer is their chief platform for experimentation, creation, and presentation. When my classroom is not being used for a course, it is full of students using our computers to prepare projects and presentations for their other classes.

To prepare them for this, consider requiring one assignment in each unit to be created and presented on a computer. It can be a slide show for science done with PowerPoint, or a quantitative graphic for history prepared with Excel, or an illustrated report for English written in Word, or a short health education video composed in iMovie, or a web page on Pythagoras assembled in Dreamweaver. With careful structuring on your part and a clear rubric for evaluations, these multimedia projects can allow students to tell their stories in a manner fitted to their future. (More information on this aspect of computing can be found in Chapter 13 in the section on Evaluating Multimedia Projects.)

The College Experience

Students still linger in lecture halls, combine compounds in chemistry labs, and surmise in seminar rooms. But more and more of the college students' work is accomplished with the help of the computer and the network it's connected to. By arranging your classroom and curriculum to prepare them for this world, you can at the same time create a livelier K–12 learning experience.

HOW TO . . . PREPARE YOUR STUDENTS FOR THE FUTURE IN TODAY'S CLASSROOM

You need: A classroom with at least one computer and a good Internet connection.

You get: A classroom environment that prepares students for college or work.

Here are some practical ideas for making your classroom into a properly preparative environment.

- Make sure that email and instant messaging are available to all students.
- Develop some curriculum assignments that employ messaging between students to investigate issues and solve problems.
- Get your students using the web browser for serious academic and administrative functions in the classroom.
- Send students off on a webquest that you guide with provocative questions and suitable sites.
- Encourage your school to do its attendance, lunch count, and other sign-ups on the Web.
- Post your worksheets, assignments, readings, calendars, and other class materials on the Web, either on your own site or the school's site.
- Create at least one assignment a week that causes students to apply an analytical software tool, such as an index, a spreadsheet, or a simulation.
- Require one assignment in each unit to be created and presented on a computer.

■ ■ ■ ■ ■ ■ ■ ■ ■ ■

LEARN MORE . . .

About Instant Messaging in the Classroom

www.aim.com

America Online is the most widespread of the instant messaging services.

http://messenger.yahoo.com

This messaging service is free from Yahoo.

www.apple.com/ichat/download

Apple iChat AV works on both platforms and allows text, audio, and video.

About One-to-One Computing

www.state.me.us/mlte

The project site for the Maine Learning Technology Initiative explains the project, gives lots of resources, and gives you some of the research results.

About Online Discussions

www.blogger.com

Here, you will find resources and free blogging tools.

PART II

HOW TO BEGIN

Chapters 4 and 5 show you how to begin setting up your technology, and how to start rethinking the way you teach so as to take full advantage of computers, networks, and the communication skills of your students. It includes a detailed description of a new process for student research, thinking, and publishing: the paperless paper.

CHAPTER FOUR

GETTING STARTED

IN THIS CHAPTER

- **Desktop or Laptop?**
- **Computer Ergonomics**
- **Wireless Networks**
- **Mass Storage**
- **Organizing Your Files**
- **When to Call for Help**
- **Learn More . . .**

This chapter provides practical advice on how to select and set up your own computer, or those in your classroom, so that they are easy to use and well-connected. It covers the choice of whether to get a desktop or laptop, and then shows you how to install it ergonomically. In this chapter you will also learn about wireless networks and the various new storage devices that are becoming more and more necessary in the world of educational multimedia. Finally, you will get some concrete ideas on how to organize your files, and what to do when things stop working.

DESKTOP OR LAPTOP?

You can find them on the train, on the plane, in the backpack, in the library, and in the lecture hall. They're getting smaller and smaller. And more powerful. And less expensive. Half of my students bring theirs to class. You'll find six of them in my house, including the one I'm using to write this chapter. Some teachers, and many students, could not survive the day at school without theirs. Though they cost more, the store sells more of the new book-size models than the old desktop appliances.

It's the invasion of the laptops. This section considers whether or not we should welcome this trend, and whether or not it bodes well for the work of the teacher and the student.

One-to-One Initiatives

Imagine every student in your class with his or her own laptop computer, connected wirelessly to the net, usable both in school and at home. Imagine that the district or the college has provided these at no cost to the student. In many schools, this is not a pipe dream but an accomplished fact. And in many cases, they're not the wealthiest schools. In rural Maine, suburban Virginia, and dozens of other places, a one-to-one initiative is taking hold—that's one computer for each student (and teacher). And in most cases, the "one" is a laptop.

You need no imagination to picture the actual situation today in many colleges and universities, where most of the students arrive at school, and in the classroom, each armed with a laptop, that can connect to the Internet anywhere and at any time through the wireless network. This is the reality on many campuses today. And the trend is spreading quickly as computer prices drop and networks proliferate.

As a teacher, how should you react to this invasion?

Not in My Classroom!

In some schools, students must check their laptops at the door, along with their iPods, MP3 players, cell phones, and PalmPilots. These are considered distractions to the learning process. (Imagine a business that banned its employees from using these devices in the office. How long would it last in the competitive marketplace?) While this restriction is understandable, it's probably not a wise policy for the future. Like the book, pencil, and calculator, which were, in their time, uncomfortable new technologies in the classroom, laptops can contribute to a major leap forward in the possibilities for learning.

Possibilities of Portability

The trick is to channel, co-opt, and control these new devices for the benefit of learning. The teachers in Maine, Virginia, and elsewhere who have faced the onslaught of the computers have learned to harness them for the good of their curriculum and their students. They have invented new assignments that take advantage of an "anywhere, anytime" access to information. They have raised their expectations for the intellectual level of the research their students conduct. They have cooperated with parents to provide computer-based homework assignments.

They have found that the laptop is in fact less intrusive than the desktop computer. Students can use their laptop in the normal, everyday places at the school—the library, the reading corner, the science lab, the gym, and the desk. Computer tasks need no longer restrict themselves to special times, uncomfortable places, or awkward appliances. A computer assignment is no longer something special; it happens every hour.

Connectivity

Laptops used to be difficult to connect to the Internet and to printers. Desktop computers were always more reliable for online work, web browsing, email, research, and printing. But with today's wireless networks, and laptops that automatically connect themselves to the network, laptops are no longer stand-alone devices. My students find their laptops connected wirelessly to the Internet when they are in the college library, the lecture hall, the new dorm, and at the coffee shop on Commonwealth Avenue. For a little over $100, a family can set up a wireless network at home. The connection process on a good laptop today can be, indeed, seamless.

Dollar for Dollar

A desktop computer remains less expensive, dollar for dollar, than a laptop. Today you can purchase a desktop Macintosh, for instance, with a 17-inch display, 1 gHz processor, and 256MB RAM, for about $1,000. The same power in a laptop will cost you over $1,500, a 50 percent premium. The laptop costs more because it must include a battery and charging system that the desktop does not; its display costs more to manufacture, and it's tough to miniaturize all those chips and drives. So the desktop computer is less expensive.

Steal This Laptop!

No one has ever stolen my desktop computer, but I have lost a laptop to a larcenous lout. Laptops beg to be stolen. They are more easily concealed, transported, and sold than their desktop cousins. A school that promotes portability must also study seriously the issue of security. For many students and teachers, caring for a device valuable enough to be a target of thieves is a new experience that may require some forethought and training. The good news is that the schools with the 1-to-1 initiatives have experienced very few losses due to theft.

My Desk? My Lap?

What's best for you? That depends on how you work. If you do most of your computing and connecting from your desk at school, if you have another desktop at home, and if you seldom work in other places, then a desktop may fill the bill for less money. But if you often take work home, work in different places at school, and don't have a computer at home (or at school), then a laptop may allow you more freedom and access than a desktop. If most of your students use laptops, you may find your communication with them easier if you join in their portability. If you like to write from the rocker, or surf from the sofa, you'll find the laptop to your liking.

Dick Tracy Devices

In the comic strips of the 1940s and 1950s, Dick Tracy used a wristwatch to contact headquarters, receive video transmissions, and access the crime databases. What was science fiction back then is the reality of today. The prognosticators point out that the future is in small, wearable devices that connect to the Internet and allow us to communicate or compute from anywhere anytime without a second thought. No desks, no laps, no cables. If they are right, then perhaps the way to prepare yourself for the future is to select the smallest computer you can find.

HOW TO . . . DECIDE BETWEEN DESKTOP OR LAPTOP

You need: An opportunity for deciding between laptop and desktop; this checklist.

You get: An analysis of whether a laptop or a desktop is best for you.

It's not an easy decision, and it depends on how you expect to use your computer. Take this survey to see where you stand on this dilemma. Check off the appropriate box for each item.

	AGREE	DISAGREE
I do computer work mostly at my desk at school, and hardly anywhere else.		
I seldom find myself needing to do computer work at home or in the library.		
There's plenty of extra room on my desk.		
I am willing to pay only the minimum absolutely necessary for a computer.		
Few of my students own or use laptop computers.		
I would never consider taking notes at a meeting on my computer.		
My classroom, office, and home are liable to frequent break-ins.		
I don't expect our school or home will ever install a wireless network.		
I prefer to relegate my computing work to the office, and restrict it from home.		
I already have a computer at school, and another at home that I can use.		

Count the number of checks in the left (Agree) column. Consider your results as follows:

- 0–3 checks on the left: Get a laptop, no question.
- 4–7 checks on the left: A tough decision. Consult your technology friends.
- 8–10 checks on the left: A desktop is probably right for you.

■ ■ ■ ■ ■ ■ ■ ■ ■ ■

COMPUTER ERGONOMICS

Many schools have inquired about the best way to set computers up in a classroom or an office. You'd think it would be easy just to acquire some tables, put the computers on them, and get to work. But the more time you or your students spend with these new technologies, the more important it becomes to set them up so they are easy to use and to learn with.

Ergonomics

The science of how people use tools to do their work is called *ergonomics,* and its application to computers is the subject of considerable research and interesting findings. This section provides a primer on the things you should think about when you set up a computer for your own use, or for your students in a classroom. It's not a course in ergonomics, but it gets you started thinking like an ergonomist. It also considers factors that go beyond ergonomics and are particularly relevant in schools.

User-Centric Design

No single method of setting up a computer will work well for everyone in all places working on all kinds of tasks. The setup depends on who the user is and what he or she is doing. The design should be based on the needs and activities of this person. Is the user a small child or a hefty adult? How will they use it? What will be the pattern of their activities? Will they be working alone for long stretches, or in small groups for quick researches? Will they be following the teacher's instructions from a large screen, or working from papers on the desk? The answers to these questions should determine the nature of the setup. This is called *user-centric design.* The best way to set up a computer is to determine first the needs and activities of the user, and then to follow the principles of ergonomic design.

Where to Put the Computer?

A desktop computer needs to be placed carefully if it is to be easy and comfortable to use. The best placement is as close to the normal work area as possible—isolating computers in out-of-the-way places is not wise. If the computer will be used by a student who must be able to see a projection screen or teacher, place it so that the computer's display and the screen or teacher are in the same field of view. Avoid windows behind your back—the light from the window will reflect from the display and make it difficult to read. Better to turn things around so that you look out of the window as you work. Although a laptop can be moved at will, most often we set up a desk area for it, so the same guidelines should apply to the location of its desk.

How High Should the Desk Be?

Most computers are placed on desks that are too high for comfortable use. The ideal computer desk height for an average-sized adult is about 27 inches from the floor to the top of the desk, even lower for children. But most desks, designed for writing and not for computing, are 30 or 31 inches high. And indeed, 3 inches makes a big difference, especially when you are typing or doing close graphics work with the mouse. A table that's too high cramps your arms, strains your fingers, and stretches your back. You can find lower tables and desks specially designed for computers, or you can saw a few inches off the legs of your current furniture to reach the ideal height. Even better, if you are buying new furniture, look into tables with adjustable height, and set them to fit the size of the user.

You'll know the table is at the right height for you if you can sit on a straight chair, with your feet flat on the floor, with the top of the table about two inches above your knees. This means that desks with drawers under the computer will not work well—the drawers create too much distance between your knees and the keyboard. The same height guidelines apply to tables used for laptops.

How Deep Should the Desk Be?

In most cases, you want the keyboard a few inches back from the front of the table or desk, and the display about a foot behind the keyboard. This calls for a back to front distance of at least 28 inches if you are using a desktop computer with a flat screen display, and at least 32 inches for a full-size monitor. You can get away with less—perhaps two feet—for a laptop. Using a standard 24-inch-deep table will put the keyboard and display too close to you for healthy typing and viewing.

How Wide Should the Space Be?

It's not just the computer, monitor, and keyboard that are on the table—don't forget the mouse, the mouse pad, the instruction book, the scanner, the assignment sheet, and even the backpack. In most education settings, these peripheral items are an essential part of the context of computing. You must allow room for them. This calls for a work area wide enough to accommodate the array of articles for each user. If a typical computer is 20 inches wide, a mouse pad 10 inches, an assignment sheet 8 inches, and a book 7, you'll need at least 45 inches of horizontal space for each user to be fully comfortable. A 4-foot-wide work area is ideal, a 3-foot space is cramped, and anything less is difficult to work in.

Choosing Chairs

How you sit is key to health and comfort while computing. Sitting upright but not arched, with your feet flat on the floor and your knees at a 90-degree angle, is about right for most people. To achieve this position, you will, in most cases, need to adjust your chair up or down, or find a fixed chair that's the right height for you. A slight recline, with your back against the chair, is acceptable, but it works better if the chair has lumbar support and you don't lean back too far. And a chair with wheels lets you move to a position that's easy to work from.

How's the View?

The key to effective work, a natural neck, and easy eyes is a computer display that's in the right place. For most people, it works best when it is about 20 inches from your nose and a bit lower than your face. A level line taken from the tip of your nose should hit the top of the display. This is a bit lower than you might think, but research has proven it to be the easiest to work with. The best way to achieve the ideal height and distance is with a flat screen on an adjustable stand. Lacking that amenity, you may have to devise other ways to get the monitor where it belongs.

In most cases, stacking the monitor on top of the computer on a standard table puts it much too high for comfortable use—you'll find yourself leaning your head back and looking up at the screen. And you'll develop a sore neck and an achy back. Put the computer next to the monitor, or under the table, and put a book or two under the monitor.

Adjust the brightness and resolution of the display so that standard text is easy to read. Make sure there are no windows or bright lights behind you. But don't work in a dark room—that creates too much contrast.

Additional Computer Ergonomics Information

Experts in health and industrial science have conducted research on computer ergonomics that can inform the way you set up your computer. We've covered the basics here, but you can learn more at the following sites.

- The Centers for Disease Control's web site section on Computer Workstation Ergonomics: www.cdc.gov/od/ohs/Ergonomics/compergo.htm
- The Occupational Safety & Health Administration's web site section on Computer Workstations: www.osha.gov/SLTC/computerworkstations_ecat/
- The Indiana University Model Classroom Description for a school computer lab: www.indiana.edu/~classrms/ccmodel5.html

HOW TO . . . CONDUCT AN ERGONOMIC AUDIT OF YOUR COMPUTER SETUP

You need: The following checklist.

You get: A specific analysis of the ergonomics of your computer setup.

Circle the items in the two columns on the right that best represent your situation.

My computer is located . . .	In the places where I spend most of my time and do most of my work.	In a room or lab separate from my normal everyday work areas.
My keyboard is on a table or desk that is . . .	About 27" off the floor, lower for a child or short person.	More than 27" off the floor.
My computer table or desktop is . . .	28" deep or more.	27" deep or less.
When I sit at the computer, my knees . . .	Are at a 90-degree angle with room under the table or desk.	Rub against the bottom of the desk or table.

My clear work area around the computer is . . .	48" wide or more.	Less than 48" wide.
The chair at my computer table . . .	Is adjustable and allows me to sit square and comfortably.	Is of fixed height, and forces my knees or elbows into something other than a 90-degree angle.
My computer display . . .	Is about 20" from my nose.	Is closer or further than 20" from my nose.
My computer display . . .	Is adjustable as to height, tilt, and angle.	Is fixed right where it is and difficult to move.
When I look at the center of my computer screen, my head is tilted . . .	Down just slightly.	Straight across or up toward the screen.
The windows or other light sources are . . .	To the side or in front of me.	Behind me.

Analysis: If you circled the far right column . . .

- 0–3 times: Your ergonomics are not bad, and need only a little adjustment.
- 4–6 times: You should take some time to adjust your setup for better ergonomics.
- 7–9 times: You should completely rethink the location and setup of your computer.

■ ■ ■ ■ ■ ■ ■ ■ ■ ■

WIRELESS NETWORKS

I hadn't visited Espresso Royale in six months. The old coffee shop across from the chapel and next to the CVS exuded the same pungent odors; behind the counter the same orange-haired clerks sported the same painful jewelry; and the same menu of coffees listed various Italian monikers. But something was different. Half the people at the tables were working on their laptop computers. Succumbing to the social pressure, I opened my PowerBook. Up came a message: Welcome to Espresso Royale. Today's specials include Lemon Chai and Latte Americano. *Espresso Royale had gone online. Its wireless network was available to all sippers, at no cost. I checked my email and confirmed my flight reservations.*

Montparnasse station hosts a sea of swarming commuters on their way in and out of Paris. At all hours of the day and night French men and women wend their way to the tracks and claim their chairs in the waiting rooms. With two hours to wait I found a seat, opened my computer, and saw the little AirPort icon flash on. I connected to the wireless network, and was asked to choose the

form of payment for my access. The minimum charge was five Euros for 20 min-
utes. My two hours online would cost me $35. Though expensive, the network
was fast and responsive, and enabled me to work with email, instant messenger,
and the Internet, as if I were in my office.

The speaker was boring. He was on slide number 23 of 56 of his presentation,
which used PowerPoint-lessly to restate the obvious. But like many of the oth-
ers in the room who had discovered it, I was using the wireless network to
research and write a chapter of this book, answer my mail, and carry on instant
message conversations with my daughter and one of my students. The confer-
ence center charged $9.95 extra per day for unlimited use of the network from
your room or anywhere in the center. Despite the deadly presenter, my morning
turned out to be quite productive.

These are all true events of the past month that could not have occurred a short while ago.
A new set of technologies that allow us to connect to the Internet no matter where we are
are fast finding their way into our coffee shops, public places, and hotels. And these wireless networks are appearing in our schools and colleges as well. My daughter tells me that
she can connect from anywhere in the entire library complex at her university, and my
friends in Maine tell me that more than half the K–12 schools offer the service. This section explains how wireless networks work, and how they can be useful in teaching and
learning.

Wireless What?

It's not like cell phones, it's not like walkie-talkies. The new technologies that enable the
kind of access described above are not a form of telephony or two-way radio. They are simply a way to replace the familiar Ethernet cable with a radio connection to your local area
network. The cable is replaced by a radio transmitter in the building and a radio receiver in
your computer. (Actually, both radios can transmit as well as receive.) Instead of traveling
down the copper conductors in the cable, the signals travel over the radio waves from your
computer to the local network.

   If you move too far away, and the radio signal gets too weak, you can no longer browse
the Web or get your email. Depending on the power of the transmitter and the quality of your
receiver and the number of obstacles between them, you will start to lose your connection
when you are perhaps 150 feet apart—the length of my back yard. And what you are connected to is the same local area network you'd have connected to with the cable. So the wireless networks that we found at the coffee shop and the conference center are local affairs,
short extensions of Espresso Royale's and the hotel's wired networks. This is the fastest-
growing of the many wireless technologies proliferating around us today, and is designed
especially for connecting computers. (Other wireless networks include the familiar cell-
phone networks, the portable phone in your home, and the newer BlueTooth system. Blue-
Tooth uses a different kind of radio wave, and is designed for very short distances, such as
between your cell phone and your earphone, for instance.)

The networks in the examples above all use the same radio frequency and the same method of encoding the data that travels along it. No matter what brand of computer, or operating system, or wireless transmitter is used, they all talk the same language, one that was designed and agreed upon by a committee of engineers from a wide variety of organizations and companies. This international standard is called 802.11, so named by the engineers who agreed on it. (Apparently they agreed previously on 801 other things before getting to this one.) So I can use my Apple laptop in my brother-in-law's home network (based on Cisco transmitters) while he uses his Dell computer running Windows.

Mostly Laptops

Seldom do we see desktop computers using a wireless network. Most of them were installed when wired networks were the only possibility, and most never move. So wireless offers little advantage. But the phenomenal growth of laptop computers has promoted portability and created a consistent demand for connectivity. Many laptops arrive from the factory with the wireless transmitter and receiver and software built in; for others it can be added with an accessory card that costs less than $100.

The wireless laptop provides the worker or the student with the freedom to research, communicate, create, or learn no matter where: in the library, the conference room, the classroom, the office, the cafeteria, or the sports field. It takes computing out of the lab and off the desk, and allows online work to be done wherever it's needed. It's no wonder that this sector of the computing industry is enjoying steady growth, and that more and more people and organizations are taking advantage of it.

Setting Up

For the simplest wireless network, all you need is a wireless laptop and a base station. The base station is a small transmitter-receiver, about the size of a ham sandwich, that you connect to your existing Ethernet network (or, in some cases, to your telephone line). Then fire up your laptop, connect to the base station, and you're on. You may need to do some configuring of network settings, but not much more. The least-expensive base stations cost about $100 and can handle up to 20 users up to 150 feet away. You'd need a more powerful base station, or a number of small ones, to equip an entire school.

Security

From my living room, my laptop picks up my neighbor's wireless network across the street. I can see his network in the list (it's called CasaFaccenda), but I am unable to connect, because Ron has protected it with a password. Most wireless networks are secured in this way from unwanted visitors piggybacking on your infrastructure. And some folks go even further, encrypting the data that's sent over the radio waves from the laptop to the LAN. On an encrypted network, my name would go over the waves as *hu (%rb@w or some other combination of symbols that would thwart anyone tuning in to the transmissions between my laptop and the base station.

Wireless Schools

Teachers and students in schools that have installed wireless networks tell me that it causes a change in the overall teaching and learning environment. People carry their laptops about with them all day, connecting when and from where they need to. The computer, its learning tools, its working tools, and the resources it can connect to, are available all day in all the places people might be. Students find this to be a natural extension of the communication technologies they have grown up with since birth, and quickly adapt the form of their learning to take full advantage of the constant connection. Teachers find they can rely on a library in every lap as they are teaching, and thus create more challenging assignments and class discussions that incorporate more sophisticated research and use of data. School leaders find that the learning environment seems different and more serious since the advent of the laptops with wireless access.

Wireless Warnings

But not everyone likes this new environment. Some teachers do not like to be challenged by a student who browses on the Web to a different interpretation of the topic, and poses a question in the middle of her lecture. Some administrators don't trust that all the power of the computer and the network, when freed through wireless, will be put to good use by students. Some policymakers fear that students already spend too much time in front of the boob-tube anyway, and this all-day, all-places access simply exacerbates a negative trend. Some students may be distracted by the breadth and depth of the information and communication capabilities offered by the wireless network, and may not pay full attention to the topic at hand.

But as I watched the students in the coffee shop, and wandered about to see what they were up to, none were playing online games, none were looking at naughty pictures, and none were disturbing the peace. One was reading a site on Chinese economic statistics. Another was writing a paper for English class. In the back corner the young lady was answering her email. As I send off this chapter to the publisher, I'll do it from my laptop through a wireless network at the conference center where I am working or from my sailboat using BlueTooth, or from my front porch while sitting in a rocking chair. The wireless way is winning.

HOW TO . . . SET UP AND CONNECT TO A WIRELESS NETWORK

You need: A computer with wireless capability; a wireless base station (yours or someone else's) connected to the network.

You get: Access to the network from a variety of locations.

1. **Acquire or locate a wireless base station.** (If your school or your local coffee shop provides a base station, you may skip directly to step 4.) If you are setting up your own, you must first purchase the hardware. You will find it at your local computer store as well as at the online boutiques. Best to get one that follows the newest standard.

2. **Install the base station.** Connect it to electric power and to the Ethernet network (or to your dial-up telephone line).

3. Configure the base station. The base station will come with software that you run on your computer to set the parameters of the wireless network. Follow the directions on this software to configure the base station and set its name and password.

4. Connect to the wireless base station. Your wireless-equipped computer will contain software for connecting to a wireless network. Use this software to connect to the base station you just set up.

5. Set your computer to connect to the Internet through the wireless link. Use the network control panel to acquire a TCP/IP connection from the wireless network.

6. Test the connection. Use your web browser or email application to see if you can connect to the Internet. If not, go back to step 4 and try again.

■ ■ ■ ■ ■ ■ ■ ■ ■ ■

MASS STORAGE

Between January and March of 2004, Apple Computer sold 807,000 iPods. An iPod is a pocket-sized device that can store and play thousands of songs saved in a digital music format. Your students know it as an MP3 player, even though the songs are not actually saved in the MP3 format anymore. iPods, and devices like it, are everywhere. Apple alone reports that sales of its device increased 900 percent from 2003 to 2004. The price of the information-storing devices drops precipitously as economies of scale and healthy competition work their magic. What does all this have to do with teaching and technology?

About a year ago, my iPod arrived in the mail. My daughter put a few songs on it for me. The machine worked well, the music sounded good, and it was small and elegant. But listening to music through headphones is not a big part of my lifestyle, so the iPod languished in my backpack. But this all changed on the day I confronted in my lab Phyllis, the frustrated film student.

Phyllis had been at work for hours in the back row, editing her masterpiece on one of our computers. But it was 9:00 P.M., time for me to go home and for the lab to close for the night. "Okay, save your work and get ready to go home," I announced, standing at the front with my backpack in my hand, ready to lock the door and depart. The students dutifully saved their web sites, films, videos, designs, animations, and photo essays to their Zip disks and memory sticks. All except for Phyllis. "It won't save," she lamented. Going over to help, I asked her how big her project was. She checked the file size: 3 gigabytes. This was quite a film she was producing. "What are you trying to save it on?" I asked. "My Zip disk," was her reply. "How much can a Zip disk hold?" I asked in my teacherly way. "I dunno, a hundred megabytes?" offered Phyllis. "Now do you see the problem?" Phyllis began to worry in earnest.

The next day was Saturday, and we expected a group of high-school journalism students to be using the lab, so we had to get her film off that computer and saved somehow. Dividing it up into 30 Zip disks was out of the question. Copying 3 gigabytes to the server would take at least an hour, and Phyllis did not have that much space in her allocation. Leaving it on the hard disk of the computer risked certain erasure by the undisciplined adolescent hordes that would descend on the lab in the morning.

> *Then I remembered the iPod. "Let's try this," and I connected the iPod to the computer. Up popped its icon on the desktop. Under Get Info I saw that it had 4 gigabytes available. I copied Phyllis's documentary to the diminutive iPod. All saved in less than three minutes. Phyllis agreed to acquire her own mass storage device over the weekend, and come back on Monday to retrieve her masterpiece from my iPod.*

Since that day, I have used my iPod regularly to store and back up my work. I haven't listened to a song in a long time. But I have transferred very large files, especially video and multimedia projects and web sites, from computer to computer (and from country to country) on the snappy little device. Once a week or so I copy all my important work files to the iPod so as to maintain a backup copy.

As students and teachers produce more multimedia work, large-scale web projects, and rich presentations, they encounter the need for mass storage, methods for saving and transferring these enormous files. The iPod is but one among many of the modern ways to store large amounts of digital data. Here are some of the others:

Floppy disk. Just about useless these days, given that any student project much bigger than a book report (without pictures) will exceed its 1.4 megabyte capacity. Many of the new computers no longer contain a drive for these disks. And at almost a dollar per megabyte of storage, they are relatively expensive.

Zip disk. These are overgrown floppy disks that hold 250 megabytes, enough for a hefty web site or a short video project. At $25 each, the cost per megabyte is about ten cents. Not every computer comes with a Zip drive but they are easy to add externally.

CD-R. These hold 600 megabytes, can be had for less than a dollar, and more and more computers include drives that read and write these discs. So the cost of storage is about one-tenth of a cent per megabyte. It's better to use CD-R (burn only once) than CD-RW (write and rewrite data) because the latter are not fully compatible across computers and cost more.

USB memory stick. These keychain-sized devices plug into the USB connector on your computer and can hold up to 16 megabytes for $20, a half-gigabyte for around $60. While they would not handle Phyllis's film, they are big enough to store most of the projects a student or teacher might build. And they make transferring files very easy.

Pocket FireWire drives. That's what the iPod is, a small hard drive that connects to the computer through a FireWire cable. My old iPod holds 5 gigabytes, the new ones 15, and at $300 that's two cents per megabyte, less than the USB memory stick. And you can find other pocket drives, without music-playing capability, for even less.

Phyllis the film student returned on Monday, with her new pocket FireWire drive. By now I am sure she is working in Hollywood or on location somewhere in the world, with her mass storage in her pocket. As we move into the multimedia digital age, we all need to consider how to store, transfer, and save our educational files. These technologies and products are developing quickly, and dropping in price, and are becoming more valuable to us every day.

HOW TO . . . DETERMINE THE MASS STORAGE THAT'S BEST FOR YOU

You need: The following table.

You get: A recommendation for the appropriate mass storage to fit your needs.

WHAT YOU SAVE	RECOMMENDED DEVICE	COST	COST PER MEGABYTE
Nothing more than short text documents and spreadsheets.	Floppy disk	$1.00	$1.00
All the above plus digital images, web pages, and PowerPoint presentations.	Zip disk USB Memory CD-R	$10.00 $25.00 $0.50	$0.10 $0.10 $0.00001
Files and presentations for transfer between computers.	USB Memory	$25.00	$1.00
All the above plus short video and audio clips.	CD-R	$0.50	$0.00001
All the above plus longer digital video and audio editing projects.	Pocket FireWire drive	$200.00	$0.0000014

■ ■ ■ ■ ■ ■ ■ ■ ■ ■

ORGANIZING YOUR FILES

A friend received a brand-new computer as a gift, and as I helped him to set it up and get started working with it I noticed that it automatically saved his work into pre-determined places. All of the pages he wrote with the word processor (or exported from Excel or pre-pared with PowerPoint) got saved in a folder called *My Documents;* anything from the MP3 player went by default into *My Music,* photos into *My Pictures,* and video clips into *My Movies.* I never found exactly where his emails got stored, but I suspect that somewhere lurks a folder called *My Mail.*

I predict that after a few weeks, this friend will find hundreds of items in his *My Documents* folder, hundreds in *My Mail,* and a few in *Music* and *Movies.* When he goes to locate the handout he prepared last week for his fourth-period history class, he'll find himself lost in a long list of documents, scrolling slowly in a search for what he needs. There must be a better way to organize the files he will use in his professional and personal life.

Bottles and Cans

Putting all your documents together in one place, your mail in another, and your pictures somewhere else is, for most people, not the best form of organization. Imagine at home, if you put all your bottles in one cupboard, all your cans in another, and all your boxes in a third place. When it came time to spray the ant's nest in the garage, you'd find the can of Raid stored between green beans and the motor oil. When you reached for the shampoo on the way to the bathroom, you'd take care not to grab the olive oil. And to salve the cut on your finger, you might confuse the box of Band-Aids with the package of Post-It notes.

In our homes, most of us store things where they are needed, according to their function: cooking utensils stand together on the kitchen counter, while screwdrivers stay in the garage. And for most of us, this same form of organization should apply to our computers. If we teach a class in history during fourth period, we should place all of its files in a single folder called Fourth Period History. This should store the handouts, the maps, the speeches, and the video clips we use in the course. If a student or a colleague sends us an email with a good suggestion for the course, we'd save it to this same folder. We might create a folder for each course, another folder for our personal hobby, and another for the online course that we are taking.

Organizational Schemes

On my computer you will find a folder called Franklin Institute, and inside it a subfolder for each of my projects, another for my advisees, and one for each committee I am on. You'll also find a folder called Boat Stuff, and another called Allyn & Bacon. When I create or receive a file pertaining to one of these areas, I place it in the appropriate folder. When a folder contains so many items that things become difficult to find, I create subfolders and reorganize the files. When I need to find something, I look in the folder for that topic. The organization of my files reflects the aspects of my work.

Not everyone works this way. One colleague organizes by date: he keeps everything that people send him in his email program, and looks it up by when it was received. So when it's time to find a document on a given subject, he first looks in his date book to see when he last dealt with that topic, and then scrolls his email list to that day, and searches there for the file he needs. Another colleague has a folder for each person she works with, and places all relevant documents into the person's folder.

Saving Gracefully

Few people organize their life and work in terms of Documents, Pictures, Movies, and Mail. These categories may make sense to computer manufacturers and software engineers, but not to teachers and students. So take some time to think through the categories of your occupations, and set up folders (and subfolders as necessary) for each one. Then, when you go to save a document, pay careful attention: don't save in the default folder that the computer suggests automatically; save instead in the place where you are likely to find it again when you need it. And give it a useful filename. Avoid names like *map6.gif* or *history paper.doc* or *IMG_345YG.JPG*. Rename the file, as you save it, to something that will make sense later: *Iraq Map 1967.gif,* or *Babylonian Culture.doc,* or *Grandma at the Tiller.jpg.*

The same goes for email messages and attachments: don't leave them in your email program; save them carefully (the ones that are worth saving), with a useful filename, into the folder for the project to which they pertain. Take some time in class to help your students find a suitable scheme for organizing their digital documents as well.

Finding It

So you saved that map of the Middle East somewhere in the Fourth Period History folder, but can't remember what you named it. But you do recall having found and saved it over winter break. Go to the Fourth Period History folder and click at the top of the window to list the files by date. Scroll down to the dates at the end of December and the beginning of January. There it is, *mideastmap5.gif,* last modified on December 30.

In like manner you can list the files within a folder by name, size (maps and videos and large photos are almost always much bigger than text documents), or file type (e.g., all jpeg images).

A place for everything, and everything in its place.

HOW TO . . . ORGANIZE YOUR FILES SENSIBLY

You need: The following diagram.

You get: A plan for reorganizing your files according to your work.

1. Use this diagram to set up a plan for organizing your files. See the model below for an example of how to organize things hierarchically.

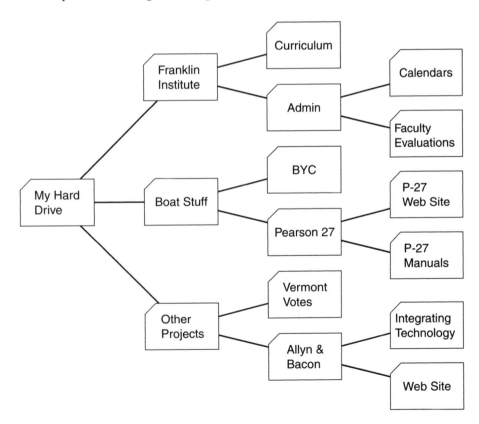

2. Copy the blank diagram, and fill in your own title for each of the folders. Draw in new folders as necessary to best represent the structure of your work.

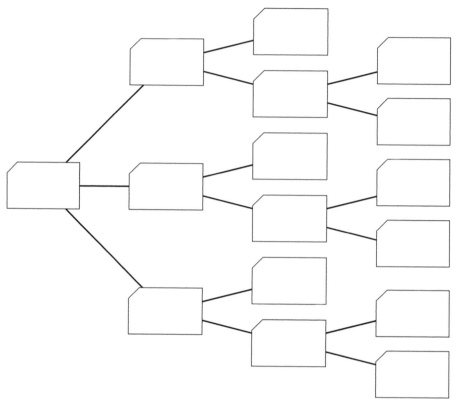

3. With the diagram in front of you, go to the hard drive or C: drive window on your computer. Choose New Folder from the file menu.
4. Name this folder as indicated on the second column of your diagram.
5. Repeat steps 3 and 4 to create the rest of the folders at the first level of your hierarchy.
6. Double-click on these new folders, and within them create the subfolders from the third column of your diagram.
7. Repeat step six to create the third level.
8. Drag the files from your hard drive and drop them into the proper folders.

■ ■ ■ ■ ■ ■ ■ ■ ■ ■

WHEN TO CALL FOR HELP

You're connected to the Internet in your classroom, but you can't send or receive your email.

The computer seems frozen—the mouse pointer will not move on the screen, and pressing keys on the keyboard has no effect.

Everything is happening slowly—the hourglass or watch is always running, clicks do not respond immediately, and windows open with great difficulty.

Nothing happens when you print. And you are sure the printer is full of paper and its light is on.

The computer seems to shut itself off in the middle of your work, for no reason. Sometimes it starts up again, sometimes it doesn't.

For most of us, these kinds of things happen all the time. They form a set of nuisances and frustrations that keep many teachers from using technology as a regular part of classroom work. And most of us do not have an engineer on call, who can come in at a moment's notice to fix things when they go wrong.

Some of these difficulties will require an expert from the computer support team, but many of them you can fix yourself. This section provides a rubric for doing your own troubleshooting, and some advice on when to call for help.

The problems described in the list above are quite different from one another, and yet the general method for solving them is similar. Here is a series of steps that you can follow in your troubleshooting that may lead to a solution and, if followed carefully, will not make things worse.

1. **Check the physical connections.** Unless you have a laptop with a wireless connection, your computer trails several cables and wires, which in a classroom or home office situation are very susceptible to disturbance. A wire that falls out of its socket can cause the screen to freeze, the Internet to disappear, or the display to go black. No matter what kind of symptoms you encounter, your first step should be to check the integrity of the physical environment.

Start with the wire that connects the mouse to the computer or the keyboard. Pull it out and plug it back in firmly. Same for the keyboard cable. Next the cables from the display to the computer: one for the power, the other for the video signal. Then the cables from the computer to the electric power and to the network. Check both ends of each cable. Make sure you hear the Ethernet network cable click itself into place. (It's best not to unplug the power cable without first shutting down your computer, but this may not be possible at times.) Don't forget to check the speaker or headphone connection. In many cases, tightening a loose connection will fix the problem.

2. **Check the system parameters.** No sound? Picture too small or blotchy? No Internet activity? It may not be a hardware but a software problem. Many of the computer's settings can be inadvertently reset or lost, especially when you move the computer to a new location or when it crashes. Here are some settings to check, depending on the problem you have:

Internet. Check your network control panel, to see if it is set to the correct type of connection. On Windows, look under Start, then Settings, then Control Panel, then Internet. On Macintosh OS X it's System Preferences, then Network. First make sure that you are connecting through Ethernet (unless you are on a wireless network). Second, make sure you have a valid IP address. IP stands for Internet Protocol; it may also be listed as TCP/IP. A valid IP address will appear like this: 128.197.190.98. If you see 0.0.0.0, or an address beginning with 169, or nothing at all, you won't be able to use the Internet. Your IP address is invalid. In most places, your IP address is reassigned to you every time you connect to the network, by a server at your Internet service provider. A sure way to get a new (and valid) address is to restart your computer as described below.

Printing. First check your print queue to make sure you haven't got the same document in line to print five times over. On Windows, go to Start, then Settings, then Printers. On Macintosh OS X it's Print Center. Click on the printer you are trying to use. Is there a list of documents waiting? Delete all of the duplicates. Start the printing. Watch for messages. If the printer is connected, and full of paper and ink, you should hear it start to print your document. (If you do not see the name of the printer you want to use in the list, click the Add Printer button.)

Display. Most modern computers can be set to display in several different resolutions and color depths. To reset these on Windows, go to Start, then Settings, then Control Panels, then Display. On Macintosh OS X use System Preferences, then Displays. The resolution is expressed in pixels, such as 800 by 600, or 1024 by 768. Adjust it to better fit the software you are using—you'll be able to fit more stuff on the screen at a higher resolution. If your color depth is low (256 colors, or 8-bit), set it to millions of colors, or 24-bit. And watch the blotches disappear.

Sound. There's a control panel for sound as well, in the same place as the other Control Panels (Windows) or System Preferences (Macintosh). Open the sound control panel and make sure it's set to full volume.

3. Quit and restart the program. Sometimes the program you are using trips over itself, or loses track of its memory. Multimedia programs are especially prone to this errant behavior. You can fix this by quitting the program, and then launching it again. And sometimes you have too many programs running at once. Fix this by quitting all of the programs except the one you are using.

4. Restart the computer. Like other programs, the operating system of your computer can also foul itself up and cause things to act strangely. The only way to get it back on its feet is to restart the computer. On Windows, go to Start, then Shutdown, then Restart. On Macintosh OS X, look under the Apple menu. (If your computer is frozen so that the menus do not work, you can restart from the keyboard: use Ctrl + Alt + Delete on Windows, or ctrl + Apple + power on Macintosh. If the keyboard is unresponsive, you may have to restart by disconnecting the power cord.)

5. Check for viruses. You have tried all of the above, and still it's acting up. Maybe you have picked up a worm or virus that affects performance. (This is much more likely on Windows than on Macintosh.) Run your virus protection program, such as Norton or Symantec. See your system administrator or computer store to get such a program if you need it. Once you have killed the viruses, restart the computer.

6. Call for help. If all this has failed, it may be time to call your system administrator, the next-door neighbor's high-tech child, the manufacturer of your computer, the store where you bought it. They will probably ask you if you have tried all the items on the list above. You can rest assured that the expert help is really needed at this point.

Computers don't use jumper cables, they don't run out of gas (though laptops do deplete their batteries), and they cannot be push-started. But you'll better enjoy your voyage on the information highways if you are prepared to do your own troubleshooting, and leave only the toughest problems to the experts.

LEARN MORE . . .

About Deciding between a Desktop and a Laptop Computer

www.nfib.com/object/4293771.html
> *Desktop or Laptop: How to Decide?* by Reid Goldsborough

www.ehow.com/how_3056_decide-between-laptop.html
> *How to Decide Between a Laptop and a Desktop* from eHow.com.

About Computer Ergonomics

http://ergo.human.cornell.edu/default.asp
> This is the web site for the Cornell University Ergonomics Lab

About Wireless Networks

http://computer.howstuffworks.com/wireless-network.htm
> *How WiFi Works* by Marshall Brain

About Troubleshooting Macintosh OS Computers

http://macs.about.com/od/troubleshooting
> This web site features troubleshooting tips and articles pertaining to Macintosh OS, including a 2-minute troubleshooting guide, a key to all those Mac error codes, and much more.

www.apple.com/support
> The Apple Computer support page allows you to search for the help you need.

About Troubleshooting Windows OS Computers

http://expertanswercenter.techtarget.com/eac/home/0,295193,sid63,00.html
> IBM sponsors the Tech Target Answer Center.

http://support.microsoft.com
> The Microsoft support page allows you to search for the help you need.

CHAPTER FIVE

GOING PAPERLESS

IN THIS CHAPTER

- **Why Go Paperless?**
- **Planning Your Work**
- **Thinking, Writing, and Publishing**
- **Learn More . . .**

WHY GO PAPERLESS?

Picture this scene.

Mrs. Timmons' social studies class. Fifth Period. The lesson is about the transcontinental railroad. Mrs. Timmons assigns a short report of approximately three pages on the topic, The Importance of the Golden Spike. *She explains that the students will have two nights and the next day in class to work on it. The paper must include one or two pictures, several quotations, and at least two reference sources. "This assignment should be easy for you," she explains, "because we've been studying this topic for quite a while."*

One of the students asks if it's all right to do the research on the Internet. Mrs. Timmons says that's a fine idea and writes this URL (Universal Resource Locator) on the chalkboard:

http://shell3.ba.best.com/~sfmuseum/hist/rail.html.

She tells the students that this site is a good place to get started with their reports.

THE FIRST FAUX PAS

Sarah copies the URL to her notebook. Billy asks to borrow a pencil to copy it. He never seems to have anything to write with. Sarah goes home, types the URL into her computer, and up comes the error message "404-File Not Found" on her screen . . .

While copying the URL from the board, Sarah probably made a small error. Perhaps she substituted a capital letter for a lowercase one when copying from the chalkboard, or maybe she mistyped the URL when entering it into her computer. Then again, maybe Mrs. Timmons made a mistake when she wrote the URL on the chalkboard or when she copied it from her source. It doesn't matter who made the error; what matters is that writing down URLs in this way can lead to trouble. Had Mrs. Timmons posted the URL to a web site, Sarah could have accessed it from school or home. Then she could link directly to the site she wanted, without worrying about whether her copying was correct.

> *Sarah telephones Billy, but he can't find the paper where he wrote down the URL. Because Abby's telephone is busy, Sarah emails her. Abby sends Sarah the correct URL in an email. It's a good thing she didn't get through by telephone or she'd be copying again.*

THE PRINT HABIT

> *Sarah clicks on the URL in the email and connects—no need to write it down. She finds what she considers to be useful information on this site, and skims the content. She begins to print the information—lots of pages—on the printer at home. Alas, the ink runs out on page 7.*
>
> *Sarah's mother, who is now in a bathrobe and relaxing on the sofa after a stressful day at work, grumbles but puts on slacks and a tee shirt and drives Sarah to the store for a new ink cartridge. Sarah prints pages 7 through 12. It's 7:30 P.M.*

The print habit is an expensive habit that's hard to break. Sarah, almost by instinct, clicked the print button to save a copy of what she was looking at. Maybe she was afraid she'd miss something if she didn't. But Sarah had other options. She could have saved the parts she needed as a file on her computer simply by using Save As in the File menu. She could have skimmed the pages, highlighted the important parts, then copied and pasted them into a page in her word processor or computer note pad. She could have put the site in her Bookmarks (Netscape) or Favorites (Internet Explorer).

> *Sarah reads the printout, all 12 pages, learns a bit about the topic, and circles three quotable paragraphs and several useful photographs. She heads to another history site and prints, reads, and marks more web pages. Sarah thinks about the topic and organizes her ideas.*

At this point, many students are so swamped with information that they just start writing to get something on paper.

> *Even though it's getting late and Sarah's getting nervous about not having anything on paper, she takes time to decide how the information and her ideas will go together. It's after 8:30 P.M. Her father asks her how much longer she'll be working. She explains that she hasn't even started writing yet. Sarah writes a*

rough copy of the paper using the word-processing program on her home computer. Good thing that we can use pictures, she reasons; they'll take up some space. Sarah's far too tired to check spelling, but she's got to add quotations. She scrambles through the papers on her floor to find anything that will fit. Sarah knows she has tomorrow in class and tomorrow night to complete the assignment, but she has soccer practice tomorrow after school and a math test the next day. She's got to get as much done as she can now. Sarah types some quotations into the report, copying them from the printed pages. Her father tells her to stop working and go to sleep. It's after 10:30 P.M.

More copying. More unnecessary work. More chance for errors. More typing when it could have been avoided. More time wasted. Does any of this sound familiar?

MORE MISTAKES

Sarah goes back to school the next day with her rough copy ready. Mrs. Timmons scans the paper briefly and tells Sarah to be sure to proofread and check her quotations. It takes Sarah almost the entire social studies period to scan some of the photos that she printed from the web site, because everyone wants to use the scanner. After school, she brings the scanned files home on a floppy disk. She inserts the photos into her report. She prints the report. Sarah's mother reads the printed paper.

Her mother finds several spelling and grammar errors in the paper, including several quotes that don't seem to make sense. She also comments that the pictures aren't very good. Sarah corrects her errors on the computer. She deletes one of the fuzzy photos, but leaves in one that is supposed to show Leland Stanford hammering in the Golden Spike—it's difficult to tell there's even a train in the picture. Sarah prints another copy of the paper for her teacher.

Sarah's Work

Sarah has worked twice as hard as necessary. Think of how she flip-flopped between notes, paper, computer, disks, and even Mom. This 24-step process, or something like it, is probably occurring right now in your school or home. It's not a good one. While it might result in a decent report in the end, it wastes lots of time and energy along the way. Sarah's paper is written no better, is no broader in scope, nor any deeper in meaning than a paper written before there were computers in our schools or homes. This process simply repeats the old way of doing papers using a new technology. And by our count, Sarah printed over 30 pages at home and school, all or most of them unnecessary.

How do you expect your students to create their papers? Do you expect them to work like Sarah? Describe the steps your students typically go through in researching, drafting, writing and publishing a 5- to 10-page paper, and estimate the number of pages of paper they generate at each step.

Going Paperless

There is a better way—the Paperless Paper. The new technologies in our schools and homes allow us to achieve the same intellectual and curriculum objectives of an assignment like Sarah's, without all the paper and wasted effort. The paperless process has but ten steps:

1. Planning and Organizing
2. Preparing to Search and Searching
3. Finding Text and Media
4. Inspecting and Analyzing
5. Taking Electronic Notes
6. Citing, and Avoiding Plagiarism
7. Thinking
8. Writing
9. Editing
10. Publishing

At each step, you use the computer and its connections to accomplish the work more efficiently. There is less wasted effort, less chance for error, and the process frees up time and energy that can be used to make your paper, report, or presentation better. Going paperless means saving rather than printing, committing your work to a file rather than to paper, copying and pasting rather than scanning and printing, and using the computer display rather than the sheet of paper to deal with your work. And it means more careful planning and organization. The next section gives you more ideas on eliminating the paper and focusing on the content.

PLANNING YOUR WORK

The last section set forth the argument for assigning paperless papers—student assignments that take full advantage of the computer, networks, and communication tools to produce works of research and writing with stronger ideas and better quality, but with less waste of time and resources. This section takes you through the first steps in the process of developing a paperless paper.

1. Plan and Organize

Any research and writing project should begin with a plan—and here the plan will begin and end not on paper but on the computer screen. As you will see, planning online provides flexibility and efficiency not available with paper. You'll start by brainstorming. Open a new word-processing document, then simply type ideas and questions about your topic. Don't worry about order or format or spelling at this point—just get the ideas flowing. Then you have a half-page full, save your work document as a file with the name Outline.

You can change the order of your ideas in the outline by selecting (highlighting) them and then using your mouse to drag and drop them into the place in your outline where they seem to fit. While you are at it, make sure that your list of ideas includes any guidelines or requirements for this assignment. For example, if you need an introduction, a conclusion, and a bibliography, put these in your outline as major sections. At the end, add a section called Extras into which you can place ideas that don't seem to fit anywhere else in the outline at this time, but may prove to be useful later.

2. The Outline

This first outline won't be exactly what you'll end up with, but it will serve as a map or guide for your work. Change your outline whenever you want and add ideas to it as you progress through your assignment. An outline will help you keep your focus throughout your work.

Your first outline or plan might look like this:

TITLE OF ASSIGNMENT

   I. Introduction
  II. Ideas or topics
.........A. Idea 1
...............1. Picture you might find or look for
...............2. Graph you think you could make
.........B. Idea 2
.........C. Idea 3, and so on
 III. Conclusion
 IV. Bibliography

3. Create Your Online Workspace

Once your outline is started, it's time to create your online or on-the-computer workspace, just as you would with any other workspace. The difference is that you'll do this without paper. A conscientious student of the Paper Age would begin by finding a cardboard file folder, paper, and a place to stack all notes and books. The paperless student, however, will set up a workspace on the computer. Create a folder for your assignment. Into this folder place all the items related to the assignment. The folder can sit on the internal hard drive of a desktop or laptop computer, on a floppy or Zip disk, on a memory stick, on a pocket FireWire drive, or in your space on the network server.

To create your folder, go under the File menu on your desktop and select New Folder. Name the new folder, open it, and then add and name your subfolders.

No matter where you save your folder, it must be easy to find and use as you do your work. Depending on the nature of the assignment, the folder can be further divided into subfolders. These subfolders represent the different types of information you plan to gather or the various topics that you plan to cover. For instance, suppose you've been assigned to do a presentation on the Battle of Gettysburg. Inside your Gettysburg folder, you add subfolders for each type of information you plan to gather, such as Pictures, Text, Audio, Maps, and Outline. These folders are empty right now, but they form an organizational scheme for your work. As you gather information and ideas, you'll place them in their proper folders. Make sure you save your outline into this folder as well.

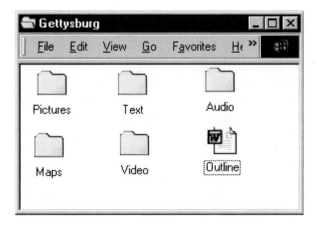

These folders may reflect the way you might organize the topics for your report. Suppose your topic is the planet Jupiter—you'd place information on the size of and distance from Jupiter in one folder, information on the atmosphere in another, and the composition of the planet's surface in yet another.

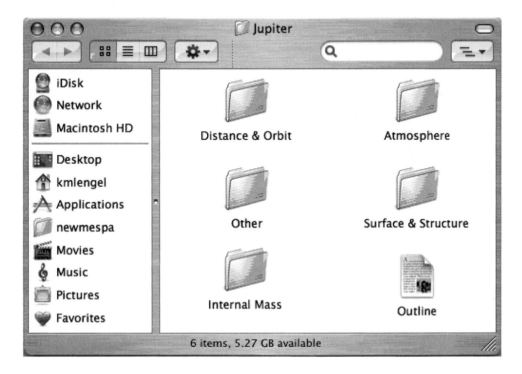

Note that your computer workspace setup is done in advance, before the actual research begins. Organizing in this way helps to make the next steps easier. If you need to change the names of the folders or add folders, you can do that later.

4. Research Your Topic

In order to fill the folders you created for your assignment, you'll need to search the online universe to find information that fits. Many teachers provide for their students starter web pages, posted on school or class web sites, that point to useful online resources related to the topic. Other teachers expect students to find useful information on their own.

And many students immediately go to one of the web search engines, such as Google or Yahoo. Following the topics listed above, they'd find more than 90,000 web sites that contain at least some information about Gettysburg and almost 300,000 sites with something about Jupiter. Only a small portion of these sites contain useful material for their assignment. Simply entering a topic word into a search engine is seldom productive.

Searching strictly for a topic like "Gettysburg" or "Jupiter" or simple words like "painting" often uncovers too broad or even irrelevant information. It's best to search for words that are unique to your topic. But how do you discover those words?

Try looking up the topic in a general reference work such as an online or CD encyclopedia where you'll not only find text information, but also media and links to related sites on the topics. Skim the article and make a list of unique terms—people, places, and things—that might be useful to search on.

Talk about your project with others. What special people, places, and things come up in your conversation? Make note of them for your search.

A general search engine such as Yahoo or Google may not be the best place to start your search. Try starting from more focused sites such as:

Trusted URLs. These are sites suggested by librarians, teacher, parents, or friends who are web savvy. They are likely to contain reliable and relevant information. For instance, at the NASA site (www.nasa.gov) you'll find descriptions and images of Jupiter; the Library of Congress (www.loc.gov) and the National Park Service (www.nps.gov) sites might help you with the Battle of Gettysburg.

Specialized Search Engines. Another method for finding relevant information is to use a search engine specifically designed for students completing school assignments. While general-purpose search engines such as Google find everything that's out there, other sites such as Yahooligans (www.yahooligans.com), Homework Central (www.bigchalk.com), and the Apple Learning Interchange (ALI) (www.ali.apple.com), limit their searches to sites that are likely to be useful to you. Instead of finding 90,000 sites on Jupiter, for example, you'll find just 19 with Yahooligans. Not every site that Yahooligans finds is on target for your topic.

Teacher and Museum Sites. Where do teachers and librarians get their information? Look for useful links from sites such as the American Library Association (www.ala.org/parentspage/greatsites/amazing.html), Apple's ALI (mentioned above), Kathy Schrock's Guide for Educators (www.discoveryschool.com/schrockguide/

index.html), Teachers' Hot Lists from the Franklin Institute (www.fi.edu), and museum sites like the Smithsonian's (www.si.edu).

5. Read the Sites

You've found some useful sites. But they contain much more information than you can use in your report. Many students at this point print out these web sites. That's not a good idea. Hold off from pressing Print, and instead skim the material on the sites to see what fits. Read over the parts that seem promising. Search through the picture and other media options to see if anything looks worthwhile. As you go along, don't forget to add ideas to your outline.

Add the best pages you find to your Bookmarks or Favorites in your browser in case you need to go back and check on some of the information. This can be a real time saver and invaluable when you need to cite a site in your bibliography.

Not everything you need for your report will be found online. But you can remain paperless even in a library full of books. Take a laptop computer with you, and take notes on separate word processing files that match the names of your project folders. Then save these files in the proper folders.

6. Take Electronic Notes

It's time to add something to those empty folders you created when you first got your paperless paper organized—you'll download exactly what you want from the Internet to your computer. At this point you should also open another working folder with a blank word processing document where you can start your bibliography. Copy and paste—don't type—the URLs you visit and use for note taking, and remember to record the date you visited the site, because the Web is an ever-changing body of knowledge. Add whatever other references you use—books, emails, and magazines—as you finish with them, and your bibliography will be a breeze to put together at the end of your project. To capture the text from Web pages, simply save it to the appropriate folders. Follow these directions:

1. Choose Save As from the File menu.
2. Choose Plain text (Explorer) or Text (Netscape) from the pop-up menu.
3. Navigate to the folders you set up earlier.
4. Enter an appropriate filename.
5. Click the Save button.

To capture images from these pages, simply download them to the appropriate folder on your computer. Follow these instructions:

1. Place the cursor directly over the picture.
2. Click and hold down the mouse button (right-click on Windows), until a pop-up menu appears.

3. Choose Download image to disk (Explorer) or Save image to disk (Netscape) from the pop-up menu. Downloading to disk means saving it to your hard drive. You can save it to a floppy disk or Zip disk instead, if you wish.
4. Navigate to the appropriate folder you set up earlier.
5. Enter an appropriate filename.
6. Click the Save button.

No copying in longhand. No retyping. No scanning. No paper. Everything remains in digital electronic form as you work.

6. Save Entire Pages

Both images and text can be cut and pasted from web sites on the Internet using the methods described above. With some computers you can also save an entire web page, including both text and images. If you're using Internet Explorer on a Macintosh or Windows XP computer, you can save a Web Archive by choosing Save As . . . from the File menu, and then choosing Web Archive or Web Page Complete from the pop-up menu.

7. Save Notes

If you don't need the entire web page or even all the text on a page, you can copy the text you want by selecting it on your computer screen. Once it's selected, go to the Edit Menu and select Copy. Open a word-processing document where you can paste what you copied. If the note is a quote, put quotation marks around it. Don't forget that besides the note, you'll want to save information about where you got the note. This means the URL (or web address) at the very least, and if you can find them, the author and date. Save the information into the appropriate folder.

You can save your own ideas into the proper or designated folders in much the same way. Open a word-processing document, write your ideas, and save into the appropriate folder.

8. Cite Your Sources

Whether your reference materials are collected on paper or on the computer, you have a responsibility to keep track of where you got the information and who authored it. Online sources are treated no differently than paper sources. You should note the source and author of each item. Using the sources without documenting them is plagiarism—a type of stealing.

You'll want to make sure that you're quoting correctly and giving credit for the ideas of others. Sometimes students take notes in a hurry and forget to add specifics about where the information came from. Later, when they write their paper, they can't remember whether the note is a quote or not. It's important to be careful with your note taking, even with electronic note taking. However, if you're saving web text or pages into your folders, you'll know what's yours and what's not. With your own notes, it's a bit more difficult. Be careful!

Next Steps

Going paperless, you have planned and researched your topic, and have a disk full of resources, all in digital form, all on the computer, nothing on paper. The next section will show you how to think about, write, edit, and publish your ideas—without printing a single sheet of paper.

THINKING, WRITING, AND PUBLISHING

The first two sections in this chapter about the paperless paper helped you lead your students through the process of planning, brainstorming, searching, and taking notes, all without printing a single page. This section will help you take them through the final steps in the process: thinking, writing, and publishing.

Let's look back at the process so far. By searching for resources and then inspecting them, your students have had the opportunity to think about the topics they're working on. They've read text, looked at pictures and diagrams, and learned some new vocabulary. They've added to their outlines. Now it's time for them to think.

Thinking

Thinking is the most important part of the process. Many ideas about Gettysburg or Jupiter or other research topics are flying about in your students' minds, ready for analysis, which is good. It's even better if they talk about what they found and why it's important, with other students, with you, or with their parents. This free thinking is a precursor to the more careful thinking that must come later in the process of creating the paperless paper. When faced with a particularly good idea during their free thinking, remind them to make a note of it by opening the outline file that they created earlier and typing in the idea at the appropriate spot.

Writing

By now your students should have done their research and taken notes without using a single sheet of paper. By now they've probably filled their folders with relevant information in many forms—text, images, multimedia, and sound—all of it now stored on their computers. The next step in the process of developing a paperless paper is to do the actual writing. Most students know how to use a word processor, and appreciate how much more efficient it is in composing, editing, and publishing papers. But many students do not use this readily available tool to the fullest. Some write their words first on paper, and later copy them over to the word processor. Some type with the word processor, then immediately print a copy to read and edit.

A better way for students to use the word processor is to let it help them through the entire process of writing. They can use it to document their ideas as they read and observe the materials they researched. They can use it to arrange and rearrange their ideas and examples. They can use it to form these ideas into an outline. And, of course, they can use the word processor to compose their sentences. But there's more. While most students print their final work, more and more of them use the word processor to publish their work in other multimedia formats, such as presentations and web pages. Here are some suggestions on how your students can take full advantage of your word processor as a writing and publishing tool-without resorting to paper.

HOW TO . . . WRITE THE PAPERLESS PAPER

You need: The folders full of researched material described above.

You get: A completed report ready to publish.

1. Read and note. With folders full of raw material, students should begin writing by first opening their outlines. They should look at their ideas and add notes on the materials that they've been gathering. At this stage, tell them not to worry too much about organization. That will come later. The first task is to add ideas that come from the text, pictures, and other content in their folders. They might begin, for example, by opening one of the articles on Jupiter and reading about how large it is and how many moons it has. Then suggest that they summarize, in their minds, the vast array of facts in the article. Get them to type their summaries into the word processor.

Let students work through the material in their folders, thinking about each one as they examine it and taking note of the ideas that come to mind. Some may become new ideas. Others become additional evidence to support an existing idea. They'll find some text and pictures, for example, that extend their concept of the vast differences between Earth and Jupiter. Reflecting on that could give them new material to add to their paper.

2. Arrange ideas. Tell your students to think of a paper not as a string of sentences, but as an arrangement of ideas. An author presents her ideas to the reader in a certain logical order so that her argument flows from one concept to the next. With a word processor, it's easy to place ideas into an order that makes sense to the reader. Once the ideas are in order, the writing of sentences becomes much easier.

Tell students to look through the list of ideas on the screen of the word processor. If they had to explain the planet Jupiter to someone else, which idea would they present first? Show them how to select that idea by highlighting it with their cursor, and drag it to the top of the *Ideas* or *Topics* section in their outline. Once they've selected an idea for the beginning, they'll choose another the idea that best follows this one logically. Show them how to drag that one directly under the first. Let them continue arranging their lists until they have put together a story about their topic in outline form.

3. Submit the outline. Many teachers require outlines as part of a paper, presentation, report, or project. Show your students how to do a Save As . . . of their outline and create another document with a different name. This way, they'll have their outlines saved separately, and will be able to work on their writing without changing the outline. They can send their outlines to you by e-mail, on a floppy disk, USB memory stick, or through the school network.

4. Tell a story. A good way for students to begin their writing is for them to sit down at the computer, with their outline of ideas on the screen, and talk with another student sitting right across the desk from them. Tell them to begin to tell their story to the other person (the listener), as if they were in a conversation. This exercise will help them put their ideas into words, and let them know if their story makes sense. If possible you might want to have them record this exercise using a tape or digital recorder. When they're done, the listener can explain which ideas seemed strongest, which needed more work, and which were most interesting. Then tell the writer to select the weak ideas and change their text color to red, and to select the strongest ideas and change them to blue. Direct them to change the text color of the interesting ideas to green.

5. Strengthen their ideas. Back working on their own, tell writers to find a way to fix the red items. Perhaps they need a better example. Perhaps they need to be reworded to make them clearer or explained in a different way. Or perhaps they're just not that important, and should be moved to the Extras section. Next, have your students look at the green and blue items, making sure they're well distributed throughout the outline. They don't want all the interesting points to be bunched up at the beginning or end of the report. Give students time to edit and review these items to make sure they're the way the writers want them to be.

6. Write. Now the writing should be easy. Discuss with students how to write a sentence that explains each idea in their outline. Direct them to type the sentences right under the ideas. Urge them to remember what they said when they told their story to the other student, and type those words into the word processor. Suggest that they compose two or three sentences for each idea. If an idea has several supporting examples, they can write a sentence about each one. Encourage them to keep writing until they've composed a paragraph for each idea.

Once their ideas are explained in sentences, show them how to add an introduction and conclusion. When they're done, instruct them to go back to the beginning of the document and read their sentences aloud. How does it sound? Encourage them to fix any sentences that don't roll easily off the tongue. Discuss how to reword sentences that don't flow logically from the ones before them.

When they're happy with their writing, show them how to go back and delete all the original outline listings, leaving just the freshly written paragraphs. Their outlines are quickly transforming into reports.

7. Don't print! Remind your students that they don't need a paper copy to do any of this. In fact, printing their work can make it seem complete and permanent, which is definitely not the case at this point. It must be human nature, but once students see their words on paper they often have a hard time changing them. Help them to resist the urge to print! Keeping their work in digital form, where it's easily modified and changed, makes them more likely to continue to make improvements. At this point in the process, it's a good idea to make sure each student saves a backup or duplicate version of their report. In the next step, they'll be adding pictures and quotes.

8. Add pictures and quotations. Student folders contain many quotes and pictures that can be added to their reports. Now is the time for them to insert them into the report where they belong. Remind them that not every item needs to be included. Instead, encourage them to find one good quote or image to exemplify each idea in the paper. Show them how to take the first paragraph, and go through the folders looking for the best supporting example. This should be easy, because they kept notes of where they found each idea. When they find the text or image they want to use, demonstrate how to select it and copy it from its original source. Then show them how to go back into their word processing document, place the cursor at the end of the paragraph they're working with, and choose Paste from the Edit menu. They'll see the item appear right in their paperless paper. They may need to adjust the text font or the image size to make it fit well. Give students time to do this for each idea in the report until they have embedded at least one example for each paragraph.

9. Cite. Students don't need to cite the sources of their own original ideas, but they do need to show the source for each quotation or image. Show them how to copy the citations from the sources in their folders, and paste them into the word processor document right after each example. If appropriate, provide students with guidelines for creating a bibliography as well as for citing sources.

10. Check it. Remind students how to do a spelling and grammar check in their word processor and correct any mistakes. Then ask them to reread carefully what they have written.

11. Publish. Of course, now that it's finished, the assignment should be printed, right? Wrong. The best place to publish student work might not be on paper. As an alternative, have your students email their papers to you. Show them how to compose an email message to you, then to add the report they just produced as an attachment. You will be able to receive and read their papers right on the computer screen. Without any printing.

It's just as easy, and more versatile, for them to continue in the paperless mode and publish their work as a web page. They can simply go to their word processor's File menu, choose Save As . . . , then choose Save as Web Page from the pop-up menu. Saving as a web page creates a folder full of files that contain the text and images from the project. To see what their papers will look like on the Internet, they can open this HTML file with their web browser (Netscape or Explorer). They'll see both pictures and text. Anyone with a browser on their computer can see their papers in this form. Students can also put the folder with the HTML files on a floppy disk and mail it to someone. Or they can put the folders onto the school's Local Area Network so anyone on the LAN can read it. If your school has a web server, students can copy the folder there and anyone on the Internet can read it. This is by far the most universal—and most paperless—method for publishing student papers.

Your students have made it through the process of writing a paperless paper. Encourage them to use this process for every writing assignment. They have learned how ideas can be found, arranged, and published all in digital form, without resorting to paper, and how the process of doing so leaves them more time and energy for thinking, with fewer chances of mistakes. So when you assign a paper, think paperless. Eventually everyone will—but by then, your students will be the masters of this latest game in town.

■ ■ ■ ■ ■ ■ ■ ■ ■ ■

LEARN MORE . . .

http://coe.sdsu.edu/eet/Articles/Paperless/start.htm
The Paperless Classroom from the College of Education at San Diego State University

www.education-world.com/a_tech/tech059.shtml
The Paperless School of the Future Is Here Now! from Education World

www.newyorker.com/critics/books/?020325crbo_books
A review of *The Social Life Of Paper* by Malcolm Gladwell, in *The New Yorker,* March 25, 2002

www-writing.berkeley.edu/TESL-EJ/ej09/int.html
The Paperless Classroom? by Thomas N. Robb

PART III

THE INTERNET

Chapters 6 through 8 start with the basics of browsing the Internet. Here you'll find much practical advice on how you and your students can become online authors, using the Internet as an educational medium.

■ ■ ■ ■ ■

CHAPTER SIX

USING THE INTERNET— BEYOND BROWSING

IN THIS CHAPTER

- **Better Browsing**
- **Finding it on the Web**
- **Understanding URLs**
- **Learn More . . .**

Many of us these days spend most of our computer time with a web browser—we use Netscape or Explorer more than we use any other software program. The browser has become our window to the world of information and communication. But have you looked at your browser lately? Is it set up properly for the best browsing experience? Is it letting you work quickly, easily, and powerfully to find, view, and save information?

This section will help you configure your browser for optimal usability. Better Browsing helps you make sure your browser is as new, big, and fast as possible; easier to use, and more capable of displaying the kinds of information you need. The last two sections show you or your students how to find what you are looking for on the Web, and how to understand the URL that denotes each page on the Web.

BETTER BROWSING

Two Surfers

Willy Wavetumble wondered why he couldn't surf as well as the other surfers on the beach. They could ride faster, on the bigger waves, stay atop their surfboards longer, and more fully enjoy their sport. "Maybe," he thought, "my surfboard is too old—the newer ones evidently incorporate some technical innovations in shape and materials that are lacking in my ancient model. Or perhaps it's too small. After all I've grown a bit over the last few years and may be putting too much weight on it. On the other hand, my board is not easy to ride. I've noticed that my board always wants to turn to the left, maybe because the fins on the bottom are crooked. And I've noticed that the other surfers spend a lot of time on the beach waxing and polishing their boards to make them go faster. And they never lose their surfboards in the sea—they have safety straps and footpads that make their surfing safer and more comfortable. Maybe I should think about updating my surfboard . . ."

E. C. Ryder races toward the shore on her swift surfboard, sure of foot and fleet of flight. She rides the latest model, with all the technical innovations, in a size and weight that's just right for her. The fins are straight, and the bottom is waxed clean for speed. Hers is a useful board, with all the necessary safety straps and current capabilities. She rides the waves with speed, confidence, and control. And she surfs wherever she wants.

Which surfer has the most fun? As you surf the Web, are you working as fast and as efficiently as possible? Perhaps it's time to look at your virtual surfboard—your web browser—and make sure it's more of an E. C. Ryder than a Willy Wavetumble.

Is Your Browser Up-to-Date?

Browser technology advances quickly. A new version emerges almost every year. Are you using the most recent version of your browser? You need the latest version to take advantage of the new web technologies found in some web sites, such as cascading style sheets, Javascript, and multimedia data types. Older versions can't handle these, and so you don't experience all that the site has to offer.

And the newer computer operating systems, such as Macintosh OS X and Windows XP, don't work well with the old browsers. Maybe that's why you experience all those little unexplainable glitches. The newer versions of the browsers also display text and images faster than the old ones, making your experience more responsive. And they contain the latest plug-ins and players, those little extra programs that you need for video and animation: you need the latest browser to use the newest plug-ins.

You want to make sure that what you have is the latest normal version of the browser—not the experimental beta version, but the most recent fully-supported release. You can learn about and download the latest versions on the web sites of Microsoft (www.microsoft.com), or Netscape (www.netscape.com), or Apple Computer (www.apple.com).

Please note: At your school you might find that there are some constraints on what browser you can use. If you have questions, be sure to check with the technology resource teacher or other instructional technology staff at your school or district before making any changes in the browser(s) available on your classroom computer.

To find out which version you are using, first open your browser, then:

- On Macintosh OS 8 or 9, choose About Internet Explorer or About Netscape from the Apple menu.
- On Windows, choose About . . . from the Help menu.
- On Macintosh OS X, choose About . . . from the Explorer or Netscape menu.

When you download the latest version, a new file will appear on your computer's hard disk. Depending on its operating system, the new version of the browser may automatically install itself, or you may need to double-click the installation file. In most cases, you will find this file on your Desktop. It will be called something like *i.e. setup.exe* or *Netscape Installer.*

Once you've installed the latest version of the browser, make sure you know where it is, and that you use it from now on. The section Customize Your Browser, later in this chapter, will help you ensure that you are launching the newest copy.

Give Your Browser Space to Work

Browsers need all the memory they can get. There's a lot of stuff going on when you are viewing web pages in a browser, and everything you see (or hear) demands RAM (random access memory) for speed and smoothness of operation. Browsers need big memory spaces. So before you launch your browser, take a moment to quit any other programs that you don't need. This will leave more room in memory for the browser to do its work.

You may not even be aware that you have other programs running. To check, do this:

- On Macintosh OS 8 or 9, click and hold the finder icon at the top right of the menubar. It will show a list of programs currently running.
- On Windows, look in the Task bar at the bottom of the screen. Each program that's running will show an icon and its name.
- On Macintosh OS X, look in the Dock for any programs labeled with a little black triangle.

Quit or exit these programs. Then launch your browser, so it can enjoy a clean and full slate of memory for itself.

Tip for Mac OS 8 and 9 Only: Set the Memory Allocation

If you are using Macintosh OS 8 or 9 and your computer has at least 128 megabytes of built-in memory, you can set the amount of memory that your browser will allocate to itself when it starts up. Here's how:

1. Click once on the program icon of your browser. (Don't launch it, just click once to select it.)
2. From the File menu, choose Get Info, then Memory.
3. You will see three numbers. Change the bottom number (Preferred Size) to 30,000.
4. This will allocate 30 megabytes to your browser whenever it opens.

Consider Your Connection Speed

Now matter how new or big your browser, if your connection is slow your surfing will suffer. For many people, the Internet connection speed is the biggest bottleneck to efficient browser performance. Three levels of connection speed, or *bandwidth,* are available:

■ **Slow: telephone modem.** You use your telephone line to connect to the Internet, which gives a maximum bandwidth of 56k—56,000 bits of data per second. At this speed, it takes ten seconds to download a small photograph. If your computer is connected to a telephone jack with a skinny flat wire (usually gray or beige) less than a quarter-inch wide, terminating in a standard four-conductor RJ-11 phone connector, then you have this slow connection.

■ **Fast: DSL or cable modem.** If the wire from your home computer is fatter than a quarter inch, and terminates in a fatter eight-conductor RJ-45 connector, then you probably have this medium-speed connection. It can be ten times faster than the telephone modem connection. DSL stands for Digital Subscriber Line, and is most often arranged through the phone company. A cable modem connection—same speed—is arranged through your cable television provider.

■ **Fastest: LAN or Ethernet connection.** If you're in a modern school or office, this is what you most likely enjoy. LAN stands for Local Area Network. It can download that photograph in less than a second, and play MP3s at the same time. It uses the same Ethernet cable (also called Category 5) as the medium connection, but most often goes directly to the Internet without being slowed down by modems or other interface units.

Moving up to a faster connection is like waxing your surfboard—only more so. You will notice the difference right away. At home, a DSL or cable modem connection will cost less than $40 per month, and will significantly improve your browsing experience. At school or at the office, get yourself connected to the LAN—it will do wonders for your web work.

The Slowness of Sharing

Just because you have a LAN or DSL or cable connection doesn't mean you'll enjoy the full benefits of the faster connection. If a thousand other browsers are connecting at the same time on a shared connection, the bandwidth will be so split among them that you'll find yourself back in slowsville. If you are stuck on a slow shared connection, try browsing at a better time, perhaps when the others are at breakfast.

Your browser should, like E. C. Ryder's surfboard, be newer and faster and bigger than before. In the next section, you'll learn how to make it easier to use and more capable.

Customize Your Browser

When browsers come from the factory, they are not always set up to make your life easy or efficient. Often they come set up with advertising that you didn't ask for, features that you don't need, and settings that send you back to the manufacturer's marketing sites. Take a moment to remove the things that can make a browser harder to use.

Baffling buttons. Look at the navigation buttons at the top of your browser window (Back, Forward, Stop, Refresh, and so forth). Do you really need these at all, since all these functions are also available from the menubar? Many people remove the button bar completely in order to enjoy a less cluttered display. Even if you decide to keep the button bar, you probably don't need both the icon and the name of every one. This will give you more space to display the content of your web pages.

- To remove the button bar in Explorer, uncheck Button Bar under the View menu. In Netscape, choose View, then Show and uncheck Navigation Toolbar.
- To remove the icons of the buttons in Explorer on Macintosh, choose Edit, then Preferences, then Browser Display, then Toolbar Style—Text only.
- On Explorer in Windows, you'll find these preferences under Tools, then Internet Options. In Netscape choose Edit, then Preferences, then Appearance, then Show toolbar as—Text only.

Meaningless menus. In Explorer, the Favorites Bar and the Explorer Bar do little more than send you to marketing sites, while taking up lots of valuable space. The same is true for the Personal Toolbar in Netscape. You can remove them easily under the View menu. Your browser will get bigger and cleaner.

Tiring text. With all that new screen space, you might want to reconsider the nature of the text that your browser displays. Words that appear too big or too small or in a bad font are much harder to read, especially in a long surfing session. The default settings for text display are often not well chosen. To set the display for easier reading:

- On Explorer for Macintosh, choose Edit, then Preferences, then Language, then Fonts.
- On Explorer for Windows, choose Tools, then Internet Options, then Fonts.
- On Netscape, choose Edit, then Preferences, then Fonts.

Try different fonts and sizes until you find settings that are easiest for you to read. Many people find that 14-point Georgia is best for the proportional (variable) font and serif font; Verdana for the sans-serif.

Simple startup. Since you use your browser so much, make it easy to launch. Here's how:

- Put its icon on your Desktop. Find its icon, click once, then choose File, then Make Alias (Macintosh OS 8 or 9) or File, then Create Shortcut (Windows). Drag this new icon to the Desktop.
- Put it under the Start or Apple or Dock menu. On Macintosh OS 8 or 9, make an alias of your browser's program icon as described above, then drag it to the Apple Menu Items folder inside the System folder. On Windows, drag the icon to the Start button. On Macintosh OS 10, drag the browser's program icon to the Dock.

Enhance Your Brower's Capability

It's not only having the latest version of the browser that makes it more capable of displaying the best that web sites have to offer—it's also installing the right browser plug-ins, support programs, and return address information. These are the little extras that allow video, sound, animation, and interactivity to work on a web page.

Video. The three most popular ways of displaying video on a web page are Quick-Time, RealVideo, and Windows Media. All three require a plug-in. If you don't have the plug-in or player, you won't see the video. And since web sites use all three, you need to make sure you have installed the latest versions of each. The best way to do this is to visit the web sites of the three publishers and download the most current (not experimental) version. The downloads are free.

- QuickTime: www.apple.com/quicktime/download
- RealVideo: www.realnetworks.com/products/free_trial.html
- Windows media: www.microsoft.com/windows/windowsmedia/download

These three video plug-ins also work for playing sound from a web page, so with all three installed you should be able to hear whatever the we page is sending.

Animation. The key plug-in for web animation is Macromedia Flash. Flash is the fastest-growing method for putting high-quality movement onto a web page. Download the latest version at www.macromedia.com/downloads.

Interactivity. Flash can handle some interactivity, but the more powerful plug-in is Shockwave. Make sure your Shockwave plug-in is up to date by connecting to www.macromedia.com/downloads and downloading the current version. Once you download the plug-in, it will sometimes automatically install itself. If it does not, double-click the install or update program that downloads to your desktop.

Return Address. When you submit a form from a web page, the information is often sent to the recipient in the form of an email. But this mail will not travel through the web without a return address. And your return address is set in the browser preferences. To set it:

- Choose Edit, then Preferences, then Email from Explorer's menubar
- Choose Edit, then Preferences, then Identity and—Mail servers in Netscape

Then fill in the blanks for email address and SMTP host. (SMTP stands for Simple Mail Transfer Protocol, and your SMTP host is the server that handles your email. If you don't know your host, look for it on the preference or setup screen of your email program.)

No Barnacles

By taking some time to clean up and customize your browser, you will enjoy a more efficient and more useful web experience. It's like removing barnacles from a surfboard—your trip through the sea of information will be faster and less painful. But navigating the sea can be tricky, so the next section gives you some guidance.

FINDING IT ON THE WEB

Each of us has stashed things everywhere at our house. We are not a super-organized household, and we have collected many items over the years and put them wherever they fit without a plan or a scheme. Nothing is indexed, nothing in order, not our CD collection, not our books, not the skis and poles and boots we just put away for the summer.

Our house is something like the World Wide Web—a huge collection of resources, arranged at random, unplanned, with no overriding organizational focus. A librarian would go crazy at our house, as many of them do when faced with the uncataloged, Dewey-decimal-free zone that is the Web. Many of us struggle to find what we are looking for on the Web—we know it must be there someplace but we can't find exactly the idea or factor picture or quotation we need for our schoolwork. And yet we all know someone who somehow knows how to find anything, and find it quickly, without scrolling through long lists of likely sites. How do they do it?

Not by following the old library rules learned by their teachers long ago. The World Wide Web is not like a library. In a library each book is selected by a librarian, cataloged, and put on a shelf along with other books on the same subject. The librarian knows everything that's in the library, why it's there, and where it is. On the Web, anyone can post a document and remove it whenever they please. Moreover, they don't have to tell anyone where it is. Nobody keeps track of everything that's on the Web, why it's there, or where it is. So finding things on the Web is quite different from locating things in a library.

The Internet Generation

But as everyone knows, the new post-Internet generation never goes to the library—they find everything they need on the Web. In our house, if you need something from the Web, you ask Molly, born in 1983 and raised with computers from her first year. Molly somehow locates those lost lyrics, critical quotes, and intriguing images that you missed. And she finds them in seconds. There is considerable truth to the claims of the capability of young people to tame the technologies invented in their lifetimes—and to use them more easily than their parents or teachers. But facility does not equate to efficiency. Molly can find simple things faster on the Web, but confront her with a deeper historical or scientific issue, where the resources are more subtle and complex, and her bravado will bog down, her search speed will slow.

The school-aged generation knows how to use the new search tools, but they lack the intellectual frameworks for understanding and interrelating the ideas they are seeking and items they find. Their parents and teachers possess the conceptual frameworks but lack facility with the new tools. This section should help both generations do a better job finding school-related ideas, facts, and objects on the Web.

Search Engines

Although there are no official librarians for the World Wide Web, there are indexers who offer librarian-like services to you. These folks have searched the Web (more accurately, they've programmed their computers to do so) and have compiled lists of what they found. They let you look through their lists to help you find what you're looking for. Without using these lists, it's virtually impossible to find things on the Web. Many such lists exist on the Web, all in competition with each other. None of them are official, and new list makers crop up each week. These services fall into two basic categories: subject directories, and search engines.

Most people who read this chapter are familiar with search engines, and use them every day. Google, Yahoo, Alta Vista, and Lycos let you enter a word or phrase, from which they produce a list of web pages that might contain what you are looking for. Powerful software at the search engine headquarters searches the Web each day looking for new materials. When it finds a new document, it reads every word (ignoring words like a, an, and the), taking note of each one and where it's located. It then adds these notations to a keyword index that also lists other documents where the same words can be found. This is called an *inverted index.*

When you connect to a search engine, you use this index to find documents that contain the keywords you're looking for. For example, if as part of a science report you enter the words *planet* and *Jupiter,* the search engine looks through its index and finds all documents that contain the word planet and all documents that contain the word Jupiter. It then compares the two lists and culls from them a single list of documents that contain both words.

Some of the documents listed will be relevant to your research—for example, a document about the atmosphere of Jupiter and a report on the planets by a student in Vermont. Both contain the words planet and Jupiter. Some of the documents, however, will no doubt be puzzling—for example, a description of Roman mythology, and a review of a motel in Florida. What do those have to do with your science report? Looking closely, you discover that Jupiter was the name of one of the Roman gods, and that the Lonely Planet Travel Guide to the Southeast covers lodging in Jupiter, Florida, among other places. The search engine cannot judge the relevance to your needs of the documents it finds. It can only report that it found the search words you requested. To the computer, the document about the Roman myths is no more or less important than the document about the Jovian atmosphere. As a result, you don't always get what you want.

Directories

Web directories generally organize topics or sites by subject. The best-known web directory is Yahoo (www.yahoo.com). The folks at Yahoo search the Web for sites which they think contain useful information. They then place the site in a topic category along with other sites on related subjects. For example, if they find a site with information about the planet Jupiter, they place it in a category named Solar System. They might also list it in a category called Planets.

Yahoo does not list every site it finds, only those that seem useful (or that pay to be listed in its directory). Over the years, Yahoo has developed an extensive list of sites, all categorized by subject. Each of its main categories—such as Arts, Business, Computers, and Education—also contains subcategories that you can access as well. For example, Arts contains subcategories such as Art History and Artists, each of which may include hundreds of web sites.

Browsing versus Searching

Both search engines and directories can be used to find what you need on the Web. Directories are better for browsing, and search engines are better for searching. Browsing is what you do when a new clothing catalog arrives in the mail—you leaf through it looking for what's new in the categories that interest you. You know you need to replace those worn trousers soon, and you are browsing around to see what's available. Searching is what you do when the headlight burns out on your car and you rush off to the auto parts store at dusk—you know exactly what you need, and just want to find it as quickly as possible.

Most school-related projects involve a little of each. A wise student will first use a web directory to browse a bit in the assigned subject area to familiarize herself with the way things are organized, learn the vocabulary, and understand where the topic fits in the hierarchy. Then she'll visit a few of the listed sites and perhaps find exactly what she needs. Then perhaps later in the development of the report, she will conduct a very specific search to find the percentage of hydrogen in Jupiter's atmosphere. Successful researchers combine browsing and searching as part of an overall strategy to finding what they need.

Find What You are Looking For

Browse first. Begin your search by browsing through a directory such as Yahoo or Homework Central and investigating the categories related to your topic. This will reveal a broad array of web sites related to the topic and may get you thinking about different approaches to the subject. While browsing through a list of planets, for example, you'll find sites for some of Jupiter's neighbors, which will allow you to compare them. While browsing, you'll find sites that might contain the information you're looking for, as well as sites that may lead you to other, better information. Take time to explore some of these other sites. Make note of where your topic appears in the various hierarchies of the directory structure.

Search narrowly. When you need to find something specific, conduct a narrow search. Don't type Jupiter into the search engine and press Return—in Google you'll get more than 2 million documents, including in the first ten the Jupiter, Florida town hall and the Jupiter media company. If you need to know the percentage of hydrogen in the atmosphere of Jupiter, you'd be better to enter +atmosphere +Jupiter +hydrogen +%. This results in only 28,000 documents, and any of the first ten contain the data you are looking for. (But there's some dispute—depending on which site you consult, Jupiter's atmosphere might be 90% or 86% hydrogen.)

In Google, those little plus signs, and the long string of words, are the key to a successful search. The + immediately in front of a word tells the search engine that the word that follows *must* occur on the page. And if you "plus" all the words, the search engine will return only those web pages that contain all four words.

A minus sign in front of a word has the opposite effect—it excludes any pages that contain the word. So adding a –Roman to the search string will result in fewer sites dealing with ancient religious beliefs. The + and – system works in Google, AltaVista, and Yahoo.

Use quotes. Putting a name or phrase in quotation marks tells the search engine to look for only those documents that contain the full phrase. For example, "Leonardo da

Vinci" will find documents containing that exact wording. Without the quotes, the search engine will look for documents that contain Leonardo plus documents that contain da plus documents that contain Vinci—over a million in all.

Use Advanced Search. All of the search engines offer an advanced search page, which makes it easy to construct a narrow search, even if you can't remember the special plusses and minuses and quotes. The more boxes you complete on the advanced search page, the narrower the search will be.

Search what you find. So you've found ten web pages that seem to contain the percentage of hydrogen on Jupiter. But when you go to the site, the number you are looking for is not immediately visible. An easy way to locate the specific item is to choose Find from your browser's Edit menu, and enter a keyword, such as hydrogen. This will search the text of the page until it finds hydrogen. Much faster than scrolling.

You Can't Always Get What You Want . . .

But if you search carefully, you might get what you need. Not everything you seek can be found on the Web. And not everything you find is what you sought. But if you apply some of these understandings and strategies to your next research visit to the Web, you might find your time better spent and your results more useful. For more detail on this topic, get a copy of *Student Guide to Research on the World Wide Web,* published by Children's Software Press.

UNDERSTANDING URLS

Most people don't know that URL stands for Universal Resource Locator. Even those who know that don't always know how to read a URL, or what its parts mean. Some URLs are easy to understand, such as *http://www.nytimes.com* or *http://www.harvard.edu* or *http://www.whitehouse.gov.* Most of us can figure out that these lead to popular and well-recognized web sites. But how about these URLs, which I saw in my browser today:

> *http://199.239.136.200*
> *http://www.bu.edu/jlengel/Websem/menu.html*
> *http://www.google.fr/search?q=harvard+university&ie=ISO-8859-1&hl=fr&meta=*
> *http://www.amazon.com/exec/obidos/subst/home/home.html/002-2590296-3818411*

What do all those letters and numbers mean? Whose sites are these? This last section of Chapter 6 looks at the syntax of URLs, helps you to make sense out of them and shows you how to use this knowledge to help yourself and your students make better use of the Web.

URL, DNS, What's Your Internet Address?

Look at the first URL in the preceding list, *http://199.239.136.200*. What does it signify? Entering this into the address bar on a browser tells a computer to use the HyperText Transfer Protocol (HTTP) to connect to a computer whose Internet Protocol (IP) address is 199.239.136.200. Very simple. Every computer (and every other device) on the Internet uses a unique number to identify itself, similar to a telephone number. No two computers can use the same number at the same time. The routers on the Internet keep track of which IP addresses are connected where, and send messages to them accordingly.

If you click on the address above, you end up on the front page of the *New York Times*. How can that be? I thought the URL of the *New York Times* was *http://www.nytimes.com*. The truth is that the computer that serves up the *Times* has an IP address of 199.239.136.200. To the routers on the Internet, that's all that matters. They use these numbers to route the connections automatically. But to the humans on the Internet, these numbers are not so useful. So we developed a way to use common words as URLs, such as *www.nytimes.com*. Much easier to remember than a 12-digit number. When I enter *http://www.nytimes.com* into my browser, my computer first looks up this URL in a Domain Name Server (DNS), a computer that keeps track of which name goes with which IP address, like a telephone directory. So my computer asks the DNS, "What is the IP address of www.nytimes.com?" and the DNS replies, "It's 199.239.136.200." Now my computer can send its request through the Internet to the right computer. A URL can be letters or numbers or a combination of the two; it can identify a computer, such as http://www.bfit.edu, or a particular document, such as http://www.bfit.edu/jlengel/Websem/menu.html. Let's analyze this last URL to understand how it is constructed.

http: This first part of the URL identifies the protocol of your request. In this case, the letters tell the receiving computer that you want your answer back using the HyperText Transfer Protocol. Most of the communication you do on the Web uses this protocol. Other protocols include FTP (File Transfer Protocol, used to move files back and forth) or RTSP (Real Time Streaming Protocol), used to play videos over the Web in real time.

www.bfit.edu: This second part of the URL identifies the computer you want to connect to. Because computers are actually referred to by number, this phrase must be looked up (automatically) in a DNS in order to make the connection. The last two pieces of this part, the bfit.edu, is the domain name. Benjamin Franklin Institute of Technology has registered this domain name officially with the authorities who manage the Internet. In the DNS directory, bfit.edu is linked to the computer with the IP address of 128.197.27.7.

jlengel: This refers to my directory on the Benjamin Franklin Institute web server, my very own folder where I put all of my web files. BFIT lets me set up this folder, and put whatever I like into it. There are hundreds of directories like this on the server.

Websem: This is one of the subfolders (subdirectories) that I have created to help me organize the many things I keep in my BFIT web folder.

menu.html: This is a document, a web page, that sits in the Websem folder on my part of the BFIT web server. It's a document I created with a web page editor and saved, in HTML format.

So this URL, when activated, tells the routers on the Internet to use the HTTP protocol to go to the BFIT Web server (at 128.197.27.7), and get the document menu.html, which is sitting inside the Websem folder, inside the jlengel folder.

So far, so good—this is logical, and you can figure out many URLs by analyzing the words. But what about the third URL in the list:

http://www.google.fr/search?q=harvard+university&ie=ISO-8859-1&hl=fr

What's this all about? This URL, like the two shown below it in the list, contains a *script.* It's easy to figure out that this URL refers to the Google web site (French version), but the rest of the URL is a mystery. That's the script part.

Scripts

A URL can not only identify a particular server on the Internet, it can also tell it what to do. The URL listed above tells Google to search for web sites that contain the words *harvard* or *university,* using standard codes. It also identifies me as coming from a French-language web site. This is called a *script.* When the Google computer receives this script from me, it runs its search program, using the parameters I entered. The script tells the server what to do. To analyze it:

search: This first word tells the server what program or process to use, what action to take. In this case, it tells Google to run its search program.

?: This character simply separates the action from the parameters that follow.

q=harvard+university: This tells the search program that I have made a query for the words harvard or university.

&: This is another separator that tells the search program to get ready for another parameter.

ie=ISO-8859–1: This tells Google that I am using the standard Latin characters on my computer, as opposed to Greek or Chinese. ISO stands for the International Standards Organization, the group that defines these kinds of things. The Latin alphabet is called 8859-1. Greek is 8859-7. If you want to know more about these character codes, see *http://ppewww.ph.gla.ac.uk/~flavell/iso8859/iso8859-pointers.html.* (That last URL tells me that the site is at a school the United Kingdom: .uk is the country domain; .ac in the UK stands for academic, as .edu in the US stands for education.)

hl=fr: This tells Google that I entered my search on a web page that was in French. The Google search engine is smart enough to look first for pages written in this langauge. If I came from an English page, I'd see hl=en.

You need not analyze or understand these scripts in order to use the Web. These scripts are generated automatically by your browser and the web server you are connected to. But it helps to have a clue as to what they mean.

Cookies

Some scripts contain cookies. Look at this one, generated when I connected to Amazon.com:

http://www.amazon.com/exec/obidos/subst/home/home.html/002-2590296-3818411

All I typed in was amazon.com, but somehow this long URL was generated by my browser. What's going on here? The Amazon web server is crafty. When it receives a simple request for amazon.com, it is not satisfied simply to display its home page. It secretly and surreptitiously and very quickly sends a query back to my computer to see if I have any Amazon *cookies.* A cookie is a bit of information that Amazon might have left behind on my computer last time I visited them. Really. This happens. Amazon has left several cookies in my browser, to identify me as a past customer. To Amazon, I am apparently Mr. 002-2590296-3818412, and when they look me up in their database they find that I am a good customer, they know what books I have bought, and they know my name. Therefore the top of the home page greets me with *Hello, Jim Lengel. We have recommendations for you. (If you're not Jim Lengel, click here.)*

This identifying cookie-number is passed to the Amazon server through the URL. The rest of the URL, *exec/obidos/subst/home/home.html,* simply tells the Amazon server which database to use and which home page to serve me.

The Root of the Matter

So how can this knowledge of the secrets of URL syntax help you be a better teacher? If you or your students are having trouble reaching a site with a long URL, full of specifics and cookies and scripts, you might find what you want by connecting to the *root* of the URL. In the browser's address bar, delete all the gobbledygook to the right, until you are left with only the basics. Connect there, and you will most likely find the home page of the organization that published the resource you were looking for. From there you may be able to locate the desired item, whose document name or script parameters might have changed.

You can also use this knowledge to make your students into more informed browsers. They'll be able to figure out the nature and publisher of the site they've found. They'll be able to understand the processes that are being used to connect them and to search for resources. And there'll be one less mystery in their minds.

LEARN MORE . . .

About How to Find Things on the Web

www.google.com/help/refinesearch.html
Advanced Search Made Easy by Google

About Understanding URLs

www.library.jhu.edu/elp/useit/evaluate/url.html
  Understanding and Decoding URLs from the Sheridan Library at Johns Hopkins University

Download the Latest Versions of the Web Browsers

- Microsoft (**www.microsoft.com**)
- Netscape (**www.netscape.com**)
- Apple Computer (**www.apple.com**)
- Firefox (**www.firefox.com**)

Download the Latest Animation and Video Players

- QuickTime (**www.apple.com/quicktime/download**)
- RealVideo (**www.realnetworks.com/products/free_trial.html**)
- Windows media (**www.microsoft.com/windows/windowsmedia/download**)
- Flash and Shockwave (**www.macromedia.com/downloads**)

CHAPTER SEVEN

THE INTERNET
IN THE CLASSROOM

IN THIS CHAPTER

- **An Internet Briefing**
- **Webquests: Organizing the Internet in Your Classroom**
- **Web Assignments**
- **Virtual Field Trips**
- **Kids and the Internet at Home**
- **Learn More . . .**

The following are a couple of interesting facts about the Internet:

- The Internet is alive and well.
- It was not invented by Al Gore, but government contracts played an important role in its establishment.
- Millions of computers connect to it every day, including many in schools and colleges and homes.
- I'm connected right now, and it's very likely that you are as well.

But that's not exactly what this chapter is about. Many teachers ask how they can better take advantage of the learning opportunities offered by the World Wide Web. Their classrooms connected, their students astute Internet surfers, their community expecting great things, they ask how to make it happen.

This chapter gets you started by investigating several opportunities for using the Internet in your classroom: Internet briefings, webquests, simple web assignments, virtual field trips, and parental involvement with children online. We'll start with a simple task, the Internet briefing.

AN INTERNET BRIEFING

One of my students works as an intern at an advertising agency. Her supervisor asked her to do some research on the fashion trends in Shanghai, as part of their work for a new client. "Do you know anything about Shanghai?" she asked me during a break in class. I told her what I remembered from my visit in 1980, but suggested that things had changed quite a bit since then. She told me she had until the next morning to prepare her briefing. I suggested she use the World Wide Web to learn as much as she could about the city and its current trends. At the next break, she returned with some more pointed questions:

How is Shanghai different from other cities in China?

Why does downtown Shanghai look like Chicago? (She found a picture of the Bund.)

How can I find out about China's fashion industry?

She had evidently done some online homework during class. In response, I gave her a brief rundown on China's history and geography, explained the western influence in China (especially Shanghai) during the first part of the twentieth century, and suggested she talk to a fellow student who recently arrived in Boston from China. I also suggested that she continue her online research with a new focus on keywords such as *western influence* and *Shanghai fashion*. Apparently this approach worked, for by the end of the day she showed me an illustrated briefing on Shanghai fashion trends, of about three pages, suitable for submission to her supervisor.

In today's business world, this kind of briefing, developed chiefly online, is standard fare. To help our students learn how to build them, we should consider making the Internet briefing a regular part of the curriculum. The same process of questioning, researching, and organizing information quickly and pointedly can be applied to history, literature, science, and the arts as well as to fashions in Shanghai. An Internet briefing is a short, focused summary of an issue, event, or person, developed mostly with online sources, in a limited period of time. Creating one is a good way to exercise a student's research, thinking, and writing skills.

HOW TO . . . CREATE AN INTERNET BRIEFING

You need: A web browser; a reliable connection to the Internet; a word processor such as Microsoft Word.

You get: A detailed written summary of a topic of interest, based on many different sources.

1. Limit the topic. It's tough to develop an Internet briefing on a broad topic such as the history of warfare. Better topics would be the Popes of Avignon, or animals in E. B. White's stories, or the invention of the electron microscope. The topic must be narrow enough to allow quick understanding and summary in a short period of time. It should also be a topic for which information is available online. It's best if it's not one that has been covered before, and not part of the students' general knowledge—it should require some new information not already available.

2. Provide a structure. Describe for students what the completed briefing should contain. Distribute some exemplary briefings that show the extent, style, and structure of what you expect. The structure might be outlined as:

- A topic sentence that sets forth the main idea.
- Five paragraphs that provide background, examples, and illustrations.
- A paragraph or two of analysis and evaluation of the examples.
- A paragraph listing the sources consulted.

3. Suggest a method. Most students have never developed an Internet briefing, and so will need guidance in how to proceed. Here's a set of steps that can be applied to most any topic:

Consult a general, trusted source. Don't start with a keyword search engine. Go first to an online encyclopedia, or respected online textbook in the field, a source that will summarize the issue or topic and perhaps put it in the context of its background and history. Your class startup page (see Chapter 8) should provide links to some of these. Learn the who, what, why, when, and how of the topic you have been assigned.

Browse a directory. Use an internet directory such as Yahoo, that organizes web sites by topic. Find the category where your topic appears, and examine the other entries in this category. This will help provide context and examples for your briefing. For instance, follow the Yahoo directory to Society and Culture, then Religion, then Catholic, then People, then Popes, and you will see a listing of many sites that include the history of the pontiff, a useful background to the topic described earlier. Visit some of these sites to better understand the history of the papacy. Make note of any references to your topic. Note also any key terms that you may want to search with.

Ask around, look around. An Internet briefing is not restricted exclusively to online research. As my student did, ask people who might have some knowledge of the topic to describe the general situation as they understand it. If it's possible and convenient, make a quick trip to the library, looking especially to respected reference books that will help you understand the topic in general terms. Again, collect a list of key search terms that interest you.

Focus your search. You should by now be armed with enough background to conduct a more focused search on the Web. Use the search terms that you have collected with one of the Web search engines such as Google. Use the advanced search feature to target your research. For instance, you might use the entire phrase *E. B. White* AND the terms *spider*, *mouse*, and *swan* to find only those documents that refer to many of the author's animals at once.

Collect your findings. As you search, skim what you uncover. When you find a page or paragraph that's especially relevant to your assignment, read it carefully. If it provides an example or illustration for your briefing, copy and paste it to a Word document. As you find focused resources, your Word document—your notes—will grow into a valuable collection of ideas and facts. Don't forget to copy and paste the URLs of each source, along with the content, so you can cite it later.

Look for an angle.   After a session of searching, step back and survey what you have found. Read through your Word document. Do you spot any trends, any interesting contrasts, any provocative insights, any clear categories? These can become the organizational principles of your briefing. For instance, you might discover a parallel simultaneous development, in both Europe and the United States, of the electron microscope, with both continents claiming the credit. This competition can help you organize and present the examples in your briefing. You might also uncover an apt metaphor, or a sequence of events that makes a good story.

Outline your ideas.   In a new Word document, use your angle to outline your ideas in order, like this:

- The schism in church governance: why, who, and where
- The two seats of power: Rome and Avignon
- The power of Popes before, during, and after the split.

For each idea, copy and paste an example or two from your notes. Read through this embellished outline. Then sit down with a friend and tell him the story, orally, from your notes. Ask for suggestions on making it better.

Write the briefing.   Remembering what you said to your friend, write a paragraph for each point in your outline. Write your own words; do not copy and paste from your notes. Instead, summarize the examples your sources provide. When you're done, read it over to yourself. Now go back and ask yourself, after all this, What's my main idea here? Take your answer to that question and write it as your topic sentence. Read through your briefing once more. Ask yourself, So what? Take your answer to that question and write it as your closing sentence. Don't forget to list your sources at the end.

That, in brief, is the process for creating an Internet briefing. It can be a fun way to learn, and provides students with valuable skill for the future.

Extensions.   Here are some suggestions for additional Internet briefings to assign.

- Take the lead story on the front page of today's newspaper, and develop an Internet briefing on the topic or issue at hand.
- Develop an Internet briefing centered around an event in history.
- Develop an Internet briefing that explains how a scientific process works, such as a rainbow.

■ ■ ■ ■ ■ ■ ■ ■ ■ ■

WEBQUESTS: ORGANIZING THE INTERNET IN YOUR CLASSROOM

In the beginning, most classroom teachers began using the Internet for research with their students, with little regard for quality, quantity, or purpose. Students were sent to the Internet, often to Yahoo to search for information about a topic at hand. Quickly, though, classroom teachers understood that, if their class was studying the planets, doing a search on Venus using Yahoo got lots of results but few that had anything to do with planets. Certainly, getting quality results was an issue. And, giving students the assignment to do research at home or in the school library on a given topic often resulted in reams of paper, with the students dropping the pile on the desk as a done deed. Is research about quantity? Is this what the Internet was going to do in the classroom?

Teachers, of any level, would not bring their class to the New York Public Library and leave them in the front lobby and tell them to *go do research on Venus.* Clearly, they had to find a better way of approaching the Internet and its potential. I can still remember being in elementary school and being engaged in a unit on the planets. Mrs. Barry went to the librarian a week or so before we started and gathered all the resources on a cart. The cart got wheeled down the hall and into our classroom. It included science books, the *World Book Encyclopedia,* and some 3-D models of planets. Our investigations and reports were led by what we found on the cart. This concept of gathering and organizing Internet resources just like Mrs. Barry did in the third grade, became the basis for webquests.

The term *WebQuest* was coined by Bernie Dodge in the mid90s as he worked with his graduate students at San Diego State University in California. Together, they began to develop tightly constructed units that had several features in common: efficient use of Internet resources, small collaborative learning groups of students, excellent lesson plans led by guiding questions fostering higher-order thinking skills, and an appreciation for the power of the technology available online.

Since that time, he has collected hundreds of excellent examples and made them available free for teachers around the world (http://webquest.sdsu.edu/matrix.html). They serve as models that teachers routinely use to develop their own webquests.

A Webquest on Webquests

To understand what a webquest is and what constitutes an excellent one, you can participate in one of the online activities in Bernie Dodge's web site, a webquest on webquests. This activity is best accomplished in a 2- to 3-hour session with a group of twelve to sixteen adults. However, if you are alone, you can go through the steps and gain a reasonable understanding.

Following the WebQuest model, the activity invites you to examine several classroom webquests and determine which are the best. Sounds simple, except that you'll work in a group of four and each of you will look at the examples from a particular perspective, then have a discussion to determine which examples would be successful in the classroom. The roles are the Efficiency Expert (does not like to waste time), the Affiliator (all activities must promote collaborative skills), the Altitudinist (demands higher-order thinking skills), and the Technophile (loves taking advantage of all that the Internet has to offer including animations, images, video, etc.).

Visit the site now (http://webquest.sdsu.edu/webquestwebquest-ms.html), where you'll find all the instructions, activity sheets to record your observations, links to the sample webquests, and a guide to your group's discussion. Take some time now to participate in the webquest on webquests. Note that the following "How to..." section outlines the steps for creating a hyperlinked Word document to help you construct your own webquest.

I hope you've got some great ideas for your first webquest. Remember, as you saw on the web site, the structure of the webquest is important and must include the Six Building Blocks.

HOW TO . . . CONSTRUCT YOUR OWN WEBQUEST

You need: A web browser; a reliable connection to the Internet; a word processor such as Microsoft® Word.

You get: A webquest suitable for your students to use as an assignment.

1. Open a Word document and use this outline to lay out your webquest.

   - Introduction
   - Task
   - Process
   - Resources
   - Evaluation
   - Conclusion

   The Resources section is where you'll list the web sites that your students can use to accomplish their tasks. Each of these sites can be hyperlinked right from your Word document. When you are finished, place the document on the desktop of your classroom computer(s) so that students can simply open the document and begin their work.

2. Add Hyperlinks to your Microsoft Word document.

   - With your Word document open, go on the Web and locate the page to which you want to link.
   - Select and copy the URL from the Address box (highlight the address, then choose Copy from the Edit menu).
   - On your Word document, place your cursor where you want the link to appear and select Paste from the Edit menu. Press the Return key and the link becomes live.

   It's OK to include the full URL within the text of your document. You'd want to do this especially if you plan to print the assignment so students can work at home.

3. Create a link from a word or picture in a Word document.

   - With your Word document open, click/drag to select the picture or word from which you want to link. The word or picture should be highlighted:

   > Explore Math

   - From the Insert menu, select Hyperlink.
   - In the dialog box, paste the URL to which you want to link. Click OK.

Insert Hyperlink		
Link to:	http://www.exploremath.com/l	
Display:	Explore Math	

The link is now live and the words *Explore Math* are linked to the math web site.

4. Illustrate your webquest document. You can use images from the page to illustrate Word documents and presentations in your webquest. Here are two methods that work very well:

■ With an Internet page open, simply drag the image to your desktop. It's ready to insert into your document (usually under the Insert menu). Or drag it to where you want it to appear on your slide, if you're working in PowerPoint.

■ You can save a copy of your image by pointing to the picture with your mouse. Then, on a Mac, press the mouse down without moving it. On a PC, simply right-click with your mouse pointed to the image. A dialog box appears where you can hoose to Save the Image to Disk. Choose a location for your images and click OK.

Have fun working with webquests in your classroom. They take some time to construct but you'll find the effort will pay off in efficiency, quality of your Internet-enriched assignments, and learning by your students.

Extensions.   Here are some suggestions for additional webquests to develop.

■ Build a webquest with another teacher in your department or grade level, that both of you can use.

■ Teach students to build their own webquests aimed at teaching other students about a topic.

■ Build a webquest on a topic that is completely new to you.

■ ■ ■ ■ ■ ■ ■ ■ ■ ■

WEB ASSIGNMENTS

A typical web assignment sends students out on the Internet to gather information and answer questions pertinent to the subject under study as described above. You can find some good examples of these kinds of assignments at http://webquest.sdsu.edu. You might also try a little web assignment yourself—I've posted one for you at http://lengel.net/AssignmentAmerica.doc. This topic may not be in your curriculum, but going through this assignment will help you understand how a web assignment works.

A good web assignment focuses students on ideas that are important to the curriculum. It uses web resources that cannot be found in typical school libraries. It puts the student into the role of information finder, investigator, and seeker of answers to worthwhile questions. It asks questions that take students in different directions, and that exercise a wide range of intellectual activities. It requires students to face the facts, analyze the differences, draw conclusions, and explain her answers. It is designed so that there may be more than one answer to some of the questions, and so that students may end up in different places. Most of all, it is designed to produce new learning.

Now that you have experienced some web assignments, it's time to create one of your own. Begin by making a *Hotlist* (see below) for a topic from your curriculum. Then develop the Assignment, as a series of questions that can be answered from the sites in the Hotlist. Then post or distribute the Assignment to your students, and help them work through it.

Hotlists

A hotlist is simply a list of web resources relevant to a subject in the curriculum. You develop a hotlist by searching the Web for sites that might help your students learn about the topic at hand, at a level appropriate to them. The easiest way to construct a hotlist is to embed the links to the sites you find in a Microsoft Word document. If you embed web links in a standard Word document, your students will be able to follow those links when they open your document on their computers. This is a very good way to distribute assignments and readings that contain references to online documents and web sites. These documents can be distributed through a web site, attached to an email, or saved to a disc.

An example might look like this:

> The America's Cup is a trophy granted to the winner of an international sailboat race. You can learn about the history of this cup at the Herreshoff Marine Museum (www.herreshoff.org).

This example contains two types of links. The first *implicit* link, on America's Cup, hides the URL, while the second shows it *explicitly*. These instructions show you how to create both kinds.

HOW TO . . . MAKE A HOTLIST

You need: A web browser; a reliable connection to the Internet; a word processor such as Microsoft Word.

You get: A hotlist suitable as a study guide for your students.

1. Open a new Word document. Enter the title of the document, and any introductory text.
2. When you get to the place where you want the link to be, stop for a moment. Save your document.
3. Open your web browser (Internet Explorer, Netscape, Safari, Firefox).
4. Open the web page you want to link to.
5. Select the URL of the site in the browser's address bar.
6. Choose Copy from the Edit menu. This copies the URL to your computer's clipboard (short-term memory).
7. Go back to your Word document.

If you are creating an implicit link:

1. In Word, select the text you want to link from.
2. Choose Hyperlink from the Insert menu.
3. Paste the URL into the box at the top.
4. Click OK, and watch the selected words turn blue.

If you are creating an explicit link:

1. Paste the URL into the text of the Word document.
2. Press return on the keyboard.
3. Watch the URL turn blue.

When your document is complete, save it. Then test it by clicking the links to make sure they work. You may upload this document to a web site; you may attach it to an email; you may distribute it on floppy disk or CD-ROM; you may post it to a web server. No matter how you distribute it, when your students open it, they will be able to follow your links.

Extensions.

■ With your colleagues, create a collection of hotlists for your grade or subject, and post them to the school web site.
■ Assign older students to create a hotlist that would help a younger student to learn about a particular topic.

■ ■ ■ ■ ■ ■ ■ ■ ■ ■

From Hotlist to Assignment

A hotlist can be a valuable resource for learning, but in and of itself it is not an assignment, and will not guarantee learning. What you need to add to the hotlist are the questions that turn it into a Web assignment.

The key to a successful web-based assignment is the set of questions that you pose. A hotlist, treasure hunt, sampler, or scrapbook will by itself seldom lead to learning—the student needs a question or provocation from the teacher, for which the hotlist can serve as a resource.

For your first web assignment, it's a good idea to pose a series of different types of questions, beginning with factual questions, then posing some analytical questions, then an evaluative question, and finally a question that you don't know the answer to. The purpose of these questions should be to get students to peruse, confront, and think about the content that's referred to in your hotlist.

Facts.   For example, consider the hotlist about the America's Cup that you saw earlier. It included a series of Web sites about the history of this boat race as well as references to the current competitions. A factual question for this assignment might be:

Where is the America's Cup race taking place this year?

This question can be answered easily by visiting almost any of the sites. Another factual question might be:

What countries are competing in this year's race?

By finding the answers to these questions, the students will be exposed to the content of the sites, and will peruse other aspects of the topic at hand. Most of them will succeed at this task, perhaps strengthening their confidence to tackle the next part of the assignment.

Analysis.   The next question might be analytical, asking them to compare things that they find, or draw conclusions from information found on several different sites. Analytical questions might include:

> Compare the experience of the crew of "Prada" with that of "Stars and Stripes."

> Describe the differences in performance between the British and American teams over the last month of racing.

These kinds of questions require the students first to search the Web for the relevant facts, and then to put these facts together, and finally to draw a conclusion from them. The search and the analysis will in most cases cause them to learn more about the topic at hand. It's important that the answers to the analytical questions not be found directly on the sites themselves, but require searching several sites and conducting a new analysis.

Evaluation.   Moving up the intellectual ladder, we might pose some evaluative questions that require facts, analysis, and a prediction or judgment. An evaluative question for this assignment might be:

> Based on crew experience and performance so far in the races, who do you predict to win the cup this year? Why?

or

> Explain how the technical aspects of the boats, the weather, and crew experience interact to produce a winner. Which of these three factors is most important? Why?

Answering these questions requires the gathering of facts and opinions from the sites, a bit of comparative analysis, and a judgment. It also calls for the student to explain how she arrived at her conclusion. Again, it's important that this question is not one that has already been treated on any of the sites in your hotlist.

Speculation.   A final question might explore an issue on which there is no commonly accepted answer, and which you have not fully explored yourself. Such a question might be:

> From race performance so far, can you ascertain any relationship between boat speed and the use of exotic materials in construction?

A speculative question like this puts the student in a different role *vis-à-vis* his teacher, and often engenders more interesting class discussions.

Construct the Assignment

The best way to build the Web assignment is to add to the hotlist you created in Word the questions that you developed in these categories. Format the document to appear like the America's Cup assignment you saw earlier. Distribute the document to students by email, posting to a web site, copying to all the computers in the classroom, or posting to a network server, or putting it on a floppy disk. Don't forget to tell them when the assignment is due.

Build a web assignment for a topic you'll be teaching next week. The questions you pose will make or break the web-based assignment. Take the time you need to construct these questions to fit the needs of your curriculum and the nature of the content on the Web.

VIRTUAL FIELD TRIPS

> *The third seal from the left—the students had named him Oscar—was about to move across the rock and challenge the authority of the old bull. The students in this Iowa classroom were observing firsthand, in real time, the activities of aquatic mammals off the coast of California, thanks to a live video feed from a science observation post over the Internet and into their classroom.*

These Iowa students are taking a virtual field trip (VFT) to a remote aquatic site on the Pacific coast. The information highway took them thousands of miles away to a place where they could study some important concepts in science, in ways previously impossible in the classroom. This trip needed neither school buses nor permission slips nor lunchboxes—but it did call for careful preparation by the teacher, perhaps even more preparation than a bus-and-lunchbox trip. This section provides some suggestions on working VFTs into your curriculum, and points you to some online destinations.

Identify the Curriculum Opportunity

The best way to use any field trip, virtual or otherwise, is to teach a concept or topic that's difficult to study in the classroom or the library. Something that's dry and abstract in the classroom might prove lively and concrete on site. We naturally think of geography or earth science topics, which lend themselves easily to field work, but don't limit yourself. Consider such topics as:

- **Literature.** A visit to the House of Seven Gables or Thoreau's Walden Pond or Shakespeare's Globe Theatre.
- **History.** Follow Lewis and Clark along their journey across the new continent, or tour the battlefield at Gettysburg.
- **Music.** Follow Mozart's career across the cities of Europe, or enter a museum of musical instruments.
- **Mathematics.** Visit the Greenwich Observatory in England to lean about the mathematics of determining longitude.

- **Art.** The Louvre, the Metropolitan, or the Museum of Fine Arts might contain some resources to help learn the history of art.

Think through your curriculum, and make a list of those hard-to-teach topics. Browse through the lists of VFTs at the end of this article. From all of these, identify the best opportunity to enhance your teaching with an online field trip.

Prepare the Trip

A VFT requires at least as much preparation and planning as any other trip. Simply sending students off on a bus or a web browser is not enough. Here are some steps to take to make the trip work well:

- **Purpose.** Make it clear to the students exactly why they are taking this trip. Explain in writing the purpose of the trip: "The purpose of the Lewis and Clark virtual field trip is to understand the varied geographies and cultures encountered by the explorers, through images, original sources, music, and art."
- **Provocation.** Challenge the students with a problem to solve or an assignment to complete while they are on the trip. Make it as clear and as concrete as possible, and expect them to produce some work they they can hand in for a grade: "On the trip, find three different landscapes seen by the men. Describe each one in your own words, and provide an image to accompany your description. Explain how each of these landscapes differed from what they had seen on the east coast." This provocation gets them thinking, and provides a motivation for their journey.
- **Path.** Guide them as they move through the trip. Provide a clear path, with explanations, background information, and a provocative question at each step. Few students learn at their best when left to wander aimlessly through the site. Many of the VFTs listed at the end of this article are highly structured to provide a prepared path. Others are simply collections of resources through which you must trace a path for your students. Look through the former to get some ideas on how to guide students along.
- **Prerequisites.** Before they depart on their online journey, make sure they understand the background of the event or topic they are visiting, just as you would for a physical field trip. Give them some readings, show them a film, provide a list of key questions, or have them do some preliminary research that results in their understanding where the topic of the trip fits in the larger context. Provide, in advance of the trip, a written statement of the purpose, the provocative questions, and the nature of the path they are to follow.

Take to the Highway

The virtual field trip can be an event that the entire class takes at once, or be scheduled over several days or weeks. If your school has a computer lab that accommodates all of your students at once, book it in advance and conduct the field trip on that day. If you have a cluster of computers in your classroom, let small groups of students take the trip each day until all have completed the work. Or let them follow your path at the computers in the library, or at home. There's more flexibility in scheduling the virtual trip.

Individual, Small Group, or Whole Class?

Even the one-computer classroom can host a virtual field trip. The whole class might take the trip together, as you lead them along the path and pose the appropriate question as the class views the objects on the display. You might assign one question each to several small groups, and let each take its turn at the computer to follow the path and answer the questions. You might let each student on his own take the trip, do the work, and then discuss the results with the entire class at the end. Mix your methods and groupings to match your students' needs and work styles, and to optimize your technology facilities.

Sources for Structured VFTs

As you determine the topic of your first virtual field trip, take a look at some well-structured trips, most concocted by fellow teachers and published on the Web for you to use. Take a sample trip yourself, and do the work, so that you have a feel for what the student will experience. Here are some interesting examples of well-structured trips:

- Tramline
  www.field-guides.com/trips.htm
- Surfaquarium
  http://surfaquarium.com/virtual.htm
- Big Bend National Park Geology Field Trip
  http://geoweb.tamu.edu/faculty/herbert/bigbend
- A Virtual Geological Field Trip to Iceland
  www.casdn.neu.edu/~geology/department/staff/colgan/iceland/
  welcome.htm
- The Mysterious Mayas
  www.uen.org/utahlink/tours/tourFames.cgi?tour_id=14933
- Tibet: A Virtual Field Trip
  http://jan.ucc.nau.edu/~wittke/Tibet/Tibet.html
- Pompeii: A Virtual Field Trip
  www.burlington.mec.edu/memorial/Pompeii.htm
- Digital Learning Events from the Apple Learning Interchange
  http://ali.apple.com/ali_sites/ali/new_events.html

Sources for VFT Raw Materials

You might also build your own trip from some of the unstructured raw materials available online. For most of these, you will need to develop the preparation, provocative questions, and clear path for your students to take full advantage of their journey:

- Virtually Hawaii: Virtual Field Trips
  http://satftp.soest.hawaii.edu/space/hawaii/virtual.field.trips.html

- VolcanoWorld Virtual Field Trips
  http://volcano.und.nodak.edu/vwdocs/kids/vrtrips.html
- A Virtual Field Trip of the Landscapes of Nova Scotia
  www.gov.ns.ca/natr/meb/field/start.htm
- Virtual and On-line Geologic Field Trip Guides
  www.lib.utexas.edu/geo/onlineguides.html
- Utah Education Network Virtual Field Trips
  www.uen.org/utahlink/tours
- Virtual Field Trip Sites from AEA 267
  www.aea2.k12.ia.us/curriculum/virtualtrips.html
- Race Rocks Live Ecology Video
  www.racerocks.com

Guidelines for Using VFTs

As you develop your own trip, you might want to consult these guidelines:

- Virtual Field Trip Guidelines
  http://surfaquarium.com/vftguide.htm

You may not need permission slips, lunchboxes, chaperones, and bus drivers for these field trips, but you still need to prepare for the trips carefully.

KIDS AND THE INTERNET AT HOME

Classroom teachers and parents of students at the elementary level would love to have kids go online at home but often have reservations about where to send them, what they can do when they get there, and what makes a good, kid-appropriate web site. One group of teachers got together and wrote the following letter home to parents one June, providing some much-needed guidance.

Dear Parents,

We have had such a wonderful year with our students working on the classroom laptops. As you may know, we've had 3 laptops for student use in each of our classrooms and have made great use of them. Your kids have had many opportunities to visit excellent web sites geared toward their age and interest.

We thought we'd share some of our favorites with you in case you and your child get to go online this summer! We have checked each of these sites and think your children will enjoy the topics and activities presented. We hope you will take the opportunity to visit them with your child this summer. Note that the Public Library has computers available for your use during their regular hours.

General Sites for Kids

www.eduplace.com
Create wacky Web tales, the online version of the old classic Mad Libs.

www.puzzlemaker.com
Puzzlemaker is a puzzle generation tool for teachers, students, and parents. Create and print customized word search, crossword, and math puzzles using your word lists.

www.iconn.org/index.html
iCONN is part of the Connecticut Education Network. It provides all students, faculty, and residents with online access to essential library and information resources. It is administered by the Connecticut State Library in conjunction with the Department of Higher Education. The web site includes Resources for the Public, Schools, and Colleges, Library Catalogs, Library Home Pages, and much, much more.

http://pbskids.org
PBS Kids is an excellent source for sites where students can go and explore or do a specific lesson. It is organized by character, and each page has a parent/teacher resource section. The site is free and easy to get around in. The pages are aimed at the elementary level.

www.howstuffworks.com
Kid-friendly explanations on how things work.

http://kidshub.org/kids/kids.cfm
Kids Hub is a noncommercial educational portal for upper elementary school and middle school students. It includes free online interactive learning games, puzzles, and quizzes.

www.wicked4kids.com
A very nice site with games, puzzles, and other activities.

www.timeforkids.com/TFK
Time for Kids is very easy to use and keeps your kids up to date!

www.kidsdomain.com
Lots of activities for kids.

Science Sites for Kids

www.chem4kids.com
A rich resource for elementary students.

Math Sites for Kids

http://mathforum.org/
A center for Math education on the net—weekly challenges, puzzles, and so on.

Search Engines for Kids

www.yahooligans.com
Yahooligans—The browser Yahoo has set up for Web surfers ages 8 to 14, brings up only sites that are suitable for this age group.

Jokes and Sillies

www.mamamedia.com
Silly jokes for little kids.

www.yucky.com
Explaining the mysteries of the yucky things kids wonder about.

www.bigchalk.com
Bigchalk's award-winning web site assembles the best free Internet learning resources for K–12 teachers, parents, and students. It includes:

> Homework Central—A free directory of educational web links created especially for students and teachers

> Lesson Plan Archives—Offering more than 10,000 web-based plans organized by topic and grade level

> Newsletters—Monthly email newsletters, highlighting the best educational resources on the Internet

> Virtual Field Trips—Interactive modules exploring everything from the life of slaves in colonial America to conservation efforts in the Congo

General Sites for Parents

www.edhelper.com
The site lists over 1,000 webquests and 6,200 lesson plans.

Have fun exploring the web with your kids this summer! If you find site that you think other kids might like, please let us know via email. Thanks and have a great summer!

Sincerely,

Mrs. Lengel (kmlengel1@mac.com)

LEARN MORE . . .

http://school.discovery.com/schrockguide
Kathy Schrock's Guide for Educators is a web site that was developed for and by teachers to help integrate the Internet in the classroom. It's now a commercial site, yet continues to provide excellent guidance and resources.

http://yahooligans.yahoo.com
Yahooligans is one of the best directories for classroom teachers, this is a safe place to send your kids for information, activities, and resources. The site also has lesson ideas for teachers.

www.iste.org/resources
The International Society for Technology in Education (ISTE) are the folks who set the standards for teachers and students in the field of technology in education. Their resources and Web guides are excellent.

http://ali.apple.com
Apple Learning Interchange is a site sponsored by Apple Computer, Inc. that gives many examples of technology-rich, curriculum lessons, K–12.

CHAPTER EIGHT

PUBLISHING ON THE WEB

IN THIS CHAPTER

- **An Educational Startup Page**
- **Teacher.com**
- **Writing for the Web**
- **Looking Good Online**
- **Design Principles for the Web**
- **Displaying Text**
- **Building a Web Page with Word**
- **Building a Web Page with Dreamweaver**
- **Learn More . . .**

Most of us use the World Wide Web as research tool. We look at information that others have placed there. And the last two chapters considered how to best use the Internet in this way, as a *consumer* of information.

This chapter turns the tide and shows you (and your students) how to become a *producer* of information, how to publish your own material on the Web for others to use. Those others might be only the people in your classroom or school, but it could be the entire universe of web browsers. The internet after all is a two-way street: once connected, you have the capability to *read* what's there as well as *write* your own contributions. It is in fact the first mass medium in which the barriers to entry are low—you need not own a printing press or a television station to get your own message out.

This chapter begins with two concrete ideas for you as a teacher to publish important educational documents on the Web: an educational startup page for your students, and your own web site. It then goes on to provide some practical advice on how to do this well: how to write, design, and display material on a web page so that it is effective and easy to use. The last two sections show you the mechanics of using Word or Dreamweaver to build your own web pages.

We understand that no professional web designer would use Microsoft Word to build pages. However, it's the most available software found in schools and will help beginners get started. Dreamweaver does provide many of the tools used by the pros and is available at an educator's discount to teachers. Other web page development applications, including Netscape Composer, Adobe GoLive, and Microsoft Front Page, are used by many teachers and follow many of the same steps. The Learn More section of this chapter provides links to some of these applications. These instructions will stick with Word, the simplest and most ubiquitous, and Dreamweaver, the most professional.

All of the advice and instruction here applies to you as well as to your students. They can follow the same design principles and step-by-step guides as they create their own curriculum-related publications.

AN EDUCATIONAL STARTUP PAGE

When you launch your web browser, where does it go? What web site shows up first in the browser window? Unless you've changed it, your browser will automatically connect to the web site of its publisher: a Windows computer will connect to the Microsoft or MSN site; an Apple Computer will connect to an Apple site; and the Netscape browser will launch the Netscape home page. There's not much of educational value on any of these web pages. The MSN site touts weight-loss schemes, online auctions, dating tips, and automobile reviews. The Netscape startup page shows large colorful ads for Napster, Dell Computers, and "Shy and Sexy LeAnn Rimes Top Videos." The Microsoft page is a series of advertisements for its products, including MechAssualt, in which we learn that "these lumbering giants are totally bad-ass. We guarantee that the flamethrower-toting Hellbringer is going to be popular."

Putting these pages up automatically every day in front of our students (or ourselves) is probably not a good idea. It's like placing ads for acne cream and fast cars on the blackboard. Many schools and teachers have designed their own startup pages, and set all of the browsers in their school or classroom to open up to these educationally useful sites. Some have even designed startup pages specially designed for students and parents at home. This section helps you build your own custom startup page, and to set your computer so that it takes its first step on the web journey on a good footing.

Why Start Up?

Some students need to be channeled. Others are fine once they're set off in the right direction. Many need help organizing their resources. All benefit from the guidance of a teacher. These truths are especially relevant to students' experience on the Internet. Left completely alone, with no organization or guidance, few will make a successful voyage and only a handful will arrive at the desired shore. An Internet startup page lets the teacher or the school guide and channel the web browsing experience from the very start. It organizes web resources in a scheme useful and familiar to the students and the subjects they are studying.

It makes it easy to connect to the assignments and references and indexes that are most important to academic work.

A startup page for a history class in eighth grade, for instance, might include:

- Contact information for the teacher
- A link to the course outline
- A link to the companion web site for the textbook used in the course
- A link to The History Place at (www.ushistoryplace.com), a collection of American History resources
- A summary of this week's assignment, and a link to its hotlist
- Links to the Google and AltaVista search engines
- A link to the high school History Department web site
- A link to the school's web site
- A link to the American Map Collection at the University of Texas (www.lib.utexas.edu/maps/americas.html)
- A link to HistoryPictures.com (www.historypictures.com)

. . . and other items selected by the teacher. Whenever the computers in this classroom are started, the browser automatically displays this page, and the students find it fast an easy tool to use to get their work done. Many students put this page on their list of bookmarks on their home computers as well. It took the history teacher less than an hour to put this page together, and another half-hour to set up all the computers to use it. This 90-minute investment has paid off several times over in increased efficiency for students.

A startup page can serve a course, a department, a school, or a library. Such a page is simple in design, limited in scope, and easy to use. For example, you can see the home page for my course in technology leadership at www.lengel.net/lead.html.

Not the Home Page

You might claim that your school already has a home page, and all the computers are set to bring it up. But a home page is seldom an educational page. For most schools, the home page is a publication that markets the school to its public constituents, designed for public relations and identity-building. Seldom do these home pages directly help a student get her work done. The home page for our college at www.bfit.edu is an example of a nice page for publicity, but not much for learning.

A startup page serves a different purpose from the typical home page. A startup page is for your students to guide them to the resources they need for your course or curriculum, and that's it.

Plan the Page

The first step in establishing a startup page is to plan the links. A startup page consists mostly of links to existing sites, and a good way to start planning is to list the tasks that your students need to accomplish on the Web. Your list might include the items in the first column of the following table.

TASK	LINKS
Conduct research	Search engine, subject directory, special resource collection
Contact the teacher	Email, telephone, office hours
Locate course and learning materials	Course outline, worksheets, sample quizzes
Get the latest assignment	Assignment sheets, lab outlines
Explore the topics of the course	Selected resource sites, image collections, primary source documents

For or each task listed in the first column, the second column lists the resources the students will need to accomplish it.

HOW TO . . . PLAN YOUR OWN STARTUP PAGE

You need: Microsoft Word or other word processor.

You get: The outline of an educational startup page geared to your students.

1. Create your own table, as described above, to plan your own startup page.
2. Find (or create) the best links for each task. For help in this regard, you might want to consult *A Student Guide to Research on the Web,* by Children's Software Press, or the section in Chapter 6 of this book entitled *Finding It on the Web.* You don't want to list every possible link; only those that will be of utmost value to your students and necessary to their work.
3. Locate the links, or create them in the form of assignment sheets and sample quizzes.
4. Copy its URL from the address box of your browser.
5. Paste it into a Word document.
6. After the link enter a few words describing the link. Put all the links in this Word document—you'll use it as the basis for building your startup page.

Build the Page

You can build your page in one of three ways: with Microsoft Word, with a web-page editing program such as Dreamweaver, or with an HTML editor. It's beyond the scope of this chapter to teach you all three methods, but you will find detailed information on the first method in the sections at the end of this chapter called Building a Web Page with Microsoft Word or Building a Web Page with Dreamweaver.

No matter which method you choose, the page should contain a title, such as *History 8 Resources,* and a list of the links from your planning. It's best to label each link with a descriptive name, such as *History Place,* rather than with its URL. You may also want to include an illustrative image (see Using Digital Images, in Chapter 11), but keep the design and layout simple: this is a working page, not an attractive come-on.

Using Word, you can simply format the list of links you developed in your planning. Then make links to each site:

1. Select the label of the site, such as History Place.
2. Choose Insert, then Hyperlink from the menubar.
3. Paste or type the URL of the site, such as www.ushistoryplace.com
4. Click OK, then click the new link.

The link should appear underlined in blue in the Word document. When you click it, it should open your browser and link to the desired site. Once the document is linked and formatted as necessary, from the menubar choose File, then Save for Web. Give the file a simple, one-word filename such as *history8startup.html*. Word will save the startup page as a web page, with the *.html* filename extension. You can test this page by opening it with your web browser.

Post the Page

If you or your school or your department has a web server, the easiest way to post the page is to copy it to the server. You may need to contact your school's webmaster to help you with this. Once it is posted, your webmaster will tell you the URL of this page, which might be something like http://myschool.mydistrict.mystate.k12.us/middleschool/history8startup.html. Make a note of this URL, since you will need it when you set up the classroom computers.

Even without a web server, you can post the page on each of the computers in your classroom (or in the library), and it will work just as well. Simply copy your startup page file to the browser folder—right next to the browser application—on each computer's hard drive, where it is not likely to be erased.

Set the Browser

Now it's time to set the browsers on all your computers so that they automatically open your startup page. Here's how:

HOW TO . . . SET THE BROWSER TO START UP ON YOUR PAGE

You need: An educational startup page, as described above, that's posted on the Web or saved on the local hard drive.

You get: Computers that go automatically to your startup page.

1. Go to your browser's preferences panel.
   - With Internet Explorer on Windows, from the menubar choose Tools, then Internet Options.

- With Internet Explorer on Macintosh OS 8 or 9, from the menubar choose Edit, then Preferences, then Browser Display.
- With Internet Explorer on Macintosh OS X, from the menubar choose Explorer, then Preferences, then Browser Display.
- With Netscape, from the menubar choose Edit, then Preferences, then Navigator.

2. Into the box labeled Home Page—Address, type or paste the URL of your startup page (if it's on a Web server), or its filename (if it's on the hard drive in the browser folder.)

3. Now close the Preferences window, and click the Home button on your browser. You should connect to your startup page. And every time the browser is opened on this computer, it will connect to that page.

Use it, Update it, Revise it

Once the computers are set to start from your special page, give the students an assignment that causes them to use it. Watch them as they work. Make note of what needs to be changed. To update or revise the page, open the original file in Word (or whatever program you used to create it), make the necessary revisions, save it in the *Save as Web Page* HTML format with the same filename, and re-post it to the server or to the hard disks. Let your students suggest new items for the startup page that will enable them to work better.

■ ■ ■ ■ ■ ■ ■ ■ ■

TEACHER.COM

Arnold Schwarznegger has his own web site at www.schwarznegger.com. So do Mother Theresa (www.catholic.net/RCC/people/mother/teresa/teresa.html), Stephen King (www.stephenking.com), Elie Weisel (www.eliewieselfoundation.org) and most of my faculty colleagues. They post these sites not only for publicity but to provide their followers and students the information they need to accomplish the work they inspire. A personal or professional web site is no longer the prerogative of the rich and famous nor the province of the gifted geek. Most of my students have built their own sites, and probably many of yours.

Many teachers, at all levels, find that a web site helps them to communicate with their students, organize their curriculum materials, and provide a point of contact for colleagues, family, and friends. Such a site can serve as a *pied-à-terre* in cyberspace, a personal online drop-box, and a message board on the Web. Following are some ideas on building your own personal and professional web site, and some advice on where to post it.

Post the Purpose

Make a list of the purposes of your web site. Each teacher has his own reasons for developing such a site, and you should consider a wide range of functions, such as:

- Post homework assignments in a place convenient to students and parents, to save paper and time and to avoid excuses.

- Explain classroom and course rules, procedures, and protocols.
- Share interesting lesson plans and work sheets with fellow teachers.
- Provide information on office hours, email address, instant messenger name, telephone numbers, and calendar of availability.
- Describe recreational or research interests and results, from monographs to photographs to video clips.
- Post course syllabi, or yearly curriculum outlines, for easy access by students and parents.
- Provide access to slide shows, documents, and presentations used in teaching, for your own use or by students.
- Post your résumé (perhaps you'll seek a promotion soon).
- Post samples of exemplary student work or milestone classroom events.
- Provide copies of interesting reports, artwork, poetry, essays, or other works that communicate your findings.

Few teacher web sites will include all of these purposes. And it's best at the beginning to start simply, and choose the things most important to you.

Gather the Elements

Next to each of your purposes, make a list of the items you'd like to include on your site. Don't worry about what form they are in—simply make a list of the documents you need. Your list might look like this:

- Curriculum plan for Grade Four Social Studies (word processing document)
- Map of Europe for third-week homework assignment (needs to be scanned)
- Report from last spring's Teaching with Technology conference (word processing document)
- Video clip of middle school science fair demonstrations (QuickTime movie)
- Webquest on Ancient Egypt, developed at technology workshop (HTML file)
- Slide show on the Fertile Crescent developed in summer workshop (PowerPoint file)
- Worksheets 1–16 from the Early Civilizations unit (word processing documents)
- Human Migration project for Unit 6 created by Juan and Susan last year (web site)
- Photograph of classroom mock trial of Galileo (in costume) (JPEG photo from digital camera).
- Classroom rules (HTML page)
- A picture of me at my desk at school (needs to be taken)
- A picture of me on my sailboat (in the digital camera)
- Welcome page with picture, message, and links to other material (needs to be developed)

Next, go through the elements one by one and get them into a folder on your computer, or on a Zip disk or memory stick. You may have to do some scanning, writing, picture-taking, and searching around to locate and copy the files you need. (Find instructions on how to do these things in Chapters 11 and 12.) Put a copy of each item into the folder, not the original. Make sure that each file in this folder carries a recognizable filename. (If you are using a Macintosh computer, make sure the filename ends with the appropriate file-name extension, such as .doc for Microsoft Word files, .jpg for pictures, .htm or .html for web pages, and so forth. On Windows, extensions are added automatically.)

Design the Cover Page

Most teacher web sites open with a home page, welcome page, or "cover" page that contains a bit of basic information and a list of links to the other materials in the site. Design and develop this page. Keep it simple. You can develop such a page with Microsoft Word, or with Macromedia Dreamweaver, or you can ask a student to do it for you—many of them already know how to build web pages.

To build your cover page with Microsoft Word, compose the page, then select File from the menubar, followed by Save as Web Page (or Save as HTML). Save the draft cover page as *index.htm,* and save it into the same folder that contains all the materials you gathered earlier. You can learn more about this process from the section *Creating a Web Page with Microsoft Word* at the end of this chapter. And you can learn more about building this page with Dreamweaver also at the end of this chapter.

The key work on the cover page is the links to the other materials you have gathered. To make these links, follow these steps.

HOW TO . . . MAKE LINKS FROM YOUR WEB PAGE

You need: Microsoft Word or Dreamweaver, or other web page editing program.

You get: Links from your home page to other pages and sites.

1. Type a list on the page of the items you want to link to, such as *Social Studies Curriculum Outline* or *Photo of Science Project.* This list should be in terms that your audience will understand.
2. Select one of the items in the list by clicking and dragging the mouse across it.
3. Make the link.

   In Microsoft Word
   - From the menubar, choose Insert, then Hyperlink.
   - Click the Document tab.
   - Click the Select button.
   - Navigate to the file you want to link to, in your web site folder.
   - Select this file, and then click the Open button.
   - Watch the filename appear in the field at the top.
   - Click OK, and watch the link appear in your document.

   In Dreamweaver:
   - From the menubar, Choose Modify, then Make Link.
   - Navigate to the file you want to link to, in your web site folder.
   - Click Open and watch the link appear in your document.

- Repeat steps 2 and 3 for the other items in the list.
- Save your page again into the web site folder.
- Test the page by opening it in your web browser.

Your cover page will appear as any web page. When you click a link, the browser should download and open the relevant document. (If it has trouble with some types of documents, use the File Helpers items in the browser's preferences panel.) Revise your page as necessary after you've tested it in the browser.

■ ■ ■ ■ ■ ■ ■ ■ ■ ■

Post the Site

Now it's time to find a home for your teacher site. Here are some hosting possibilities:

- **At your school.** Many schools encourage and support teachers' development of such sites, and provide teachers with space on the school's web server. Speak to the webmaster for your school or district's web server. She will show you (and perhaps help you) to get your folder onto the server under your name.
- **At your ISP.** Your Internet Service Provider—the company that provides your Internet access from home probably allows you to post a personal web site on their server, as part of your monthly fee. Go to your ISP's web site and follow the instructions for requesting a site, and then for posting materials to it.

No matter which housing arrangement you choose, you'll get a username and password that will allow you to connect to the server and to copy the materials to it from your web site folder. Your webmaster or ISP help desk can guide you through this process, or do it for you. It's a bit different depending on the systems they use.

Tell Your Friends

Once your teacher site is posted, your target audiences of students, colleagues, and friends will need to know that it exists, and its URL. (The URL is, in most cases, the name of the protocol and the name of the server, followed by your name, such as http://www.bfit.edu/jlengel). As your friends use your site, they will suggest additional items. You can add these by copying the new document to the web site folder, revising the cover page to add a new link, and then posting both the cover page and the new document to the web server.

Style on the Web

Once you've mastered the technical side of creating your own teacher site, you'll continue to build your site. Now's a good time to begin to focus on writing effectively for the Web.

WRITING FOR THE WEB

The teaching of writing is a hot topic these days. Our faculty at the college in Boston talks about *writing across the curriculum.* In France they complain that their students can't compose a decent essay. MIT hires novelists to develop the literacy of their engineers. And in the curriculum of the school district whose plans I am posting on the Web, I notice a new emphasis on writing skills. In particular, three of their goals piqued my interest:

- Grade Three: Writes for different audiences
- Grade Four: Selects genre to fit audience and purpose
- Grade Five: Drafts, organizes, revises, and publishes writing to match the format

I am sure that when I was in the fourth grade I didn't know what a *genre* was. Apparently the curriculum has moved forward, and we expect our children to realize early on that the style of their writing should match its audience and the format of its publication. This is good. And since the new technologies have brought forth new formats for publishing, new appliances for reading, and new contexts for working with the written word, we need to consider how to help our students write in styles appropriate to email notes, instant messages, and web pages. This section looks at writing for the Web.

Writing for the Web is not like writing for a magazine, or a newspaper, or a business report. Because it is read from a computer display, often at a desk or on a lap in the midst of several other activities, text on a web page should use a special style if it is to be effective. Most of us will be called on at times to compose our own words, or to prepare articles written elsewhere, for publication on the Web. As you prepare such web pages, keep the following guidelines in mind.

Keep It Short

Most people spend less time looking at a web page than at a printed page, so you should write in short paragraphs with punchy sentences. Avoid long narrative exposition. Use hyperlinks instead, to send the reader off for these kinds of explanations. Write in short paragraphs that present information in digestible chunks.

Create Self-Contained Pages

You never know how the reader will arrive at the page you are writing, so its text must contain enough information to set the context. You cannot assume that the reader has seen the previous page, or has followed the path you designed to get to this page.

Be Straightforward

Use regular words and phrases, as if you are speaking. Avoid unusual constructions such as his/her, never use the slash, avoid abbreviations, stay away from Latinate words such as i.e.

and et al. and etc., don't use ALL CAPITALS, avoid peculiar punctuation, and make sure every sentence contains an active verb.

Use Subheads

Readers of web pages often skim or scroll through text looking for the idea they are seeking—they seldom read every word. Use subheads to help them, more than you would use in printed text. A subhead every few paragraphs is a good idea.

Provide Send-Offs

It's easy to refer to other sources, to provide background information, and to supply details with hypertext links. Embed links to other pages on your own site, or to other sites, to help the reader delve more deeply into the subject at hand.

Be Stylish

The standard web browser can display text in several different styles: plain paragraphs, bulleted lists, numbered lists, and definition lists. Consider using these list styles when you prepare your text. They are easy to format in most web page editors. But remember that a pretty font face cannot hide faulty prose.

Keep It Simple

Avoid the temptation to use all those font tricks that are so easy to create with the computer but make your body text hard to read: blaring boldface, ugly underlining, annoying italics, and perturbing punctuation!!!?!. Let the words themselves do the communicating.

Writing serves little purpose unless someone reads it. Writing a web page, posting it for all to read, and letting the readers send feedback over the Web, is a good way to develop students' writing skill. The best way to learn to write is to write every day and solicit the reactions of your readers. The new technologies make this easy to accomplish.

LOOKING GOOD ONLINE

As our schools and our society become more connected, we find ourselves communicating less on paper and more on the computer. Students turn in their papers in digital form, and their teachers read them from the computer screen. Teachers reproduce fewer paper handouts but publish more documents on the Web. New resources for education often appear on the Internet first, and only much later (if at all) on paper. How can we make sure that what we publish online is as useful and easy to read as possible? How do the rules and conventions change when we move from the 8.5" by 11" page to the 1,024-pixel computer display? This section provides some guidelines for preparing works for publication online. These guidelines can apply to your own web pages, as well as to the online publications of your students.

Readability

Much of the information that teachers and students produce is in text form, destined to be read directly from the computer screen, so we should do all we can to make the text as readable as possible. When preparing documents in Word or PowerPoint or other applications in which you set the format of the text, or if you are preparing style sheets to display text from TXT, XML, or HTML files, consider these guidelines:

Text size: Use nothing smaller than 12-point, or HTML size 2, for body text.

Line width: Body text should be displayed with 10–12 words per line.

Alignment: Body text should be aligned flush left, ragged right.

Word spacing: Should be consistent throughout the text.

Fonts: Use no more than two different fonts on a page. The most readable fonts for the computer display are Verdana (sans-serif) and Georgia (serif).

Paragraphs: Separate paragraphs with a blank line. Avoid indenting the first line.

Heads and subheads: Set these in a font and style and size to contrast with the body text. Use more of them than you might in a printed book or article.

Text style: Use italic text for book titles, article titles, and foreign words. Use bold for key words that might be in the glossary. Use plain text for all the rest. Never use underline or ALL CAPITALS.

Margins: Don't run the text right up to the edge of the page. Text is more readable with white space surrounding it on all sides.

More details on displaying text in your document can be found in the section Displaying Text later in this chapter.

Screen Size

Most computer screens are wider than they are tall, as opposed to the way we use paper, taller than it is wide. And the newest displays are wide like the cinema. So we must consider anew how we format our online documents. Think of the computer display more like a television than a piece of paper. In fact, if you take a piece of standard paper, and place it sideways over your computer screen, you will see immediately the difference. Design your documents for this sideways view.

And not all of your readers will enjoy the same size display. Computer screens are configured in several sizes, measured in pixels. If you create documents that are too big to fit on the screen, you will not serve the needs of your audience. And for web pages, the screen size is further limited by the space taken up by the edges of the browser window, which are often full of buttons and sliders and bars. Your document must fit within this smaller available window. This table shows the most popular computer screen sizes, the area remaining inside the browser, and the approximate percentage of people using each size. All sizes are in pixels.

DISPLAY SIZE	USABLE BROWSER WINDOW	% OF USERS
800 × 600	760 × 450	~40%
1,024 × 768	980 × 618	~55%
1,280 × 1,024	1,240 × 874	~5%

So if you want your web page or diagram or animation or photograph to display well for all users, keep it smaller than 760 by 450 pixels.

Simplicity

Keep documents and graphics as clean and uncluttered as possible. Avoid colored backgrounds, textures, framing, and shading unless it is absolutely necessary, to explain the content. Like the first documents out of the laser printers in the early days of desktop publishing, many early web pages display a perplexing plethora of fonts and features that while easy to create with the new media, are distracting to read. Keep your documents clean and simple. Don't use a visual device or a new font unless without a good reason.

Word Documents

In preparing documents in Microsoft Word, follow the readability guidelines above. In most cases, this will require you to set the margins a bit wider, and the size of the body text a bit larger than the default. Before saving the file, set the View to Page Layout and the Zoom to 100%. Save with a filename that will work on the Web: no spaces, no periods, no accents or special characters.

On most computers, the Word file when downloaded from the Web will open automatically with Word, in its own window, from which the user may read it or print it. To make a Word document easiest to read within the online environment, set the bottom margin to four inches. This makes the pages shorter, so that all of the text fits on the screen, and the reader can move from page to page with one click, without scrolling. Such a document, however, will waste paper if printed.

PowerPoint

PowerPoint files work best if you keep the layout simple and uncluttered. And if you are publishing your PowerPoint slides from a lecture or a student project, keep in mind that most PowerPoint slide shows that are used for classroom presentations will not be useful to users online, without the narration that goes with each slide. An easy way to add this narration is to type it into the Notes area for each slide. To add notes, choose View, then Normal from the menubar, then enter the notes in the frame at the bottom. Make sure that the document is displayed in the normal view as you save it.

On most computers, the PowerPoint file, when downloaded from the Web, will open automatically with PowerPoint, in its own window that will size the contents dynamically to fit the student's screen size. So you need not worry about document size.

PDF

When creating Portable Document Format files, first make sure the original follows the readability guidelines described above. PDF works best for files that will be printed on paper by the student. If you are creating PDF files that will be read from the computer display, consider setting the bottom margin to four inches as described above under the guidelines for Word documents. This will allow the reader to page through the document naturally, without scrolling. Test your PDF file from a browser to make sure it is useful and readable on the screen.

Web Pages

In creating HTML documents such as web pages, keep things simple. Avoid proprietary Javascript and HTML tags that only work with certain operating systems or browsers. (The rollover buttons created with FrontPage are especially suspect in this regard.) When setting fonts, HTML, CSS, or other display styles, follow the general readability guidelines above, so that the result works well within the online environment. Avoid fixed-width tables unless they are smaller than 600 pixels, as explained above under Screen Size; use relative sizing instead. If you work in a web page editor such as Dreamweaver, set the Window Size of the document window to 760 by 420 pixels, so you will see exactly what will show on your display of your least-pixeled user.

Even though the paperless school for most of us remains a dream, the forces of digital display expand daily. If we want to look good and work well in the online publishing environment, we must shift to landscape mode and develop some new rules of thumb.

DESIGN PRINCIPLES FOR THE WEB

As more and more teachers and students develop and publish their own online documents, especially web pages, it's a good idea now and then to remind ourselves of some tried-and-true principles that can lead to more useful and easy to read publications. Even though new software tools such as Dreamweaver and Flash make it easy for the novice to develop a fancy web site quickly and easily, these programs do not prevent you from violating the guidelines for good web page design. Here are some principles to consider.

Display Size

Design for the display size and aspect ratio of your user's web page. A computer screen, for instance, is wider than it is tall, while a Palm is taller than it is wide. Let your design fit the shape that most of your users will see. Understand the size restraints of your user's web page.

Make sure that key content, especially navigation information, appears within the view of the user with the smallest likely display.

Locating Functions

Place key functions of the web page, especially titles and navigation, where they are most evident and expected. If you want a certain item or message to be noticed by the user, put it near the top, or in a place with few other items competing for attention.

Certain items work best in natural locations. Titles belong at or near the top of the page, because we are so used to this placement in newspapers, books, and magazines. Buttons that navigate to the next page work best near the right side, because that's where we are used to going to turn to the next page in a book or magazine. Buttons or menu items that take the user up the hierarchy of the information belong at the top, because that's the way people think about the organization of information—up is more general, down is more specific.

Color and Contrast

Bold, bright colors may distract the user's eyes from other elements on the web page such as text and photographs. Use subtle or pastel colors for backgrounds. Text that is displayed over bold colors will be very difficult to read. Photographs will compete for attention with the background and lose their visual appeal.

Colors should fit the purpose of your web page; colors used in combination should complement each other. Some colors lend a cool feeling to the page, while others warm it up. Some colors just don't go together. A bright blue logo on a dark orange background, for instance, will cause most viewers to cringe. The color wheel can help you avoid the most glaring combinations. Some combinations can create visual contrast and discord, while others may induce comfort and harmony.

Balance

A web page display must balance many opposites: top and bottom, left and right, light and dark, bold and subtle, large and small, gestalt and detail, important and trivial. A web page that takes these all into consideration will be easier to use.

Balance items across and up and down the web page—don't crowd the functional parts all in one place. Balance graphics and text, dark and light, large objects and small ones. Let the size and location of items provide a clue as to their importance.

Alignment

The human eye likes it when things line up. It wants to see the left edge of a picture line up exactly with the left edge of the column of text in which it is embedded. The eye would prefer our web pages to display its elements along a single axis, an invisible line, usually vertical, against or around which the columns of text and edges of graphics line up.

The scheme of alignment for a web page should be consistent from page to page, for ease of use and consistency. A very simple web page, consisting of a single column of text and a few images, will form a natural axis along the left margin, where each line of text begins. The designer in most cases must use this left edge of the column as the core of the alignment scheme.

Menus and Navigation

Titles, menus and navigation provide the user with information to answer the questions,

- Where am I?
- What else is available?
- Where should I go next?

In most web pages, these questions are answered through a menu that lists the navigational choices that the user can make. As in a restaurant, the menu lists the items that are available, and lets the customer choose which to enjoy next. Not all menu items will be clicked by the user, and not all users will visit the various sections in the same order. A good designer will make it easy for the user to view the menu, perhaps by keeping it always visible, or by making it just a click away. A menu can be displayed across the top, at the bottom, or down the sides, but it's best if it shows up in the same place on all pages.

Scrolling

As you read a book, you turn the pages one to the next. This is a familiar and comfortable way to read. The text stays still, and it's easy to keep track of where you are. But on some digital web pages, we are often expected to scroll down through the text to follow the story. Scrolling is unnatural and inefficient process. Few users ever get to the materials that lie "below the scroll" on a web page.

The computer screen is more like a television than a newspaper. What if the anchor on the evening news, after showing the first story, told the viewers to get up off the couch, walk over to their televisions, and click on the screen to scroll down to the next story? Then repeat the process five minutes later in order to see the weather report. This would not be considered user-centric design.

User Control

A web page should offer as much control as possible to the users, letting them choose what to view, in whatever order, at whatever level of detail. We are dealing with interactive media, and user control is a central aspect of this interactivity.

If a web page were a restaurant, it would be a 24-hour buffet rather than a multi-course *prix fixe* banquet. The sign on the wall would read, "Life is short, start with dessert." The menu would stay on the table. The waiter would not scold you if you asked for your dessert before your cheese. An effective web page puts the user in the driver's seat.

Simplicity

Putting all these principles to work in a single web page can make a very complex presentation. But most users seek simplicity. When confronted with a page full of diverse colors and choices and frames and menus and text and images and links, they are taken aback and often confused. A complex and cluttered web page is not kind to the user.

Kindness can breed happiness, and a happy user is more likely to harbor positive feelings toward the web page, and the organization that sponsors it. To be kind, the designer must distill the complexity of design issues into a simple presentation that makes sense to the user at first glance. Designing an web page that seems simple and straightforward to the user, and yet takes into consideration the full gamut of design issues mentioned here, is more art than science.

Learn More

Want to learn more about these principles? Connect to the Cornell University Ergonomics Lab (http://ergo.human.cornell.edu/ahtutorials/web page.html), and read their Guidelines for User Web Page Design. For a slightly different point of view, consult the Design Basics from the IBM design lab (www-306.ibm.com/ibm/easy/eou_ext.nsf/Publish/6).

DISPLAYING TEXT

Teachers and students more and more are called upon to publish their works for the computer screen. Whether they are putting them on a web page, a word processor, or a PowerPoint slide, the words they type are destined to be read from a computer screen. What's the best way to make this text easily readable by the audience?

There is an art to making text on a computer easy to read. Much of the text we see on the computer is not nearly as easy to read as it could be. The quality of the display of the text can go a long way to helping students read and understand the material the encounter. Even though the computer screen's low resolution does not allow us to display text as nicely as in a printed book, we can go a long way to making the best of what we have to work with. Here are a few guidelines for displaying text.

Black on White

Black text on a plain white background is by far the easiest to read. We may be tempted to use the school colors as the background for our pages, and to display the text in a contrasting white. But most of our audience will find this difficult to read. Our eyes and are minds are used to reading black letters on a white page. This produces the most contrast, and the least strain on the eyes. It also prints much better on paper. Never display text (that you expect the viewer to read) over a background photograph or drawing. This makes the text almost impossible to read.

10 to 12 Words Per Line

People read best with 10 to 12 words per line. A line of text any wider than that causes the reader to have difficulty capturing all the words in a single glance, and makes it hard to keep track of which line is next. Look at a well-printed and well-designed hardcover book, and you will see that it averages 10 to 12 words per line. Young children and old folks might be more comfortable with an average of 8 to 10 words per line. All word processors and web page editors let you program the page to regulate the number of words per line so that users will find the text easy to read and comprehend.

System Fonts

Stick to 12 point system fonts and plain text. Most standard system fonts were designed to display well on a computer screen and to be easy to read. They have the added advantage of ubiquity—everyone's got them on the computer, whether Windows or Macintosh, Netscape or Explorer, old or new. The system fonts include Times, Helvetica, Arial, and Times Roman. Verdana and Georgia are two new font families designed especially for ease of reading from a computer screen. For the body text of a web page, it's better in some cases to specify no particular font at all, letting the user choose the most appropriate font.

Body and Titles

Use a serif font for body text, sans serif for titles. The serifs are the little feet and caps on the bottoms and tops and ends of the letters. Georgia is a serif font. Verdana and Arial are sans-serif (without serifs) fonts. Serif fonts are easier to read in standard narrative text in paragraphs. Sans-serif fonts are easier to read in short and single-word titles and signs. Word processors and web page editors let you to specify and control font display.

Two Styles

Don't mix more than two fonts or two sizes on a page. This confuses the user. Stick to one font for titles, and another for body text. Make all titles the same size, and make all body text a consistent smaller size. 12-point type displays well on all computers, and for most people is easy to read from the screen. Use this size for body text whenever possible.

Lowercase

Avoid words set in all caps. The purpose of uppercase letters is to denote the beginning of a sentence or to indicate a person or place-name by serving as the initial letter. They should not be used for anything else, except for single-word emergency warnings such as DANGER or STOP. People read standard lowercase-lettered words easier because they are used to it. Displaying words in all caps makes readers think THAT YOU ARE YELLING AT THEM!

Contrast

Make sure titles contrast with body text. Titles and subtitles make a page of text easier to read, by letting users glance quickly through the material to find the topic they are interested in. This random-access style of reading is far more prevalent on the Web than in newspapers or books, and so more subtitles should be designed into the text that's displayed on the screen. To stand out, the tiles and subtitles should be larger (bigger point size) and heavier (boldface) than the body text on the page. You may also use a contrasting font for the titles—if you used Georgia for the body text, use Verdana for the titles. Leave some extra space around the titles, to make them easier to find at a glance.

Paragraphs

Separate paragraphs with line space or indents, but not both. Look at a well-printed book, and see how the publisher separates the paragraphs. Some use a blank line between the paragraphs, while others indent the first line of a paragraph. Either method will work on a web page, but it is not wise to use both a line space and an indent.

White Space

Leave plenty of white space around the text. The human eye needs room to roam while it is reading. It likes white apace above, below, and especially to the left and right of the column of text. It abhors text that is penned in by the edge of the window, surrounded by boxes, or nudged by graphics. A 10-word-wide column of text with substantial white margins will be easiest to read.

Single Axis

Build your page around a single axis. Our minds seek order and organization. We like things to line up. We read easier if the page is formatted around an axis, an invisible line to which the text, images, and graphics align. The axis can be near the left, at the center, or to the right, but the page should have only one.

Simplicity

The simpler the better. Chaos and clutter are the opposites of order and organization. A simple page with a few visual and text elements will be easier to read than a page with a plethora of items competing for the viewer's attention. Keep the number of items on the page as small as possible. Divide the contents into two pages if necessary. One way to make sure that the user pays attention to your text is to keep other distracting items away from it, off the page.

BUILDING A WEB PAGE WITH WORD

> *There must be fifty ways to make a web page. Mel might use HTML. Dave might try a little Shockwave. Mr. Cleaver might use Dreamweaver. Clive might do it with GoLive, Rip might write some JavaScript, as Phil makes it with PageMill. While Ferd might export from Word, a sage would try FrontPage. Just pick a tool and go.*

The web page has become the fastest-growing, most universal, and easiest method for distributing information. Everybody's computer can open web pages, they are small and compact, and they can travel easily over networks. Many teachers have turned all their learning materials into web pages to make them easy to find, easy to retrieve, and easy to use by students. But how do you create a web page in the first place?

One of the easiest ways to make a simple web page is with Microsoft Word. Word is familiar to many, and its recent versions include a simple Save as web page or Save as HTML menu item. These instructions get you started using Word to create a simple web page.

HOW TO . . . CREATE A WEB PAGE WITH WORD

You need: Microsoft Word, and a good idea for a web page.

You get: A web page that can be opened with any web browser.

What you are going to do is to create a standard Word document, add a few hyperlinks, and then save it in HTML (Web) format. Follow these steps:

1. Enter the text. Type the text of your page as in a standard Word document. You may also paste text from other sources. If you are entering URLs (web site addresses), it's best to copy and paste them from the browser, since it's quite difficult to enter these strange strings of letters and symbols accurately from the keyboard. As you enter the text, avoid using certain characters that do not translate well to the Web:

- Don't use the Tab key.
- Avoid quotation marks (use italics for book and article titles).
- Don't enter a string of spaces.

At this point, it's a good idea to save your work so far as a standard Word document, with the .doc filename extension.

2. Make hyperlinks. Many web pages include hyperlinks, blue words that link to other documents on the Web. Once your text is entered, it's time to create those links. Here's how:

- Select the word or phrase you want to link from.
- Choose Hyperlink from the Insert menu.
- Enter (or paste) the URL of the link. It should be in the form http://web.server.net/document.html
- Click OK.

You will see the link turn blue, indicating that this word or phrase will link to another document on the Web. You can create as many hyperlinks as you want from a document.

3. Format as necessary. Use standard Word editing and formatting tools to make your document look that way you want:

- **Font, size, and style.** You may adjust these as necessary, but remember that any nonstandard fonts will not display properly for most viewers of your web page. It's best to stick with standard fonts such as Times, Helvetica, Arial, Georgia, or

Verdana, which most computers and browsers can handle. The size, style, and color of the text will translate well to the Web.

- **Alignment.** You may center, left-align, or right-align the text. But don't justify both right and left—that will not translate well to the Web.
- **Lists.** You may use the standard Word tools to create numbered and bulleted lists—these will translate directly to the Web.
- **Tables.** Simple tables created in Word will translate well to the Web, but complex table styling and formatting may not.

Please avoid multiple columns, adjusted margins, text boxes, word art, graphics, and tabs. These will not translate well to the Web.

4. Save as Web Page. When all is entered, linked, and formatted, you can save the page in a format suitable for the Web—in Hypertext markup Language (HTML). Here's how:

- Choose Save As HTML or Save as Web Page from the File menu.
- Enter a proper filename. A proper filename contains only letters, numbers, and periods—no spaces, no slashes, no funny characters. The filename must end with .html or .htm.
- Save the file in a place on your computer where you can find it again easily. (Later you will copy this file to a web server.)

5. Test with browser. To see what your page will look like to viewers on the Web, you need to open the file that you just saved with a web browser such as Internet Explorer or Netscape Navigator. Here's how:

- Open your browser.
- Choose Open File (Explorer) or Open Page in Navigator (Netscape) from the File menu.
- Find the web page file you just saved.
- See what it looks like in the browser.

You will notice that its appearance is not identical to the Word document. That's because the browser interprets the HTML code in a slightly different way than Word. As long as your page is useful and readable, it's OK. But if it appears unusable, you'll have to go back to Word, fix it, save it again, and test it again in the browser, until you get it right.

6. Distribute the page. Once your file appears acceptably in the browser, you can distribute it in several different ways:

- Save it on a floppy disk and distribute it to others.
- Attach it to an email and send to others.
- Post it to a file server on the network, and tell the others where it is.
- Post it to a web server, so that others can view it through the Internet. There are several ways to do this, depending on the nature of the server and where you are sending from. Your school's webmaster will provide further information on this process.

■ ■ ■ ■ ■ ■ ■ ■ ■ ■

BUILDING A WEB PAGE WITH DREAMWEAVER

As the Web becomes the publishing medium of choice and efficiency for educational works, teachers and students will be called upon more and more to build their own web pages. This section gets you started building your own web pages using one of the most popular and easy-to-use software tools, Macromedia Dreamweaver. If you don't own a copy, you can download a trial version from the Macromedia web site. Dreamweaver is used widely in schools and businesses around the world, and can be used by beginners as well as experts to create web pages and sites. Macromedia offers a site license that allows Dreamweaver to be used on all of a school's computers at a very reasonable cost, so it's a good choice for web publishing.

This section shows you how to build a simple web page with text, images, multimedia, and links. Before you start building your page, you might want to locate some multimedia files: an image, a sound, a video clip, and a Flash animation. If you don't have these readily at hand, you can download some samples from my web site at www.lengel.net/dwsamples.

HOW TO . . . BUILD A WEB PAGE WITH DREAMWEAVER

You need: Macromedia Dreamweaver, and a good idea for a web page.

You get: A web page that can be opened in any browser.

1. Open Dreamweaver. Open Dreamweaver and close any windows other than the Document and Properties windows. Use the Window Size box at the bottom of the document window to set the size to 760 × 420 pixels. Choose View, then Design from the menubar to get the WYSIWYG (What You See Is What You Get) view. This is an important feature of Dreamweaver, letting you see exactly what your web page will look like as you build it.

2. Insert text. You will see the cursor flashing in the upper left corner of the page. Enter some text from the keyboard, or copy it from another source and paste it in. The text will appear in Dreamweaver's default font style and size. To change the appearance of the text, select it, and then use the items under the Text menu to modify the size, style, alignment, or color. To start a new paragraph, press the return key. To start a new line, but not a new paragraph, press Shift+return.

To make a headline, put the text on a line by itself, then set it to bold and to a larger size such as 5. To make a bulleted list, enter each bullet item as a new paragraph. Then select all the bullets, and choose Text, then List, then Unordered List from the menubar. To indent a paragraph, select it and choose Text, then Indent from the menubar. As you can see, Dreamweaver here is working much like a word processor. The controls over text style, and the means of modifying it, are similar to those in Microsoft Word.

To see what this page would look like to your audience, choose File, then Preview in Browser, then Internet Explorer (or Netscape Navigator).

3. No browser? Select one! Before you can preview your web page in a browser, you need to tell Dreamweaver where your browsers are located. Choose File, then Preview in

Browser, then Edit Browser List. Use the "+" button to add a browser to the list. If you have both Internet Explorer and Netscape on your computer, add both of them to the list.

Notice that your page does not look exactly the same in the browser as it does in Dreamweaver. That's because the browser interprets the page a bit differently than both Dreamweaver, and other browsers. Your text may appear a little larger, or in a different font. Insert enough text to make a simple web page, perhaps two paragraphs. Then it's time to save the page.

4. Warning: Filenames. Whenever you save a file that will be used in a web site, you must take care to use a filename that will work well on the Web. Such filenames should contain only letters and numbers—no special characters and no spaces. And they also must end with an appropriate filename extension, in this case, .html or .htm. Create a new folder called *samplesite,* and save the file there.

5. Prepare image. Before you add an image to your web page, you need first to prepare the image in the proper format. The images on my web site, boat.jpg and logo.gif, are all set, but if you prepare your own image, you must make sure that it's saved in a proper form for the Web. If you are not sure of the format of your image, open it in a program like Photoshop or PaintShop Pro, and choose Save for Web from the File menu. Save it into your samplesite folder with a filename extension that matches the file type. A GIF image must end in .gif, and a JPEG in .jpg, but you can't change the file type simply by changing the filename extension. For instance, to change an image from JPEG to GIF format, you need to open it in an image-editing program, and then choose the new format in the Save As dialog box.

6. Insert image. Click the mouse to place the cursor at the point where you want the image to appear. Choose Insert, then Image from the menubar. Navigate to the image, click Open, and watch your image appear on the Web page.

Your page might be more useful if the image were aligned to the left, with the text next to it on the right. To align the image to the left of the text, select the image, choose Align, then Left from the popup menu at the lower right of the Properties window. Save the page that now contains text and a picture by choosing Save As from the File menu, and saving the page into your samplesite folder.

7. Insert multimedia. Most web sites rely on text and images to carry the message to the audience. But in some cases, the user needs to hear a sound, see an animation, or watch a video clip to fully understand the content. These kinds of media are more difficult to prepare, and more difficult to receive over the Web, than their static counterparts. Multimedia may be used sparingly, and Dreamweaver can handle these media well.

Inserting a video, sound, or animation into a web page works very similarly to inserting an image. First, place your cursor at the point where you want the media to appear. Choose Insert, then Media from the menubar, then indicate the type of media you want to insert.

To insert a Flash animation, for instance, choose Insert, then Media, then Flash from the menubar, and select a Flash (.swf) file. The animation will appear as a gray box in the Dreamweaver document window—you won't see the animation playing in Dreamweaver unless you click the green arrow in its Properties window.

8. Preparing media files. Each type of media that you want to import into Dreamweaver—animation, video, and sound—must be prepared and saved in a format that works with Dreamweaver as well as the browsers of your audience. You may use the files already prepared for you at www.lengel.net/dwsamples. To see the page with its animation, you must choose File, then Preview in Browser, then Internet Explorer (or Netscape Navigator) from the menubar.

9. Plug-Ins for media. All of the multimedia types require browser plug-ins in order to work. For instance, without the Flash Player, your browser will not be able to display the sample animation that is part of this exercise. Text and images require no browser plug-ins, but animation, sound, and video do. Make sure you have the latest Flash and QuickTime plug-ins installed in your browser, so that you can try out these samples. You may can download these for free at www.macromedia.com and www.apple.com/quicktime.

To insert a sound on this page, place the cursor where you want the sound controller to appear. Choose Insert, then Media, then Plugin from the menubar. Select the sound file, click Open, and watch as a small, square, gray plug-in icon appears. To make the sound easier to control, stretch this icon out so that it's about 200 pixels wide. When the page displays in the browser, the icon will be replaced by a standard sound controller bar.

Before you add a video to your web site, you should save the page you are working on and create a new page. It would be confusing to the viewer to see an animation, hear a sound, and watch a video all on the same page. To create a new page, choose File, then New from Dreamweaver's menubar. Make sure Basic HTML page is selected, then click the Create button. You will see a new Dreamweaver document window appear, with the text cursor blinking in the upper left corner. Enter a heading for this page, and add some text that explains the video.

To insert the video, place the cursor where you want the video to appear. Choose Insert, then Media, then Plugin from the menubar. Select the video file, click Open, and watch as a small, square, gray plug-in icon appears. Stretch this icon to fit the size of the video plus 16 pixels. The extra 16 pixels are for the controller bar. If you are using the sample shark video from my web site, set the size of the plug-in icon to 160 pixels wide and 136 pixels high. It's easiest to enter these numbers directly into the Properties window for the video.

Preview this page in the browser. The video should play automatically, with a standard controller bar at the bottom. Save this second web page with a proper filename. Be sure to save it in the same folder as your other Dreamweaver web page.

10. Link the pages. You need to provide a way for the viewer to get from one of your Dreamweaver pages to another, with a hyperlink. Open the first page in Dreamweaver. Select a word or phrase to link from. Choose Modify, then Make Link from the menubar. In the Select File dialog box, choose the file you want to link to.

When the dialog box disappears, you will notice that the words you selected have turned blue. From a browser, clicking these words will link to the other web page. Preview the page in your browser and try it.

You now have a web site with two multimedia pages and a link. And you are finding your way around Dreamweaver, learning the ropes as you take this vessel on an introductory sail. Dreamweaver can take you on a much longer voyage as a web author, past the shores of formatting tools, colors, forms, flashy buttons, templates, style sheets, site management, and many other web features.

■ ■ ■ ■ ■ ■ ■ ■ ■ ■

LEARN MORE . . .

About Design Principles

http://ergo.human.cornell.edu/ahtutorials/web page.html
> Cornell University Ergonomics Lab has guidelines for user web design.

www-306.ibm.com/ibm/easy/eou_ext.nsf/Publish/6
> IBM's design lab has some pointers for effective web page development.

www.hwg.org/resources/accessibility/sixprinciples.html
> Creating accessible web pages is a skill. This site suggests six principles to guide you.

About Assessing Classroom Web Pages

http://school.discovery.com/schrockguide/assess.html
> Kathy Schrock's site has rubrics for evaluating student web pages, classroom web pages and webquests. From the bottom of this page, you can also go to sample classroom web pages.

About Building a Web Page with Word

www.spebsqsa.org/web/groups/public/documents/pages/pub_id_042666.hcsp
> This page, entitled *Using Microsoft Word—Five Things Every Writer Should Know,* gives clear, easy to follow instructions for using styles, creating bullets, and so on.

About Building a Web Page using Dreamweaver

www.macromedia.com
> Download a trial version of Dreamweaver.

www.lengel.net/dwsamples/
> Here you will find some sample media elements provided by the authors.

About Other Web Authoring Tools

http://wp.netscape.com/communicator/composer/v4.0/index.html
> Netscape Composer

http://wp.netscape.com/communicator/composer/v4.0/index.html
> Adobe GoLive

http://office.microsoft.com/en-us/FX010858021033.aspx
> Microsoft FrontPage

PART IV

THE MEDIA

Chapters 9 through 15 each look at a particular type of media—words, images, video, numbers—and provide practical ideas for reaping the full educational opportunities of each one.

CHAPTER NINE

WORDS

IN THIS CHAPTER

- **Correcting Papers**
- **Newsletters in Word**
- **Brochures in Word**
- **Beyond Words: Using Tables and Diagrams**
- **Accentuate the Positive: Foreign Words**
- **Math Equations in Word**
- **Learn More . . .**

This is the first of the media chapters of this book. We begin here with words, specifically text, the medium most familiar to most teachers and most likely to be found on your computer. This chapter starts with the everyday task of correcting the text of papers (without using paper at all.) It goes on to show you how to use your computer and its word processor to prepare widely-used text documents such as newsletters and brochures that can provide you or your students with a creative outlet with many applications to teaching and learning. The chapter closes with three sections about special kinds of texts that are often treated with word processors in schools: tables, foreign words, and math equations.

You need no special software or programming skills to work with the examples in this chapter—throughout you'll use Microsoft Word to prepare the examples.

CORRECTING PAPERS

It's the burden that every teacher bears. It's the often late-night shuffle of worksheets and essays that demand attention and evaluation. And yet its results are essential to students' learning, and its process forms a kernel of student–teacher interaction.

No matter how you go about correcting papers, to do it well takes time, energy, and judgment. Most teachers have learned how to make the process as efficient as possible, by setting rules for the appearance of student work, by quantifying the grading criteria, and by developing a standard set of symbols and abbreviations to communicate their corrections to students. We all search for a way to provide the most feedback in the least amount of time. This section looks at how technology can help with the quotidian task of correcting papers.

Avoid Printing

At the Liberty Mutual insurance company office in New Hampshire, trucks full of claims mailed in by customers arrive at the loading dock each day. Before the day is out, all of the claim papers are destroyed. Shredded. The claims, some handwritten, some typed on standard insurance forms, are opened, scanned, and saved in digital form on a server. The originals go into the trash. From here on, all the work is done with the online electronic copies. Claims are processed and checks issued without any printing whatsoever. The company looks forward to the day when all claims are filed directly online, thus avoiding the scanning.

As more and more student work is submitted in digital form, as a file instead of a sheet of paper, we may follow the example of the insurance company, avoid the natural tendency to print the students' work, and then correct the printed copy. As you will see, it's much easier and more efficient (and environmentally proper) to correct the digital copy, and avoid printing altogether. And if a student submits a paperless paper, as described in Chapter 3, it's only natural that you return the favor with a paperless correction.

The first step in computerizing the correcting of papers is to structure your assignments so that the students' work can be submitted as a Word document, a PowerPoint slide show, a web page, a video clip, or other type of digital document. The rest of this section shows you how to work with these files to perform the various tasks we associate with the correction of papers.

Editing versus Commenting

Let's start with a typical example: a student essay submitted as a Word document. Depending on our teaching style and objectives, we may want to *edit* the paper: change the words and punctuation to show the student the way it should have been written. Or we may want to *comment* on the paper: tell the student what we think about certain passages. Microsoft Word provides tools for both of these processes. We open the student's document in Word, and begin our work.

How to Edit with Markup Tools

You want the changes that you make to the student's paper to show up in red. This is easy. From the menubar, choose Tools, then Track Changes, then Highlight Changes. In the dialog box that appears, check off all three boxes, including Track changes while editing. Now go ahead and edit the document as you normally would, by selecting the mistakes, and entering in the corrections from the keyboard. Watch as your corrections show in red, and the student's original words remain crossed-out. When you save the edited document, and send it back to the student, she will see the edits in the same manner. This turns out to be much faster and easier to use by both student and teacher than the old process of correcting with a pen or pencil.

How to Add Comments

Suppose you find a sentence that's missing its verb. Select the sentence. Then from the menubar, choose Insert, then Comment. You will see a box open up at the bottom of the screen. Enter your comments into this box, such as *This sentence is missing its verb.* Your comment will be saved, and the student will see the errant sentence highlighted. When he clicks the sentence, he will see your comment. You may in this same way insert as many comments as you like into the document.

HOW TO . . . CORRECT WITH DRAWING TOOLS

Suppose you are correcting a diagram or a drawing created by the student in Word. The editing and commenting tools may not be the best for this. Better to use the circles and arrows of the drawing tools to add your comments. Make sure your drawing toolbar is showing: choose View, then Toolbars, then Drawing from the menubar. Now you have three different ways to add comments:

- Text Box
  1. Choose the text box tool (letter A).
  2. Click and drag in the document to draw a text box.
  3. Enter your comments into the text box.
  4. Click the Lines button on the drawing toolbar.
  5. Choose the arrow tool from the collection of lines.
  6. Click and drag the mouse from the text box to the appropriate place on the student's document.
  7. Use the Line Color button on the drawing toolbar to make the arrow red.
- Callouts
  1. On the drawing toolbar, click the AutoShapes button.
  2. Choose Callouts from the list of possibilities.
  3. Select one of the callout types (these are little speech bubbles and boxes, like you see in the comics).
  4. Click and drag on the student's document to draw the callout.
  5. Enter your comment into the callout.
- Circles and Arrows
  1. From the drawing toolbar, click the Lines button.
  2. From the six possibilities, choose the scribble tool.
  3. Draw a circle around the item you want to identify on the student's document.

4. Choose the text box tool (letter A).

5. Click and drag in the document to draw a text box.

6. Enter your comments about the circled item into the text box.

7. Click the Lines button on the drawing toolbar.

8. Choose the arrow tool from the collection of lines.

9. Click and drag the mouse from the text box to the circle you just made.

How to Correct Math Equations and Plots

The last three methods above can be applied to text documents, diagrams, drawings, and even pictures. They can also be used to comment on students' math equations and plots. (The last section of this chapter shows how to use Word's Equation Editor and drawing tools to work with math equations and plots in Word.)

With all these methods of correcting documents, you must save the commented document and return it to the student by email or through a class server or learning management system.

Correct Work, not Papers

So you're not correcting papers anymore—you are editing, commenting, and remarking your students' work in digital form. With a little practice, this can be a faster, neater, and more useful process.

■ ■ ■ ■ ■ ■ ■ ■ ■

NEWSLETTERS IN WORD

Picture this:

> The assignment for the social studies class involved creating a three-page newspaper from July 5, 1776. In small groups, students researched the events and studied the context. Now they were arranging the stories on the page and placing the pictures next to the text. They had studied the format of the journals of the late eighteenth century, and were doing their best to mimic the old style.

> The Director of Curriculum wanted to publish a monthly newsletter for a wide audience, from parents to pupils, in a format that could be simultaneously emailed, printed, downloaded, and placed on the district's web site. She wanted it to look professional, but easily available and readable for all. And she only wanted to develop it once, and have it work well no matter how they received it.

> The Music Association wanted to develop its newsletter in a round-robin fashion, where each member of the executive committee contributed one article, then passed it along to the next member until the newsletter was complete. Then

it could be distributed to the entire mailing list of parents, teachers, and students. But they all seemed to have different brands of computers and operating systems, so they were not sure how to make this work.

All three of these educational vignettes involve the *news,* and how to assemble and distribute it. And all three look to technology to provide the methods and efficiencies to publish and distribute the news. This section provides practical advice on using Microsoft Word to create newsletters for educational and administrative purposes that can be published in a variety of ways. Since most people have a copy of Word on their computers and Word files can be moved easily from Macintosh to Windows to Linux and back, it's a practical solution to the problem of publishing the news. Newsletters for educational purposes are the province of students as well as teachers, and these instructions can be used by both. Here's how to get started.

HOW TO . . . CREATE A NEWSLETTER WITH WORD

You need: Microsoft Word, and an idea for a newsletter.

You get: A good-looking document that can be printed, mailed, or distributed online.

1. Sketch your ideas. Who is your audience? What are the ideas you want to get across to them? What elements do you need in your newsletter to communicate those ideas? Answer these questions, then list the elements of your newsletter: stories, photographs, headlines, graphics, and so forth. Next, sketch out the placement of these elements. Consider the principles of balance and contrast as you do this.

2. Set up your page. Create a new Word document. Use Format, then Document from the menubar to set all of the margins to 0.75 inches. Use Format, then Columns to create two columns.

3. Create a footer. Many newsletters show a footer with title and page numbers at the bottom of every page. Set up the footer now, using the View, then Headers and Footers from the menubar. Footers can be aligned left, right, or center just like regular text. They are usually set in very small type. A typical footer for a newsletter might read, *Philadelphia Gazette, July 5, 1776, page 1.*

4. Create the masthead. This is the title that appears at the top of page one. All of the parts of the masthead—title, lines, logos—should be created as text boxes. To do this, use Insert, then Text Box from the menubar. Then enter the title from the keyboard, such as *Philadelphia Gazette.* Select the text and set its size to spread across the page. Stretch and adjust the size of the box itself as necessary, using the handles around the edge. Choose Format, then Text Box from the menubar, then choose the Layout tab and click the Square text wrap button. This will cause any text that you type in later to wrap around this masthead.

5. Place your graphic elements. Place your pictures and diagrams onto the newsletter. You may copy and paste them from another program, using the Edit, then Paste Special command to make sure it appears as a picture. Or use Insert, then Picture to bring it in from a file on your disk. Once you have imported the graphics, move them around the screen to the place you want. Select each picture in turn, and then use Format, then Picture from the menubar, then choose the Layout tab and click the Square text wrap button. This will cause any text that you type in later to wrap around the picture.

6. Enter your stories. You can type stories right into the columns, or you can paste text from another source. Your words should automatically wrap around your graphic elements as you type them.

7. Add headlines. Type the text of the headline. Select it, and then adjust size (such as 18) and weight (bold) and font (Arial) to look like a headline.

8. Adjust the text to fit. Select the body text. Adjust font, size, line spacing, and style so that it is attractive, readable, and fits into the space you have. Edit the content if necessary to make it fit. Check the spelling. Body text reads best if it is aligned left, in 10- or 12-point serif type such as Times or Georgia.

9. Review your work. Use the View menu to Zoom out and look at your newsletter in a full-page view. How's the balance? The contrast? Adjust these as necessary, then print a copy. Look at it one more time for balance, contrast, and readability. Go back and adjust as necessary.

10. Publish your newsletter. You may publish it on paper by printing the file. You may distribute by email by attaching the *newsletter.doc* file to an email message. You may create a link from a Web page directly to the *newsletter.doc* file. When the readers click on the link, the browser will download the newsletter file and open it in Word. They may then read it directly from the computer display, or print a copy.

These same steps can be used by eighth-graders preparing their social studies project, as well as by the district administrator creating the monthly communications bulletin. If all the news is fit to print, then your technology is ready to make it happen.

■ ■ ■ ■ ■ ■ ■ ■ ■

BROCHURES IN WORD

How did Lewis and Clark recruit explorers for their mission to open up the West? Following the recent bicentennial of this historic trip, our students can explore many aspects of the journey by creating multimedia projects on the computer. This section shows you how to create a brochure, perhaps one that might have been used by Lewis and Clark to gather companions for the trip. Future chapters will show you how to create the slide shows and video commercials that the explorers might have used, had they access to today's communication technologies.

A brochure assignment can fit into many subjects and topics. Students could create a brochure that:

■ Introduces one of the elements in the periodic table
■ Recruits soldiers for the Confederate side in the Civil War

- Promotes a work of literature, a favorite book
- Supports a candidate for president in the election of 1860
- Announces a school club, event, or organization

The construction of a brochure involves research, gathering materials, writing, design, decision making, and the relation of all to the context. Such a project requires the student to explain a complex issue through a small selection of words and pictures in a standard format. It promotes good thinking and organization, as well as creative planning and careful technical execution. Many teachers have found the brochure to be a useful educational project.

These instructions show how to use Microsoft Word to create a standard three-panel brochure, to be printed on regular 8.5 × 11 inch paper. You will see that they are similar in form but different in detail than the instructions above for creating a newsletter.

HOW TO . . . CREATE A BROCHURE WITH WORD

You need: Microsoft Word, and an idea for a brochure.

You get: A three-column brochure that can be printed, mailed, or distributed online.

1. Sketch out your ideas. Who is your audience? What are the ideas you want to get across to them? What elements do you need in your brochure to communicate those ideas? Answer these questions, then list the elements of your brochure: text, titles, photographs, diagrams, and so forth. Next, sketch out the placement of these elements. Consider the principles of balance and contrast as you do this.

2. Gather your materials. For each of the elements you listed, locate a source for them and get them onto your computer. This may involve research in the library, searching online, scanning, copying from the Web, drawing, or using a digital camera. Organize all the elements into a single folder on your computer. (For tips on gathering images, see Chapter 11 on working with images.)

3. Set up your page. Create a new a Word document. With Page Setup under the File menu, change the orientation of the page from portrait to landscape. Next use the Document item under the Format menu to set your margins to 0.5 inches all around: top, bottom, left, and right.

4. Create three columns. Use the Columns item of the Format menu to create three columns of equal width. Set the spacing between columns to 0.9 inches. This will set up your document so that the folds in a three-panel brochure land more or less in the center of the gutters between the columns.

5. Place your graphic elements. Put your titles, pictures, and diagrams onto the brochure.

If your picture is a file on the disk, use the Picture command under the Insert menu to bring a picture from a file into Word. Make sure that the Float over text box is checked as you choose the image. The picture appears as a graphic element. You can tell if it's a graphic element by its handles—a graphic has four white squares in its corners when it's selected. If your picture appears with black handles and you can't move it, that means that it has been inserted as a text item. To bring it back as a graphic item, select it, then choose Cut from the Edit menu. Then choose Paste Special from the edit menu, and insert it as a picture. Now it will show white handles and be moveable. Once you have imported the graphics, move them around the screen to the places you want.

6. Make your titles. Titles should be placed in text boxes, not typed in as part of the text. To create such a title, Choose Text Box from the Insert menu. Then click and drag to draw a box across several columns. Type the text of your title into the box. Select the text of your title, then adjust the font and size as necessary. Move and stretch your title to its desired location.

To get rid of the line around the text box, double click on the edge of the text box, then choose No Line from the Line Color box. While you're here, you might also want to change the Fill Color to No Fill, in order to make the text box transparent.

7. Enter your text. You can type the body text of your brochure right into the columns, or you can paste it from the something you copied from another source, or insert it from a file. Your text may appear underneath or over some of your graphic elements. Don't worry. You'll fix that next.

8. Make the text wrap around the graphics. Select the graphic element by clicking it once so that its handles show. Use Picture under the Format menu. Select the Wrapping Tab. Click on the kind of wrapping style you want, then click OK and watch the text wrap around the graphic. Do the same for the text box containing the title, and for the other graphics.

9. Adjust the text to fit. Select the text, using Select All from the Edit menu. Adjust font, size, line spacing, and style so that it is attractive, readable, and fits into the space you have. 10-point text seems to work best in a brochure like this. Edit the content if necessary to make it fit. Check the spelling, under the Tools menu.

10. Review your work. Use the Zoom item under the View menu to zoom out and look at your brochure from a distance. How's the balance? The contrast?

11. Print a copy. Look at it again for balance, contrast, and readability. Fold it and see how things line up. Go back and adjust as necessary. Beyond distribution in print, this brochure can be attached to an email, or posted on a web site, for others to open and print.

■ ■ ■ ■ ■ ■ ■ ■ ■ ■

BEYOND WORDS: USING TABLES AND DIAGRAMS

Nearly everybody uses Microsoft Word. While it does not enjoy a complete monopoly on the word processing marketplace, it's hard to find many people who use a competitor. And this ubiquitous tool is more than something to write papers with. It includes many capabilities, hidden to many of us, that enable it to be used as a general media editor. This section shows two ways in which Word can be used in ways that go far beyond the simple processing of words. Use Word to create tables and diagrams.

Tables

The students found it very useful in studying for the test. Mrs. Young had prepared a study guide that showed for each of the countries of the European Union the chief economic and social facts, organized in rows and columns on the page in a way that made them easy to compare.

Shauna was taking virtual notes from her research. Into the first column she pasted the URL of her source. The second column contained a summary, in her own words, of the key ideas she found there. In the third column she pasted a quotation or image from the site. The layout helped her to organize her work and to make it useful later when it came time to write her report.

The substitute was armed with a neatly presented page that showed thumbnail pictures and names for each of the students in this "difficult" class. Arranged in rows and columns, in alphabetical order, she quickly learned with whom she was working.

All of these people were using documents prepared with Microsoft Word, using tables to organize information so it is easy to use. A table is a grid of rows and columns into which information can be typed or pasted. Whether displayed on the screen or printed or sent over the Internet, these tables maintain their form and keep everything nicely lined up. Headings and labels make it easy to cross check and compare information. Tables like these are used widely in publishing of books and magazines, and in professional web sites.

HOW TO . . . CREATE A TABLE IN WORD

You need: Microsoft Word, and an idea for presenting information in rows and columns.

You get: A document with a neatly formatted table that lines up all your information so that it is easy to use.

To create a table in Word, follow these steps:

1. Before you insert the table, do a little planning. Sketch out the table you need, with headings for each row and column to indicate the categories of information that it will contain.

2. Choose Table, then Insert, then Table from the menubar, and then set the number of rows and columns. Your table will appear on the page. When you create a table, it will show lines around each of the cells of the table.

3. Enter text from the keyboard into a cell, or paste text copied from other sources. (You may also paste images into a table.)

4. Change the size of the columns and rows as necessary by clicking and dragging on the lines.

5. Use the text alignment tools to change the way the words (or pictures) appear in the cells.

6. When your table is complete, you may change its format by selecting the table, and then choosing Table, then Table Auto Format from the menubar. Choose an appropriate format from the list and Word will change the appearance of your table.

Teachers can use tables to help arrange material for students (or for themselves), and students can use blank tables that you set up for them, or tables they create themselves, to organize the materials they are working with.

■ ■ ■ ■ ■ ■ ■ ■ ■ ■

Diagrams

> *He had read three times the paragraphs on how a bill becomes a law. But he never really understood the process until he worked through the diagram (with boxes and arrows linking the key steps) that Mr. Steadwell had prepared.*

> *She was a good reader, and fast, but she had some trouble creating a flowchart that summarized the main events in the plot. It forced her to remember the facts and to organize what she read, in a way that was new to her.*

> *It was a classic brainstorming lesson. But this time Mrs. Jabbour displayed on the big screen a new box for each student idea, and linked it to the other boxes with lines and arrows. When the lesson was over, each student walked home with a printed copy of the results.*

All of these examples use the drawing capabilities of Microsoft word to create a diagram that explains or illustrates an important concept.

HOW TO . . . CREATE A DIAGRAM WITH WORD

You need: Microsoft Word, and an idea for a diagram.

You get: A good-looking diagram that can be printed, mailed, inserted into another document, or distributed online.

The fastest way to create a simple diagram involves these steps:

1. Choose Insert, then Text Box from the menubar.
2. Watch the cursor turn into a crosshair.
3. Click and drag the mouse to form a rectangle of the size you need.
4. Enter from the keyboard the text that you want to appear inside the box.
5. To move a text box, click on its edge and drag it.
6. To change the size of a text box, select it and then drag its handles.
7. Repeat steps 1–6 to create and arrange the other boxes you need for your diagram.
8. To connect the boxes, choose the lines tool from the Drawing toolbar.

9. Choose an arrow or line.

10. Click on the edge of one text box, and drag to another.

Once created, diagrams are easily modified by clicking and dragging the elements around the screen, or using the standard text editing tools to change the appearance of the words. Diagrams can be used in a wide range of subject areas, for a variety of purposes.

A good way to teach this process to students is to create a diagram in front of them as part of a lesson, so they can see what you are doing. Then assign them a task that requires a diagram that they turn in for a grade.

Word documents with tables or diagrams can be printed (make sure to keep your boxes and arrows within the printable portion of the page), they can be saved and shared, they can be emailed, and they can even be saved as web pages (choose Save as Web Page from Word's menubar.) For organizing, recording, and publishing educational materials, tables and diagrams can help you and your students move beyond words and into the realm of organized ideas.

■ ■ ■ ■ ■ ■ ■ ■ ■ ■

ACCENTUATE THE POSITIVE: FOREIGN WORDS

We don't use many accent marks in English. Our words, for the most part, just contain plain old letters. We have 26 letters, and 26 keys on the keyboard with which to type them. But other languages make extensive use of accent marks. At some point you may find yourself at a loss as to how to add those marks to materials you are preparing for your students, or to help your students prepare these kinds of materials for an assignment, whether it is in social studies, math, or a foreign language class.

This section gets you started using the most common accent marks. We'll assume you are using Microsoft Word as your word processor, on either Macintosh or Windows, with the standard U.S. English keyboard and operating system, and that you are working in a European language that uses the Roman alphabet. This overview, therefore, does not apply to Greek, Russian, Chinese, or Urdu, for instance, but should work for words that come from European languages such as German, French, Italian, and Spanish.

Most of the accents you need are little marks that appear on top of the letters, such as é, à, ü, î, and ñ. But we will also consider the ç, the ø, the ¿, the ß, and the œ, which are not accents at all, but nonEnglish characters. You don't need any special software or new keyboards to produce these accents and special characters—everything you need is already present in the keyboard, programs, and systems that you already have. The best way to read this material is to try out the typing of each letter as it is described. Open Microsoft Word on your computer and get ready to give your fingers a workout.

HOW TO . . . CREATE ACCENTED LETTERS WITH WORD

Two-Step Accents

Most of the accented letters are created in two steps: the first step creates the accent, and the second step creates the letter. The accent is usually chosen by holding down the option or control key while you type another key; then you type the letter. For example, to make é, you would do this:

Macintosh:

1. Hold down the option key.
2. Continue holding down the option key as you press the e key.
3. Notice that nothing happens on the screen—all you have done is chosen the accent.
4. Release the option key.
5. Press the e key (again.)
6. See your é on the screen.

Windows:

1. Hold down the control key.
2. Continue holding down the control key as you press the apostrophe key.
3. Notice that nothing happens on the screen—all you have done is chosen the accent.
4. Let go of the control key.
5. Press the e key (again.)
6. See your é on the screen.

Try this several times until you get the hang of it. The pressing of option+e at the same time chooses the accent; the pressing of e the second time puts the letter under the accent. Here's another example: making the à:

Macintosh:

1. Hold down the option key.
2. Continue holding down the option key as you press the "`" key. On most keyboards, this is next to the numeral 1 in the upper left.
3. Notice that nothing happens on the screen—all you have done is chosen the accent.
4. Let go of the option key.
5. Press the "a" key.
6. See your à on the screen.

Windows:

1. Hold down the control key.
2. Continue holding down the control key as you press the "`" key. On most keyboards, this is next to the numeral 1 in the upper left.
3. Notice that nothing happens on the screen—all you have done is chosen the accent.
4. Let go of the control key.
5. Press the "a" key.
6. See your à on the screen.

In the same way, you could also create í, ó, ú, è, ì, and ù. Try it until it works for you. As you can see, the trick is to figure out the "accent selection" key for each platform. Here is a summary table:

ACCENT	DESCRIPTION*	SPECIAL KEY MACINTOSH	SPECIAL KEY WINDOWS
´	*accent aigu*	option+e	control+' (apostrophe)
`	*accent grave*	option+`	control+`
^	circumflex	option+i	control+^ (control+shift+6)
¨	umlaut	option+u	control+: (colon) (control+shift+;)
~	tilde	option+n	control+~ (tilde) (control+shift+')

* That's what the French or Spanish or Germans call these accents. Other languages may call them by other names.

Remember that you type the special keys first, then type the letter that will go underneath the accent mark. Some accent marks apply to only one letter, such as å, ç, and ø. And these are made differently depending on whether you are using Macintosh or Windows. In Windows, you need two steps, as with the characters in the preceding table:

- To make å, press control+@, then press a.
- To make ç, press control+, (comma), then press c.
- To make ø, press control+/, then press o.
- To make ß, press control+&, then press s.
- To make œ, press control+&, then press o.

In Macintosh, these and other characters are made in one step.

- To make å, hold down the option key as you type a.
- To make ç, hold down the option key as you type c.
- To make ø, hold down the option key as you type o.
- To make ß, hold down the option key as you type s.
- To make œ, hold down the option key as you type q.
- Other special characters that are made in this one-step method on the Macintosh include ¿ (option+shift+/). This can also be made in Windows (alt+control+?).

■ ■ ■ ■ ■ ■ ■ ■ ■ ■

MATH EQUATIONS IN WORD

Mathematicians use their language to describe and predict the phenomena of the universe, from the forces in the atom to the movement of the planets. But it is a strange language, often using symbols that don't appear on the keyboard. Many math teachers, from elementary school through university level, find it difficult to write math on the computer, so they revert to pencil and paper. This section looks at how anyone, from math specialist to primary teacher or middle-school student, can use ubiquitous tools like Microsoft Word or PowerPoint to create and work with the symbolic language of mathematics.

Because this is a plain-text page you are reading, I can't show you directly the symbols that we can create with Word. But you may download a sample Word document containing all the examples I cite, and consult it as you read this book.

Picture This

Al J. Brahe teaches engineering at Frenchville Community College. He is preparing a problem set for his students, in which they must adapt and modify some complex math equations that involve summation and integration. He cannot enter these symbols from his keyboard, no matter what special combinations of keys he presses.

Kelly Kounter is doing her fifth-grade math homework on the computer, and wants to show how she can add and subtract fractions with different denominators.

Cal Q. Luss is preparing a presentation for his twelfth-grade class, to help them review for the big math test at the end of the semester, and needs to show differentials and integrals.

Though they are working in very different situations, all of these people face the same problem: how to create accurate and easy-to-read math equations that can be included in a standard document or slide show, saved, printed, and transmitted electronically to others. And the solution for each is the same: use the Microsoft® Equation Editor® that comes with Microsoft® Office®. This little tool helps you to create the language of math that does not appear on the keyboard.

Installing Equation Editor

The Equation Editor does not arrive automatically on your computer with Microsoft Office. It's on the Office installation CD, but may not have been installed on your computer. First, find out if it's installed on your system:

1. Open Microsoft® Word® or PowerPoint®.
2. Create a new blank document with an empty page or slide.
3. Choose Insert, then Object from the menubar.

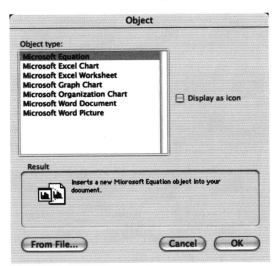

Look at the list of Object types in the window. Do you see Microsoft Equation? If so, you are all set, and you may forgo the installation process and proceed to the next section.

If Microsoft Equation does not appear in the list, you must install it from the Office CD:

1. Insert the Office CD into your computer.
2. Find the Equation Editor file in the folder called Value Pack.
3. Copy this file to the Office folder inside the Microsoft Office folder on your computer. In most cases, the Microsoft Office folder is in the Applications or Programs folder on your hard disk.

Now the next time you open Word or PowerPoint, it will see the Equation Editor and add it to the list of object types. To make sure it's installed, quit Word or PowerPoint, and repeat steps 1 through 4 above.

Making Math

Let's start with Kelly Kounter's problem, writing fractions. She is wrestling with one-third plus five-sixths. She wants to write it in good math format, as it appears in her textbooks. So she follows these steps:

1. Place the cursor in the document where you want the math to appear.
2. Choose Insert, then Object from the menubar.
3. From the list of object types, select Microsoft Equation, and click OK.
4. In a moment, you will see the Equation window appear, along with a small gray box in the document.
5. In the Equation window, click the type of math you want to make. (In Kelly's case, it's the fraction template, bottom row, second from the left.)
6. From the pop-down menu, choose the exact format you need. (Kelly chooses the full-sized vertical fraction format.)
7. Watch the template appear in the Equation window.
8. Enter the numbers into the template. (Kelly enters 1 into the top and 3 into the bottom of the fraction template.)
9. Enter the next item in the math sentence—the + symbol—from the keyboard.
10. Create the second fraction (five-sixths) in the same way.
11. Enter the = symbol from the keyboard. (We now have one-third plus five-sixths equals . . .)
12. Enter the result, one and one sixth, by entering 1 from the keyboard, and then entering another vertical fraction.
13. Close the Equation window, and watch the math appear in the document.
14. Drag the handles of the math in the document to make it appear larger or smaller as necessary.

The math is actually an image, a little picture that contains all the special symbols.

$$\frac{1}{3} + \frac{5}{6} = 1\frac{1}{6}$$

More Math

Now let's visit Brahe, who needs to show the integral from minus infinity to plus infinity of the Dirac impulse x(t). He starts the same way as Kelly, but chooses a different template. Picking up at Kelly's step 6, the engineer follows these steps:

1. From the integral templates, choose the integral with superscript and subscript template.
2. Enter plus-infinity and minus-infinity into the super- and subscript, respectively.
3. Use the Greek letter tool in the Equation window to enter the lowercase delta symbol.
4. Use the keyboard to enter the rest.
5. Close the Equation window to see the results in the document.

$$\int_{-\infty}^{+\infty} \mathrm{d}(t)\, dt = 1$$

Plotting

Cal Q. Luss, the high-school teacher, in addition to these kinds of math sentences, also wants to include some sample plots on an x, y axis. He won't use the equation editor for this; instead he'll use the drawing tools. He follows these steps to make a simple plot of a curving function:

1. Make sure the drawing toolbar is showing, by choosing View, then Toolbars, then Drawing from the menubar.
2. Choose the Arrow tool from the Lines button.
3. Click and drag the crosshair in the document to create the arrow for the x-axis.
4. Choose the arrow tool again, and create the y-axis. Remember that the head of the arrow appears at the end, not at the beginning of the line.
5. Choose the Curve tool from the Lines button.
6. Draw the curve, clicking once to create the belly of the curve, and twice to end the curve.
7. To label the plot, use the Text Box tool (letter A in the drawing toolbar). Choose the Text Box tool, click and drag in the document to create a box, then enter the label into the box from the keyboard.
8. To remove the line around the text box, select the text box, then choose Forma, then Text Box from the menubar, and set the Line Color to no line.
9. The size and position of all of the items in this plot can be adjusted by selecting them and dragging their handles.

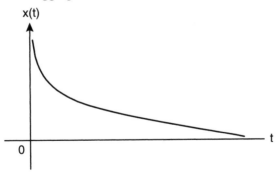

Powerpoint and Excel As Well

The equation editor and the drawing tools work the same way in PowerPoint and Excel as they do in Word. So you can include the language of math in a wide variety of documents. And with PowerPoint, you can make the elements of a plot, or the list of equations in a proof, appear one after the other in an animated fashion by using Animation function under the Slide Show menu. These tools work as well on the Windows versions of Office as they do on Macintosh.

On the Web

Once you create a Word or PowerPoint document containing math sentences or plots, you can post it to the Web by choosing Save as Web Page . . . from the File menu. The text of the document will be saved in HTML format, and the equations and plots as images. Make sure you copy to the web server the image folder that Word created when it saved the file. Sometimes Word has trouble getting the equations in exactly the right places, so you may want to open your HTML file with a web page editor such as Dreamweaver, and adjust things accordingly.

The Microsoft Equation editor is a relatively simple and straightforward tool for creating math symbols and writing math sentences. More sophisticated tools exist that perform the same function, such as MathType, which you can learn about at www.dessci.com/en/products/mathtype. The tried-and-true users of math documents swear by this tool. The language of math is full of work and wonder, and as you have now seen, is no stranger to the world of computer documents.

LEARN MORE . . .

About Symbols for Correcting Student Work

www.victorianweb.org/courses/nonfiction/correct.html
> This site features a list of symbols and abbreviations for adding your comments to student papers, created by George P. Landow, Shaw Professor of English and Digital Culture at Brown University.

About School-Home Communication with Newsletters

www.eduscapes.com/sessions/publishing
> This site walks you through the steps for student- and teacher-created newsletters. It also provides rubrics for evaluating student newsletters.

About Using Brochures in the Classroom

http://coe.west.asu.edu/students/dmatousek/webquest.htm
> This is a webquest on biomes that uses brochures as a culminating project. Can be easily adapted to other subjects and grade levels.

About International Accent Marks

www.starr.net/is/type/kbh.html

The International Accent Marks and Diacriticals web site explains the basics, covers other programs beyond Word, and provides an excellent set of links to other sources of information on this topic.

About Creating Mathematics inside Microsoft Word

http://spot.pcc.edu/~ssimonds/thisandthat/msword.htm

This page provides more information about the equation editor, including shortcuts and tips.

CHAPTER TEN

NUMBERS

IN THIS CHAPTER

- **Math Teachers**
- **Spreadsheets: Getting Started with Excel**
- **More Work with Excel Graphs**
- **Learn More . . .**

Numbers aren't just for math teachers. We all communicate with numbers, even in the softest of subjects. And our students need to learn to express ideas with numbers as well as nouns, with ciphers as well as sentences, with graphs as well as grammar. This chapter begins with a description of some of the ways that math teachers use technology for their work, and then goes on to show how any teacher (or student) can use a spreadsheet to organize information and create graphical representations.

MATH TEACHERS

In the beginning, computers in schools tended toward the math department. They were, after all, devices for *computing,* which is what math teachers do. Math teachers were always in first place with computing in our schools. I was a social studies teacher in the early days of computers, and never did much with math. But recent encounters with math teachers and computers have led to this chapter.

In helping a school of engineering to put their teaching program online, I have enjoyed the opportunity to work with teachers who use mathematics every day in their work, a high level of math of a type I never expected my sixth-graders to learn, and that seldom confronts a professor of communication. Integrals, sums, sinusoidal functions, and fast Fourier transforms find their way into the everyday speech of these teachers. Through my work with them, I have found that while the rest of us have all become computer users over the last two decades, the math teachers have maintained their lead. They use computers in ways that go far beyond what the rest of us do.

The Tools They Use

They've come a long way from paper, pencil, chalk, and blackboard. The math teachers, the engineers, and the mathematicians that I see do much of their work on the computer. There's a computer on their desk, and one in the classroom. More often than not, it's the same one, a laptop that they take with them wherever they go. And the software effects I see them using include the following.

Animation.   The sine function seemed to draw itself across the x and y axes, like a wave swooping up and down in a smooth continuous motion. But now the wave is sampled into a series of discontinuous dots, thus teaching an important concept in signal processing. The teacher built this animation in Flash to help him teach students a difficult but basic idea in a memorable way. The animation proved the concept in ways that would have been impossible on the pages of a textbook or on the chalkboard.

Simulation.   The same teacher wanted to go farther, and let his students change certain factors, such as the frequency of the sine function or the rate of sampling, to see the results for themselves. So he modified the animation to turn it into a simulation that allowed students to test the concept interactively. This too was built with Flash, but here he needed a Flash programmer—one of his students—to help him with the scripting. Going deeper, this teacher then assigned his students to use MatLab, which can simulate just about any mathematical process on the computer screen, to explore the concept in more detail.

Equations.   Math people use equations to tell their stories. While the rest of us use words made up of the 26 letters on the keyboard, the mathematicians use equations made up of strange symbols that you will be hard-pressed to find on your keyboard. Seldom do they write these equations with pencil on paper—I see them instead composing the equations for their students' homework problem sets with Microsoft Word, using Word's Equation Editor to enter their favorite math symbols carefully organized on the page to tell the story. (Chapter 9 shows how to do this.) And apparently the more dedicated among them use a more powerful equation-writer called MathType.

Calculators.   Yes, they still use the computer to compute, but ever since mathematics moved beyond arithmetic their calculations became more than mere numbers and sums. They enter an equation and see it calculated and graphed in an instant. They change a variable and see the display of the function move on the display. They cut, copy, paste, print, and email the results of the calculations. The graphing calculator, all the rage in the high school math classroom a few years ago, has given way to the personal computer with built-in calculation software that's more powerful and flexible.

Spreadsheets.   When they do work with numbers and quantities and statistical data, I see them using as their tool of choice the lowly spreadsheet. The same copy of Microsoft Excel that came with your computer is used by the math mavens to organize information, numbers, names, data, anything they can enter into the cells. And then to work with the data: apply formulas to it, add, subtract, sum, and compare it, and graph it. I've even seen math lessons built on the spreadsheet, for students of all ages.

Presentation.   Another tool from the Microsoft Office suite, PowerPoint, shows up on their math desks and in their classrooms. I see the engineers prepare their lectures not for the chalkboard but for the projector, delivered as PowerPoint slide shows. With the same equations, beautifully scaled and presented and visible across the classroom. With text that explains the math. And with graphs copied from the calculator to illustrate the concepts. The PowerPoint file ends up on the Web, where students may access it from anywhere, at any time.

Where did they learn all this? Not from their own math teachers, in most cases. They went to the Web, to places like the Math Forum at http://mathforum.org. And when they want to help their students learn, they send them to the Web also, to programs like MathXL at www.mathxl.com/support/features.htm, that provide tutorials and tools for learning math with these new-fashioned tools.

You may not be a math teacher, but your field most likely has developed some new tools of the trade over the last few years, based on the personal computer. How do you learn about them? How do you learn to use them? How do you bring them into the act of teaching?

Today's Tools, Yesterday's Teaching

What do these new tools portend for the future? When all the math teachers and all the math students bring computers into the classroom, what will it look like? How will the environment change? How will teaching be different? "I'm not sure I like it," remarked a math teacher sitting in his office. "They'll be paying attention to what's on their computer rather than looking at me. I'm afraid I'll lose control of their train of thought. I think I'll stick to paper and pencil and chalk in the classroom."

If this teacher's view results in a banning of the new tools from the math classroom, we will see a disconnect between the tools of math used in labs and on the desks of real mathematicians, and those used for teaching in the classroom. Will this be good for our students?

These tools are not just for solving math problems. The spreadsheet has become an all-purpose data organizing and graphing and problem-solving tool that we all should know how to use.

SPREADSHEETS: GETTING STARTED WITH EXCEL

What is a spreadsheet and why should you care? We usually think about mathematics or accountants when we think of spreadsheets: columns of numbers, budgets spread over many pages, complex formulas that only mathematicians understand, and obscure functions totally removed from most classrooms. This section introduces two simple and practical uses of spreadsheets that can be helpful to students and teachers: creating simple graphs of mathematical data, and managing text in the form of lists. If you combine the two, you can create your own grade book!

Put simply, a spreadsheet is a matrix of columns and rows into which you can place data. Once the data is in the spreadsheet, it's possible to manipulate the data using simple commands, create charts and graphs, reorganize your data in alphabetical or numeric order, and work with your data using formulas.

To get started using Microsoft® Excel®, the most commonly available spreadsheet program, we'll use a simple problem found in many upper elementary school classrooms: estimating, measuring, and analyzing what's in a bag of M&Ms. In this exercise, you'll learn how to:

- Place data in a spreadsheet
- Change the format of the text in a spreadsheet
- Use a formula for addition
- Create a chart

Of course you may eat the M&Ms when you're finished!

HOW TO . . . GET STARTED USING A SPREADSHEET

You'll need: A bag of M&Ms, and a computer that has Excel installed.

You'll get: A simple spreadsheet with data, formulas, and graphs.

1. First, without opening the bag, estimate how many M&Ms you think you have. Make a guess about which colors are in the bag and if there's a dominant color.
2. Take your bag of M&M's and spread them out on the table next to the computer.
3. Sort them by color into piles.
4. Open an Excel worksheet.
5. Type the word *Color* at the head of the first column (Cell A1).
6. Type the word *Number* at the head of the second column (Cell B1).
7. Click your mouse in cell A2. Type each color in column one, pressing Return to register the names of each color.
8. Count the number of each color and enter each into column B, pressing Return to register the number of M&Ms for each color.

	A	B
1	Color	Number
2	Blue	7
3	Green	12
4	Yellow	9
5	Red	8
6		
7		
8		
9		
10		

FORMAT TEXT

1. Select cell A1 and change the font and size of the text using the format menu.
2. Change the text for each color to reflect its own color.

CREATE A CHART

1. To create a chart of your data, select all cells that you want to include (click/drag from the lower right corner to the upper left corner).

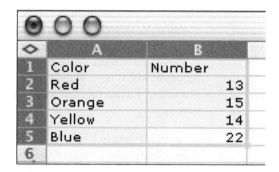

2. Next, choose Chart from the Insert menu.

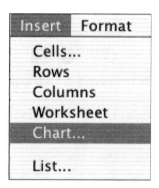

3. From the dialog box, choose the chart that best tells your story.

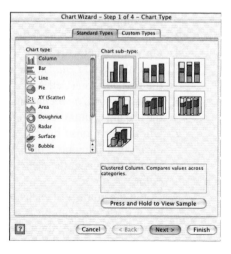

4. Click Finish. Your chart is ready!

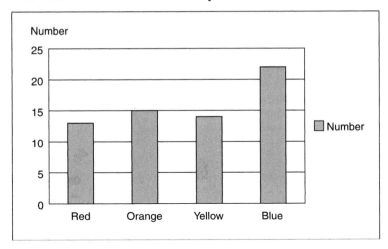

You'll find more details on working with graphs in the next section of this chapter.

■ ■ ■ ■ ■ ■ ■ ■ ■ ■

USE A FORMULA

Excel makes data analysis very easy. What if you wanted to know how many M&Ms are in your bag? If you have a small bag, it's easy to just count them but, since you have the individual colors all counted, we'll use a formula to get the total.

1. Click in the destination cell (where you want your answer to appear):

2. Type = and notice that the program assumes you want to find a sum.

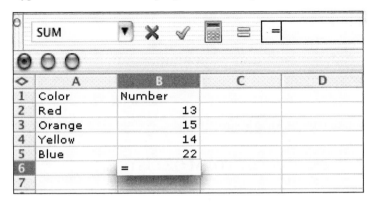

3. Click Sum and a dialog box appears asking which cells you want to include (note that it assumes you want to include all the cells above the destination cell).

4. Click OK and the answer appears in the destination cell.
5. Notice that if you change any of the numbers, the total changes as well. This is one of the features of spreadsheets that make them so useful.

REPLICATE A FORMULA ACROSS SEVERAL COLUMNS OR ROWS

Excel lets you repeat a formula across columns or down rows. What if we have several columns of data and have used a formula to get the sum of one column?

1. Beginning with the cell containing the original formula, select the cells you want to have use the same formula.

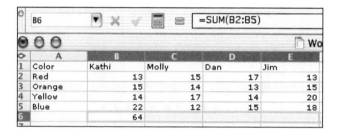

2. From the Edit menu, choose Fill, Right. Instantly all the columns are totaled.

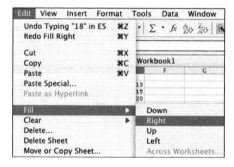

3. You can eat the M&Ms now!

MANAGE TEXT IN THE FORM OF LISTS

Spreadsheets are more than number analysis tools. Many classroom teachers use spreadsheets to create sortable lists. Here's an example: Mr. Brucelle has 15 students in his eighth-period science class. When it's time to dismiss them, there's always some confusion about who goes where. So, he's going to create a spreadsheet that will allow him to sort the students quickly in a variety of ways.

1. The first thing he does is type in the student names, using a separate column for last and first names, and entering the bus number for each student:

	A	B	C
1	Last	First	Bus Number
2	Ahearn	Allison	5
3	Harb	Eileen	2
4	Young	Ellie	2
5	Leist	Jacob	3
6	Haselman	Janet	2
7	Lawrence	Jimmy	1
8	McCorkle	Julie	7
9	Fisher	Mary	1
10	Dupont	Molly	walker
11	Dubois	Patrick	7
12	Andrews	Sam	4
13	Jabbour	Sara	3
14	Thomas	Simon	walker
15	Rota	Tom	5

2. Right now, nothing is in order but he doesn't worry about that. He'll use the sorting feature of the spreadsheet to create a more organized list.
3. The first list he's going to make will alphabetize the students by last name.
4. First, he'll select all the cells that have data in them so individuals' data stay together:
5. Click/drag the mouse to select the cells:

	A	B	C
1	Last	First	Bus Number
2	Ahearn	Allison	5
3	Harb	Eileen	2
4	Young	Ellie	2
5	Leist	Jacob	3
6	Haselman	Janet	2
7	Lawrence	Jimmy	1
8	McCorkle	Julie	7
9	Fisher	Mary	1
10	Dupont	Molly	walker
11	Dubois	Patrick	7
12	Andrews	Sam	4
13	Jabbour	Sara	3
14	Thomas	Simon	walker
15	Rota	Tom	5

6. Next, he chooses Sort from the Data menu. Notice that the program assumes you want to sort using column A. He clicks OK and the list is now sorted by last name.

7. To sort by a different column, such as Bus Number, he'll again select all the cells containing data, choose Sort from the Data menu, and then change the Sort By to the column he wishes.

Once you have begun to use spreadsheets for numbers and text, you can easily create simple gradebooks for yourself by setting up lists of your students, placing assignment titles across the top row, then entering grades for the students. To average their grades, you'll simply select the destination cell, type =, then choose Average from the list of formulas.

Spreadsheets provide an easy and interesting way for both students and teachers to analyze and present data. This chapter demonstrated two, very simple uses for spreadsheets. Microsoft Excel has many features that allow you to complete complex tasks. It is worth the time to explore the Help menu to learn about what Excel can do for you.

MORE WORK WITH EXCEL GRAPHS

Numbers appear all around us. They trace the rise and fall of the stock market, they record the progress of our students, they list the distances to the planets, and they weigh the guinea pig in the back of the classroom. Our students spend a good deal of their time in school learning to work with numbers, and to understand how numbers help explain how the world works. Computers need numbers in order to operate, and in fact in the early days of computing you needed to feed the machine numbers—it did not understand text, nor images nor sound.

Collections of numbers, like the results of an election, or the batting averages of a team, or the growth of a population over the years, are often used to communicate important ideas in school and in public communication. But it takes a lot of work on the part of the viewer to interpret these numbers to understand what they mean. It's often more efficient to use a graph to show the "story behind the numbers." And in most math curricula, the making and understanding of graphs is an important skill. This section gets you started making graphs from collections of numbers.

The instructions here refer to Microsoft Excel, which is the program most people use to organize their numbers and to create graphs quickly. Other spreadsheet programs that might be found in a school, such as AppleWorks, operate in similar ways and will require few modifications to the steps listed here.

How Tall?

The best way to learn to make graphs with a spreadsheet is to build a small collection of numbers, and then experiment with various graphs. Open your spreadsheet program and create a new blank document.

Into the spreadsheet enter the names of the members of a family and their heights. Your collection of data should look something like this:

	A	B	C
1		Height	
2	Molly	49	
3	Jimmy	68	
4	Kathi	64	
5	Annie	66	
6	Ben	73	

In this example, the numbers that represent height are called *values,* and the words that represent names are called *labels.* Each label and value is entered in one cell of the spreadsheet. The label Jimmy, for instance, is in cell A3, column A, row 3, while the value 73 is in B6. And cell C7 is empty. (Of course you may use any kind of data you like for this exercise, but keep it small and simple to begin with, with short labels and straightforward values.)

HOW TO . . . MAKE A GRAPH

The process of making a graph from data like these takes four steps:

1. Select some data. Click and drag the mouse to select the numbers and words that you want to include in the graph. In this example we will graph all of the data, but in many situations you won't want to include all the information in the graph. Select only what you need, in this case selecting the area from A1 to B6.

2. Create a chart. From the menubar choose Insert, then Chart. Then choose the type of chart you want (column, bar, line, pie, and so forth). Then click the Finish button. (Notice that Excel refers to what you are making as a chart, while most teachers would call this a graph. Don't let the terms fool you.)

3. Examine your graph. Excel will construct your graph automatically, but not always in exactly the way that you might wish. Does it appear as you had planned? Does it include all the necessary information? Will it make sense to the audience? Does it include any extraneous or distracting elements? Make a note of what needs changing.

4. Modify the graph. For a simple graph like this, you may not need to change anything. But if you do, simply double-click the item you want to change, and you will get a dialog box that lets you change it. To get rid of an item on the graph, you simply select it (one click) and press the delete or backspace key.

■ ■ ■ ■ ■ ■ ■ ■ ■ ■

Types of Graphs

For displaying the comparative heights of the members of a family, a column graph is appropriate, because the vertical columns in the chart appear similar to people standing up next to each other. If we were graphing the distances to various cities, we might best show it as a horizontal bar graph, because we move horizontally when we travel to them. A pie graph is best used when we are showing the parts of a whole, such as the proportions of a population with various color of eyes. A line graph might best represent data that shows a continuous trend or flow over time, such as air temperature.

To change a graph from one type to another, select the graph, and then from the menubar choose Chart, then Chart type. Notice that Excel provides two levels of choice here, a general graph type on the left, and a specific format on the right. The best way to understand how this works is to make a graph of your own, and then try changing the type to see the results.

Avoid the tendency to make the graph too fancy. Excel provides many formats, some of which are over-decorated and make your graph hard to understand. Choose the simpler formats and your graph will communicate better to its audience.

Complex Graphs

To make a more complex graph, you would add more columns of values to your spreadsheet, and then show them all in one graph. For instance, in the example shown above you might add a column for weight and another for girth. But be careful—a graph that compares widely different measures is hard to make sense of. In this case, you would avoid including a column that showed the annual income of each person on the list, because the numbers would be way off the scale and the comparisons with height and weight irrelevant.

To make a graph from a spreadsheet with multiple columns, carefully select all the data that you need, and then from the menubar choose Insert, then Graph. All of the selected data will be shown in the graph, each column of numbers with its own line or box.

Sometimes the values of the various measurements are out of proportion to each other, such as heights that range from 50 to 70 inches next to weights that range from 150 to 300 pounds. The graph produced by such data might not be easy to interpret if both measurements are plotted on the same scale. Excel lets you construct a graph with two different axes, each with its own scale of values. To create such a graph, choose the Custom Types tab in the Chart Wizard window, and then scroll down to the Line-Column on 2 axes type. This will scale the heights from 0 to 80 on the left axis, and the weights from 0 to 300 on the right.

Saving Graphs

When you save an Excel document, the graph is saved with it, and whenever it is opened the graph will appear where you left it. You can also save the table of numbers and the graph as a web page, by choosing Save as Web Page from the File menu. You can also copy the graph alone by selecting it, and then choosing Copy from the Edit menu. From here it can be pasted into any document, such as a report in Word or an image in Photoshop.

Printing Graphs

To print the graph along with the table of numbers on the same page, first deselect the graph (this is best done by clicking the mouse in one of the cells of the spreadsheet), and then choose Print from the File menu.To print only the graph, select it by clicking once on the graph, and then choose Print from the File menu.

Students and teachers both can find many ways to use graphs for teaching and learning. The best way to get started is to experiment with your own collections of numbers, graphing them every chance you get, and trying different types and formats until you find the ones that work best.

LEARN MORE . . .

http://mathforum.org
The Math Forum is a tremendous repository of math-related resources for K–12 teachers.

www.mathxl.com/support/features.htm
MathXL is a powerful online homework, tutorial, and assessment system designed specifically for Pearson Education textbooks in mathematics and statistics.

http://illuminations.nctm.org//index2.html
The illuminations site, sponsored by the National Council for Teachers of Mathematics, includes a rich set of virtual manipulatives and lessons.

www.sabine.k12.la.us/class/excel_resources.htm
This site has an extensive collection of lesson plans and tutorials for classroom teachers.

CHAPTER ELEVEN

IMACES

IN THIS CHAPTER

- **Gathering Digital Images**
- **How Digital Images Work**
- **Editing Digital Images**
- **Publishing Digital Images**
- **From Camera to Computer: Macintosh**
- **From Camera to Computer: Windows**
- **Learn More . . .**

We are all using digital images more and more in our work, in school, and at home. That's because they are faster, cheaper, more creative, and easier to copy and distribute than older types of pictures. The arrival of the digital camera as an inexpensive consumer item, along with the growing collection of images on the World Wide Web, has made it important for educators to understand how best to work with these new kinds of pictures.

Teaching and learning thrives on images. Picture this:

A student in the social studies class finds a map from 1803 in the town library, scans it, and displays it next to a current map of the same area (found on the Web), and explains the differences.

A science teacher takes a digital photograph of a tropical flowering plant in the school greenhouse. Then she searches for a photo of the same species from a book, and scans it. She edits them to the same size, and displays them for comparison in her next lecture.

Fourth graders shoot digital photos of their dramatization of a scene from Charlotte's Web, *arrange them into a slide show, and narrate the story to the second-grade class.*

The art teacher gathers a collection of digital images of paintings and buildings for use in an online quiz, in which students place these examples in historical order.

Images can make the job of the teacher or of the student more interesting, more creative, and more effective. This chapter shows you how to *gather* digital images from cameras, scanners, and the Web; how to *edit* them so they conform to your educational needs; and finally how to *publish* them so they are useful in your teaching. The chapter closes with a detailed look at how to get the pictures from your digital camera into your computer.

GATHERING DIGITAL IMAGES

The first step is to is taking advantage of the power of images for learning is to find the picture you need, and get it onto your computer. This section reviews the many sources of images, and shows you how to capture them with a digital camera, through the Web, or by scanning.

Sources for Images

Digital images can come from many sources:

The library. Many of those books (and magazines and other resources) in the library contain the images that you might need for your work. The librarian can help you find the picture you need, but then you'll want to take a digital copy of it. A few libraries have scanners connected to computers, where you can make your own scan and take it with you on a floppy disk. Most libraries have copy machines that you can use to make a paper copy of what you found, but this is not the best way—you'll have to scan the copy at your own computer, and the quality will suffer. You may be able to borrow the book or paper that contains the picture you need, take it to your computer, scan it, and return it to the library.

A camera. A digital camera works best, but you can also use a film camera to take the photo you need. As you snap the shot, make sure the subject fills the picture, by getting as close as you can but still fitting it all in. Make sure the light is behind you, not behind the subject, and that the background is as plain and simple as possible. Take two or three shots from different angles. If you have film, you'll need to get it developed, and when you do, ask them to provide the pictures on a floppy disk or CD-ROM—most photo shops will do this for a small extra charge.

Paper. Sometimes the easiest way to create a map or diagram or sketch is with paper and pen (or pencil or chalk or paint or marker). Draw it on paper as neatly as you can, then scan it into your computer.

Your computer. Diagrams and illustrations can be drawn by hand using the software that's already on your computer. You can use text boxes and lines in Microsoft Word to create tables and diagrams, as described in Chapter 9. You can use your spreadsheet program to create charts and graphs, as described in Chapter 10. You can also use your painting or photo editing program to create illustrations.

The Internet. The Internet is full of images, and they are easy to find. Use the image-finding capabilities of one of the standard Internet search engines such as Google or AltaVista. Note that images you download from the Internet do not belong to you and can only be used in a limited way in the classroom. The U.S. Copyright Law has a Fair Use clause that defines what you can use, how you can use it, and where you can publish images and media taken from the Internet. The short answer is that teachers and students are allowed to use media downloaded from the Web for educational purposes within the classroom and school. Publishing outside the classroom or school (on your school's web site, for instance) is not permitted without permission from the owner of the media. For guidance on this important topic, see the University of Maryland article, *Copyright and Fair Use in the Classroom, on the Internet, and the World Wide Web* (www.umuc.edu/library/copy.html).

HOW TO . . . FIND AND DOWNLOAD PICTURES FROM THE WEB

You need: A web browser and access to the Internet.

You get: Images on your hard disk, that you can use in educational projects.

1. Open your browser.
2. Go to the search engine of your choice, such as Google or AltaVista.
3. Click the Images button on the opening page.
4. Enter key words for the image you are looking for. (Here you may use all the searching techniques described in Chapter 7.)
5. Watch the search engine find pictures that are relevant to your keywords. You'll see a page full of thumbnail images.
6. Click on one of the thumbnails to go to the web page where the image is posted.
7. Scroll down the page as necessary to find the picture.
8. To download the image to your computer, right-click (Windows) or click-and-hold (Macintosh) on the image.
9. From the popup menu, choose Download Image.
10. Give the image a name that makes sense, and save it in a place where you'll be able to find it again.

■ ■ ■ ■ ■ ■ ■ ■ ■ ■

Capturing the Image from a Digital Camera or Scanner

Before you can work with an image, you must get it into your computer. It's easy to capture from a scanner, a digital camera, even from a video camcorder. Each of these devices needs software to accomplish the capture. This software may need to be installed from the CD-ROM that came with the camera or scanner, or downloaded from the camera manufacturer's web site. A good source of information about which capture software goes with your camera or scanner can be found at the Digital Eyes web site, www.image-acquire.com. This site also provides links for downloading the software that you need. In most cases, using this capturing software is a three-step process:

1. Connect your computer to the scanner or camera.
2. Select the image(s) or set the parameters. If you are given a choice, set the resolution at or near 72 pixels per inch, and set the size of the image to match how you plan to use it.
3. Capture and save the image. Save to a folder on the Desktop for now; later you will copy this folder to another disk as necessary.

If you are given the choice, save photos in the JPEG format with medium compression. A scanner works best for capturing flat items, such as book pages, photographs, and drawings. A scanner can also do a good job with small objects such as cloth and keys. But even if you don't have a scanner, you can use a digital camera or video camcorder to capture these kinds of images. You can also use the cameras for capturing people, landscapes, and large objects. The last section of this chapter provides more detailed instructions on how to get the images from a digital camera onto your computer.

No matter where you capture the image, remember that the image belongs to someone else. For most school projects, you do not need to get the permission of the owner to use an image in a report. But you should keep track of where you acquired each image, and cite your source in the final publication.

After the Capture

Once the image is captured, you may be able to use it directly in a PowerPoint presentation, in a Word document, on a web site, or by printing on paper. But most images will need some editing, and to be a good editor, you need to know a bit about how images work on your computer.

HOW DIGITAL IMAGES WORK

It's good to know what's going on when you work with digital images. Here are the key concepts:

Pixels. A pixel is a point of light, so small that you can see it only if you look very closely. Images on a computer are divided up into thousands of little tiny pixels. Each pixel is a square of color. In the computer, each pixel is stored as a number that indicates its color. The image file is simply a long series of numbers, one pixel after the other. A typical quarter-screen image would contain 76,800 pixels, and so its file would consist of 76,800 numbers.

Size. The bigger the image, the more pixels, and the longer the string of numbers. Your computer displays about 72 pixels per inch, so a picture one inch square contains 72 × 72 or 5,184 pixels. A picture that filled your computer screen would contain of 480,000 pixels. Such a picture would produce a very long string of numbers, and thus a very large file on your disk. In fact, such a picture would be so large it might not even fit on a floppy disk. So you see that it's important to get the size of your image right when you capture it. If it's too small, you won't be able to see the details. If it's too big, it will take up too much room on the computer.

Resolution. Your computer displays about 72 pixels per inch. Your printer can display over 300 pixels per inch. A television screen can show about 20 pixels per inch. A good film camera can show 2,000 pixels per inch. That's why you can see more detail on paper or on a photograph than you can on a computer screen or television. The number of pixels per inch is called the *resolution* of the image. The higher the resolution, the more detail you can see, but the bigger the file. For most projects, a resolution of 72 pixels per inch works best, and results in smaller file sizes that are easier to work with. The only time you might need to use a higher resolution is when your project is going to be published on paper with a high-quality printer, and when the extra detail is necessary. Since most of the images we use in teaching are destined to be displayed on a computer, it's best to prepare all your images at a resolution of 72 pixels per inch.

File formats. When you saved your pictures from the Web, or got them from the digital camera, you may have noticed a three-letter extension to the filename, such as .jpg or .gif. These filename extensions indicate the file format of the image. Most photographic images are stored in the JPEG or .jpg format, and most drawings are stored in the GIF or .gif format. JPEG (pronounced jay-peg) stands for Joint Photographer Expert Group. GIF (pronounced with a hard G) stands for Graphics Interchange Format. You may encounter other image file formats, such as PNG, EPS, TIFF, PICT, and BMP, but it's best to save your images in the JPEG or GIF formats, because these can be read by just about every computer and software program, and they create small files.

Compression. JPEG and GIF are *compressed* file formats—they do not save every number from every pixel—and so the files are smaller. Compression works by mathematical formulas that examine the string of numbers in an image file looking for repeated numbers or adjacent pixels of similar color, or removing information your eye does not need. The result of this data compression is a much smaller file that, when decompressed, looks almost as good as the original.

EDITING DIGITAL IMAGES

Digital images are faster, cheaper, more creative, and easier to copy and distribute than older types of pictures. The arrival of the digital camera as an inexpensive consumer item, along with the growing collection of images on the World Wide Web, has made it important for educators to understand how best to work with these new kinds of pictures. The last section showed you how to capture these images with cameras, scanners, and web browsers; in this section, you'll learn how to edit the images.

Image-Editing Software

To make the best use of this section, you'll need a computer with some kind of image-editing software. Many programs can work with images in a simple way, including Microsoft Word, PowerPoint, and AppleWorks. You can do some very basic work with images if you have one of these on your computer. But to take full advantage of the power of pictures, you should use a dedicated image-editing program such as Adobe® Photoshop® Elements. Photoshop Elements will enable you to do all of the work described in this section, and more. It costs less than $50, and often comes packaged with digital cameras and scanners. To try it out, you can download a trial copy of Photoshop Elements at the Adobe web site (www.adobe.com).

Viewing the Image

Once you have captured the image, you need to open it with the image-editing software so that you can see it and work with it. These instructions are designed to be used with Adobe Photoshop Elements, which we will refer to from here on as simply Photoshop, but you will find that most of the other image-editing programs contain similar functions and menu items that you can follow along with.

HOW TO . . . EDIT AN IMAGE

You need: An image-editing program such as Photoshop Elements, and some digital image files to edit.

You get: Retouched, cropped, resized, and adjusted images oriented to your purposes and saved in a format appropriate to your method of publication.

1. **Open the image.** First open Photoshop, then choose Open from the File menu, then navigate to the image you want to work with and open it. You should see the image open in a new Photoshop window.
2. **View the image.** Make sure you are seeing the image in its actual size. The title bar of the Photoshop window should read something like myimage.jpg @ 100% (RGB). To change the magnification of the image, choose Zoom in or Zoom out from the View menu, until you get to 100%. This zooming does not modify the image itself; it simply adjusts how you are seeing it. It's best to view it at 100% at this point. You can view more than one image at once—each will open it its own window.
3. **Flip or rotate the image.** Some pictures may have been captured sideways or upside down. Now's the time to set them straight. Use Rotate from the Image menu to view the picture right-side up. You will be rotating the entire image here, everything that's in the window. Photoshop refers to this as *rotating the canvas,* the canvas being the entire window. You can rotate the canvas 90 degrees right or left, or 180 degrees (upside down). You can also flip the canvas horizontally or vertically. The Canvas custom item lets you rotate the image by degrees.

   Try these rotations by yourself on one of your images. You can choose Undo from the Edit menu to reverse any rotations that you make.

As you view the image, size it up. Does it look OK? Will it need some brightening or darkening? Are the edges clean and crisp? Will it need to be cropped to focus better on the subject? It is the right size for its intended use? The next section shows you how to make these adjustments.

■ ■ ■ ■ ■ ■ ■ ■ ■ ■

Adjusting Size and Resolution

Before setting the size and resolution of an image, you must determine where the image will be published, and exactly how big it will be in its final form. You should choose your resolution carefully.

If your image will be printed on paper, you should set its resolution—the number of pixels per inch—to match your printer. For most ink-jet and laser printers, a resolution of 300 pixels per inch will produce good results. If you have an excellent quality image, taken with a multi-megapixel digital camera, and a photo-quality printer, then you might get better results at 600 pixels per inch.

If you plan to display this image on the computer screen, in a PowerPoint show or on a web page, then set the resolution to 72 pixels per inch. Anything higher may cause problems—the picture file will be too large to fit within the memory of PowerPoint or the web browser.

HOW TO . . . SET THE RESOLUTION OF AN IMAGE

1. In Photoshop, choose Image, then Resize, then Image Size from the menubar.
2. Set the appropriate resolution by entering the number in the resolution box. (See the paragraphs above for advice on the right resolution for your purposes.)
3. Set the size of the image. The image should be set to the exact size you want it to appear in your paper or on your computer screen.

■ ■ ■ ■ ■ ■ ■ ■ ■ ■

Cleaning Up the Image

Seldom does the image appear exactly how you'd like. Often you need to adjust things and clean them up, by straightening, cropping, erasing, touch-up, cover-up, brightening, darkening, sharpening, and adjusting color and contrast. You won't need to do all of these things with every one of your images, but you should be prepared to do at least the following actions.

Straighten the image. To straighten an image, choose Image, then Rotate, then Canvas Custom. . . . Enter the number of degrees you want to rotate the image, and the direction.

Crop the image. Are its edges messy, torn, uneven? Is there a lot of wasted space around the outside of the main subject? If so, it's time to crop the image. Cropping

Move tool		Zoom tool
Hand tool		Eyedropper
Marquee tool		Lasso
Magic wand		Selection brush
Type tool		Crop tool
Cookie cutter		Red eye
Healing tool		Clone stamp
Pencil		Eraser
Brush		Paint bucket
Gradient		Shape tool
Blur tool		Sponge tool
Foreground color		Background color

involves two steps: first select the good portion of the image; then delete all the rest. To select part of the image, use Photoshop's Rectangular Marquee Tool. You'll find it at the upper left of the Tool Palette. Once you have chosen the Rectangular Marquee tool, click and drag it over the portion of the image that you want to remain. Then choose Crop from the Image menu, and the picture will be cropped and ready for the next steps.

Remove dust and scratches. In your image, do you see scratches or dust that came through with the scanning? These are easy to remove. From Photoshop's Filter menu, choose Noise, then Dust & Scratches. Adjust the slider until the scratches disappear.

Edit the image. What if there's more than just dust and scratches to remove? Suppose you have a photograph of an historic ship, but in the background is a modern bridge and in the foreground are some modern boats that distract from the old ship. Can these be removed? If you simply choose the eraser tool and rub it over the bridge, you will leave a white streak. Instead, you may remove the bridge by replacing it with something else. You might replace the bridge, for instance, with more sky. To do this, you may use the tools from Photoshop, as shown here.

HOW TO . . . REMOVE OBJECTS FROM A PICTURE

1. Choose the Clone Stamp tool.
2. Pick up some pixels to cover up the object you want to remove—for example, pick up some sky to cover up the bridge. Pickup sky by placing the Clone Stamp on the sky and then . . .
3. Hold down the option key while clicking the mouse. (This picks up some sky. You won't see it, but it will be there.)
4. Click and drag the Clone Stamp tool over the bridge.
5. Watch the sky replace the bridge. (You may need to pick up different parts of the sky to get just the right matching color.)

■ ■ ■ ■ ■ ■ ■ ■ ■ ■

If necessary, use the Blur and Sponge tools from Photoshop's Tool Palette to soften the blend of colors in the areas where you painted in new sky. The best way to learn and understand these photo-editing skills is to try them yourself. If you haven't done so already, open a picture in Photoshop and practice some of the techniques described so far.

> **Adjust brightness and contrast.** Picture too dark? Brighten it up. All washed out? Darken it and increase the contrast. Too harsh? Decrease the contrast. To do this, choose Enhance, then Auto Contrast from the menubar. Adjust what you see until you like what you see. Click OK, and your picture is enhanced.
>
> **Color adjustments.** In the same way that you adjusted the brightness and contrast of your image, you can also alter the color of your image. If the color of your picture seems to be a bit off, for instance, choose Enhance, then Colors, then Hue and Saturation from the menubar, then use the sliders to change the colors until they look more realistic.

As you are making these adjustments, don't forget that you can undo changes you don't want—otherwise you may be stuck with them. Under the Edit menu, you can use Undo or Step Backward to reverse the effects of the adjustments.

Combining Images

Sometimes you want to combine pieces from several different images. There are at least two ways to do this.

- **Copy and paste.** Use the magic wand, marquee, or lasso tool to select the area you want to copy from the first image. Choose Copy from the Edit menu. Go to the second image and choose Paste from the Edit menu. Now use the Move tool to place the pasted piece where you want it.

- **Cloning.** Another way to combine images is to clone part of one picture into another. Open both images in Photoshop, each in their own window. Choose the Clone Stamp tool. Option-click the Clone Stamp tool on part of the the first image that you want to clone. Then go to the second image, and place the Clone Stamp tool where you want the cloned part to appear. Click and drag to clone the first part onto the second picture.

Applying Special Effects

Filters and other special effects can change the nature of your image to set a tone or match a design. The best way to understand these effects is to try them on a picture of your own, and see what they do. These effects can apply to the entire image, or to just a portion that you have selected. You can see the effects—there are dozens of them -under the Filter menu.

Adding Elements

Suppose you need to add some arrows and labels to show various locations, or to circle certain areas on your image. Photoshop provides several tools for adding lines, arrows, and text. You might, for instance:

- Add a red arrow to point out a key element: use the line tool modified with an arrow-head.
- Add a green text label to an object in the picture: use the Text tool.
- Circle an area in red: use the paintbrush.

Modifying Tools

Many of the tools in Photoshop can be modified in terms of their size, opacity, and other features. The possible modifications appear in a palette across the top of the screen.

Layers

As you add each of these elements to a picture, Photoshop creates a new layer for each item you add. You can see all the layers at once, but each layer leads a separate existence and can be moved or edited without affecting the other layers. So when you create the red arrow, it does not replace the underlying parts of the map that it covers. Those underlying pixels are still there in the background layer. The arrow is in Layer 1, atop and not yet integrated into the map itself. The label is in Layer 2, and the circle in Layer 3. The layers remain separate until you merge them (called *flattening the image*), or save the file in a compressed format.

Apply these techniques as necessary until your image appears as you want it to.

Saving Images

The way you save an image depends on how you are going to publish it. If the image will appear on a web site or in a PowerPoint presentation, it should be saved at 72 pixels per inch in the JPEG or GIF format. If the image is to be printed, it should be saved in the Photoshop (.psd) format at 300 pixels per inch, or (possibly) at 600 pixels per inch if the original was from a high-resolution camera and the printer to be used supports the higher resolution.

To save an image for the Web or PowerPoint or any program that displays it on a computer screen, choose Save for Web from Photoshop's File menu. This will open a window in which you can see before and after views of the image that you are compressing and saving. If you look closely, you can see that that the compressed images are a bit fuzzier than the uncompressed. But they are also much smaller in size, and much faster to download. To save an image for printing, leave it in its high-resolution Photoshop (.psd) format.

It is often best to save more than one copy of your images, each with a different quality, and each with a different name. One might be shipforweb.jpg, while another might be shipforprint.psd. So you will find yourself often using the Save As . . . and Save for Web . . . items. Save your images in a folder where you can easily find them later.

Next Steps

Now that your images are edited so that they appear the way you want them, the next step is to publish these images. The next section shows you how to publish and employ these images in a variety of settings, from simple reports to Flash animations.

PUBLISHING DIGITAL IMAGES

By now your images have been captured, resized, edited, filtered, compressed, and saved. All that's left to do is to publish the pictures so that others can see them. There are many ways to publish your images: printed on paper, as a part of written reports, as a slide show, on a web page, in a Flash animation, or in a QuickTime movie.

Printed on Paper

Teachers often print images such as maps and diagrams on paper for students to use in the classroom. Students include photos in the reports they turn in on paper. Even though we say we are moving to an online, paperless society, the realities often require us to print our works on paper. Before printing your images, take a moment to get things ready.

First, make sure you have the right kind of paper in the printer. For photographic images, the stiff, glossy photo quality paper will produce much better results than plain printer paper. But for simple diagrams and drawings, plain paper will do. Check the orientation of the paper: for a picture wider than it is tall, use the landscape orientation; for taller pictures, use the portrait mode. These can be set by choosing Page Setup from the File menu. Then print one copy, and see how it looks. You may want to adjust brightness or contrast again once you've seen it in print. You will generally get the best printed results with high-resolution images of about 300 pixels per inch.

Embedded in a Written Report

The written report, built with a word processor such as Microsoft Word, is a staple of the educational enterprise. It's easy to embed your images into a Word document.

HOW TO . . . EMBED IMAGES IN A WORD DOCUMENT

You need: Microsoft Word, and some images suitable for embedding.

You get: A document containing words and pictures, suitable for printing, emailing, or electronic distribution.

1. Open a Word document.
2. Place the cursor where you want the image to appear.
3. From the menubar choose Insert, then Picture, then From File.
4. Find the image you saved earlier, and choose it.
5. Watch the image appear in the document.

The Word document with the embedded pictures can be sent through email, distributed on desk or CD-ROM, or printed on paper.

■ ■ ■ ■ ■ ■ ■ ■ ■ ■

In a PowerPoint Presentation

Teachers and students in many schools have learned how useful it can be to present their ideas through a slide show. Teachers illustrate their lectures with charts, diagrams, photos, and maps. Students present the findings of their research through a slide show that includes text as well as images. Follow these guidelines to import your images into a slide show.

HOW TO . . . IMPORT IMAGES INTO A POWERPOINT SLIDE SHOW

You need: Microsoft PowerPoint, and a collection of images saved on your computer.

You get: A slide show with images and text.

1. Open PowerPoint, and choose a plain slide style.
2. From the menubar choose Insert, then Picture, then From File.
3. Find the picture you want to insert, and choose it.
4. Watch the picture appear on the slide.
5. Drag it from its middle to move it around the slide.
6. Drag it from the corners to make it larger or smaller.
7. Set a background color for the slide by choosing Format, then Background from the menubar.

When complete, your slide show can contain a string of images, and can be viewed on the full screen. This PowerPoint file can also be distributed to others by email, disk, or CD-ROM. Learn more about creating a slide show in Chapter 14.

■ ■ ■ ■ ■ ■ ■ ■ ■ ■

On a Web Page

More and more teachers publish their lesson materials as web pages, even if they are used only in their own classroom. Many students are comfortable using web page software to design their own publications. These web pages can be distributed easily on disk, CD-ROM, over the local area network, or on the Internet. Web pages can include images as well as text.

To prepare a web page, you'll need a web page editing program such as Microsoft FrontPage or Macromedia Dreamweaver. Place the cursor on the page where you want the image to appear. Choose Insert, then Image from the menubar, choose your JPEG or GIF image, and watch it appear on the page. For the Web, your images must have a filename with no spaces, punctuation, or special characters, and must end with the proper filename extension such as .jpg or .gif. Web pages can, of course, be posted to a web server; they can also be distributed as attachments to email or on disk or CD-ROM. You can find more detailed information about creating web pages, and working with images, in Chapter 8.

In a Flash Animation

Animation is no longer the province of Disney and *South Park.* New computer tools make it easy for students and teachers to produce animations that illustrate important concepts for their students, from moving diagrams in science, to storyboards in literature. The images that you have collected and edited can easily be turned into animations.

Macromedia Flash is the best way to present animated sequences on the Web. You can also prepare animations with Macromedia Fireworks, or with programs such as GIF Animator and GIF Builder. Although the creation of Flash animations will be covered in Chapter 14, you can get started by opening Flash and choosing File, then Import to place your images directly onto the Flash stage. You can also copy and paste images into Flash. Macromedia Flash can easily move, dissolve, fade, and present images in an interesting sequence, accompanied by narration or music. Flash takes some time to learn, but you can find tutorials as well as a free software trial at the Macromedia web site (www.macromedia.com).

In a QuickTime Slide Show

PowerPoint isn't the only way to prepare a slide show. If all your images are about the same size, you can very quickly arrange them into a slide show that will play on any computer and can be sent over the Internet. This is especially effective for photographic images that tell a story.

HOW TO . . . CREATE A SLIDE SHOW OF IMAGES WITH QUICKTIME

You need: The QuickTime Player Pro software that you can download from the QuickTime web site (www.apple.com/quicktime), and a series of images of the same size.

You get: A compact slide show that can play on any computer and be sent easily over the Web or published on CD-ROM.

1. Place a copy of the images for the slide show into a single folder on your hard drive.
2. Rename the images in the order you want them to appear, such as picture1.jpg, picture2.jpg, picture3.jpg, and so forth.
3. Open QuickTime player.
4. From the File menu, choose Open Image Sequence.
5. Go to the folder with the numbered images.
6. Choose the first image in the series.
7. Set the Frame rate to 2 seconds per frame.

This will create a QuickTime movie that is a slide show of your images. This slide show can be shown from your computer, distributed on disk or CD-ROM, attached to an email, or embedded in a web page. These aren't the only ways to publish your digital images. Here are some more:

- If you have a Macintosh computer, you can use the iPhoto application to organize and publish your images into a book, slide show, or web site with a few clicks of the mouse.
- You can assemble your images into a digital video, using software such as Adobe Premiere, iMovie, or Final Cut Express, with dissolves between the pictures and musical or narrative accompaniment.
- Instead of PowerPoint, you can build a sequence of slides with HyperStudio or Keynote.
- You can attach your image files to an email and send them to others.
- You may copy all your images to a CD-ROM and distribute them as needed.

The possibilities are many as you find ways to improve teaching and learning through the power of images.

■ ■ ■ ■ ■ ■ ■ ■ ■ ■

FROM CAMERA TO COMPUTER: MACINTOSH

The digital camera has changed the face of photography, and made it much easier for students and teachers to employ images in their educational works. These last two sections of this chapter show you exactly how to get the images from a digital camera into your computer. For Apple Macintosh users, the software is iPhoto; Windows users should skip this section and go on to the next.

iPhoto allows you to organize and share digital photographs. It is one of the iLife suite of tools found on all new Macintosh computers. All you need to get started is a digital still camera, its USB cable, and iPhoto. Take a few pictures and you're ready to go.

Step One: Import

Connect your camera to your Macintosh with a USB cable, and iPhoto automatically launches itself. Click the Import button and iPhoto transfers the images into a master archive, the Photo Library. You can also import images from CDs, Kodak Photo CDs, or directly from your hard disk (drag them directly into iPhoto. You may also scan photos and import them into the application.

Note: It's a good idea to delete photos from the camera right after you've transferred them, for two reasons: first, to empty the camera's flashcard so you're ready to shoot more pictures; second, because iPhoto imports all the pictures from the camera every time, and when it detects duplicates, it gives you an error message. So click the button that says "Delete Originals." iPhoto does the rest.

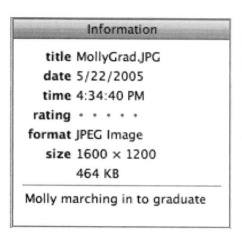

Information

title MollyGrad.JPG
date 5/22/2005
time 4:34:40 PM
rating · · · · ·
format JPEG Image
size 1600 × 1200
464 KB

Molly marching in to graduate

Step Two: Organize

It won't take long before your library has so many pictures that you'll want to begin to organize them. You organize by creating an album for each set of pictures.

Creating Albums

1. Create an album by clicking the + button at the bottom of the iPhoto window.
2. Name each new album by event, not by date—imagine what will happen when you have many albums, all by date and can't remember exactly when the event

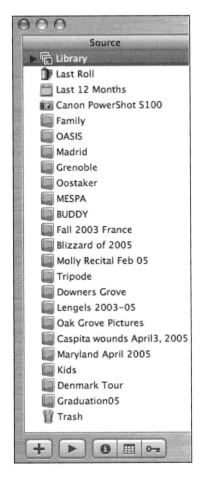

occurred. You'd have to open many albums to find the one you want.

3. To put pictures into an album, simply drag them from the Photo Library.

Note: the Photo Library has all the pictures you've imported. You can place each picture into more than one album. The original picture must remain in the Photo Library.

Naming Pictures. Just as you've named your albums, you'll want to name each of your pictures. Again, use a real name for the picture and you'll have an easier time finding it later.

To name a picture, simply click on it to select it, then type the name into the box labeled *Title*. Notice that the filename ends in .JPG. This is an important part of the file name if you are planning to export your pictures. Use a short title with no spaces or extra characters.

Go through all of your pictures after each Import and name them. This is a good housekeeping practice and will help you stay organized.

Later, you will be able to search by keyword by selecting Keywords from the Edit menu. Type the word in the box and click Search—all the pictures that include that word in the title will appear. You can also assign keywords to your albums and pictures by going to Keywords and clicking a category to assign.

Step Three: Edit

iPhoto provides many basic, easy-to-use tools that make your pictures look their best.

- To rotate your picture, click the rotate button.
- To zoom in or out to edit your picture more closely, drag the slider
- To crop the picture, click and drag to select the part of the picture you want. Then, click the Crop button.
- To brighten the picture, click the Enhance button.
- To remove red eye, select the eyes and click the Red Eye button.
- *Retouch* allows you to remove pixels (like a blemish on a face) and have the missing bit blend in with the surrounding area.
- *B&W* lets you change your color picture to black and white.
- Adjust the Brightness and Contrast with the sliders.

Step Four: Share

iPhoto lets you share your pictures in a variety of ways. From the Organize mode, click your choice.

Free Options

- *Print* lets you print your pictures in several sizes and formats.
- *Slideshow* creates a presentation that can run on its own, be accompanied by music, and run its slides at random if you wish. Note: iPhoto accesses your iTunes Library to select music.
- *Email* opens your email program and attaches the selected photos to a new message.
- *Desktop* automatically sets the selected picture as your desktop background.
- *Burn* lets you burn a CD of the selected albums or pictures.

Not-So-Free Options

- **Order Prints** is an option from Apple Computer that you can order online.
- **Book** is a hardcover book in a variety of formats that Apple Computer will sell you.
- **HomePage** and **.Mac** slides both require a .Mac account. They are extremely easy to use. A trial account and pricing information are available at www.mac.com.
- **HomePage** lets you publish your photos on the Web. You can set up a trial iDisk subscription for 30 days and publish your iPhotos. The yearly fee of $95 gives you 100 megabytes of storage on the Apple server.
- **.Mac Slides** allows you to publish slide shows on the Web with iDisk.

FROM CAMERA TO COMPUTER: WINDOWS

Import

Your Windows computer may need the driver installed for your camera, found on the CD that came with the camera. Once the driver is installed, you'll plug your camera into the USB port on the computer, switch the camera to play position, and turn the camera on. Windows recognizes that the camera is attached and treats it like any other external drive. You'll open the camera folder to find your images. These can then be dragged into your Pictures folder or directly onto a Word document or PowerPoint slide.

If you've installed Photo Story 3 from Microsoft, you'll have many of the same options found in iPhoto for Macintosh. It's a free download for XP users and can be found at www.microsoft.com/windowsxp.

Organize

Windows' users organize images in the My Pictures folder, where it's possible to create subfolders. Name the folders by event to make it easier to find the pictures later. It's also a good idea to rename your pictures as soon as you download them. They will come in from your camera with a name like IMG_3321.jpg—it's pretty hard to tell what that picture is. So, renaming the picture TobySits.jpg is a bit more descriptive. Be sure to retain the .jpg extension, which tells Windows that this is a photo.

Place and Edit

Once you've downloaded, labeled, and stored your images, they are ready to import into other documents such as Word, PowerPoint, and web pages. Microsoft Word allows you to do some simple editing of digital images after they are imported into a document. To resize the picture, select it, then click-drag from one of the corners to make it bigger or smaller.

To see other formatting tools, select the picture, and then choose Formatting Palette from the View menu. You'll be able to change the picture's brightness and contrast, fix red eye, crop it, and so on. These tools are somewhat limited, but that do allow you a bit of control over how the picture looks.

LEARN MORE . . .

About Using Images in the Classroom

http://ali.apple.com
> The Apple Learning Interchange where you can find classroom projects for all grade levels and topics.

www.kn.pacbell.com/wired/fil/pages/listdigitalphe.html
> A hotlist prepared by a classroom teacher to help you learn more about digital images in the classroom. It includes help in creating digital images, using them in your classroom, and downloadable tools to enhance your digital images.

www.bobsedulinks.com/digital.htm
> Digital still imaging and 101 uses for digital images in the classroom. This site includes a buying guide for digital cameras.

www.umuc.edu/library/copy.html
> The University of Maryland web site provides guidance for educators on the Fair Use clause, which governs how images downloaded from the Internet may be used in the classroom.

About from Camera to Computer: Macintosh

www.apple.com/iphoto
> This web site features tips and tricks, tutorials, iMovies—everything you need to get started with iPhoto.

About from Camera to Computer: Windows

www.kodak.com/global/en/service/publications/tib4211.jhtml
> This is the troubleshooting site from Kodak and will walk you through connection challenges on your Windows computer.

www.microsoft.com/windowsxp/using/digitalphotography/photostory/default.mspx
> This Microsoft site is where you can download Photo Story 3, the Windows' XP photo editing and presentation software.

CHAPTER TWELVE

VIDEO

IN THIS CHAPTER

- **Shooting Good Video**

- **Getting Started with iMovie (Macintosh)**

- **Getting Started with Movie Maker (Windows XP)**

- **Video on the Web**

- **Video Conferencing for Teaching and Learning**

- **How Compression Works**

- **Learn More . . .**

With the arrival of broadband connections in homes and schools, the growing availability of digital video (DV) camcorders, and the improvement of video editing software, we see more and more students and teachers using video as part of their computer and web projects. I've seen third-graders explain the metamorphosis of a caterpillar with a narrated video. I've seen high-schoolers shoot and edit complex dramatic history stories with dozens of scenes. I've visited schools where digital video production courses are a growing part of the formal curriculum. They're using iMovie, Windows Movie Maker, Pinnacle DV, and Final Cut video editing software, with the computer as the development platform, and output to videotape, DVD, CD-ROM, and the Web. Suddenly the generation that has grown up with six hours a day of television is enabled by new technologies to produce and distribute their own media. And many teachers are capitalizing on all this to use video production to strengthen learning. The invention of DV (digital video) that saves video information in computer form has made all of this possible.

The first part of this chapter shows you how to produce and edit your own video, right on your computer. This is followed by a section on publishing your video online. The last section looks at computer-based videoconferencing, a new and inexpensive way to teach and learn across distances.

SHOOTING GOOD VIDEO

While many of our students seem to be facile with the computer and the editing software, they often ignore the quality of the video they are editing. We've all seen examples of good content, excellent cutting and tilting and transitions, but with video that's tough to see, hard to hear, and not professional-looking. This section provides some practical advice on getting good video into your editing program. It won't teach you to be a videographer, but it should serve to improve those educational video projects.

In any multimedia project, it's a good idea to follow the Plan, Gather, Build sequence. Choose a topic, make a rough plan, shoot all the video clips, then build your movie. If you don't follow this sequence, you may find yourself having to stop and start many times, and the results will not be satisfactory. No matter what kind of DV camera you use, or which video editor you have on your computer, following these guidelines for lighting, composition, audio, and retakes will get you started in the right direction.

Phase 1: Plan

Plan the Shots.   Start with a storyboard that describes the clips you need for video and audio. You don't need long and involved clips for most educational projects. As you begin your movie-making career, it's best to make a short video rather than an hour-long documentary. A movie of 2 to 3 minutes is long enough to tell your story and to practice all the capabilities of the editing software. This means planning and shooting brief, well-defined clips.

Here's an example of the beginning of a storyboard:

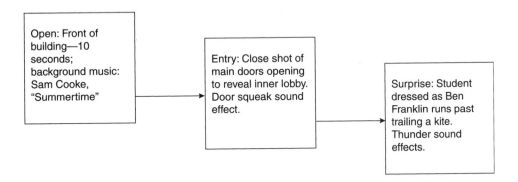

Include a box for each video clip. When you have all the clips planned, create a shot list, with approximate times for each shot. Also create a list of props needed for the scenes, and arrange for someone to be in charge of locating props and returning them to their owners. Share the storyboard with the people involved in the shot (either as actors or helpers), before the shooting session.

Plan the Lighting.   Plan for the subject to be well-lighted, preferably from behind the camera. If you are shooting outdoors in full daylight, you're not likely to need artificial lighting. In general, if your subject is brighter than the background, the lighting is probably OK. You might find it useful to reflect light upward onto faces, however, using a large piece of white cardboard held by a trusty assistant. Indoors, you may want to use an extra light that shines from the side onto your subject. Light from the side that creates interesting shadows on the subject will show off facial expressions, color, and textures better than light from directly above or straight on. Classroom flourescent lights in the ceiling can provide some light, but their color and location is not the best for video. Supplement these with an incandescent lamp at the side, and you'll get a better video.

Compose the Shots.   Plan to use a tripod, if possible, for all of your shooting. A tripod makes a bigger difference than you might think. Steady video is easier to watch, and compresses better for the Web. In a setup session before the actual shooting session, carefully frame your shot in the viewfinder from the tripod. Move in close for as tight a shot as you can get. Experts say it is better to move the camera close than to use the zoom feature. They call this "zooming with your feet." Don't be afraid to let the subject fill the viewfinder. If it's an interview, experiment with a shot that only shows the face. Plan to keep the clips short and active, avoiding rapid pans and zooms. Unless you are trying to create a mood of activity and confusion, keep the background simple.

Ensure Audio Quality.   If you will be recording an interview, plan to use an external microphone placed near the speaker's mouth. Pin the mike to the subject's shirt, or have an assistant hold the mike for you just off-camera. You can buy a standard, inexpensive microphone with a 1/8-inch phone plug connector at your local video or electronic store. Connect the microphone to the microphone jack of the camcorder. If it's impossible to use an external microphone, plan to shoot from less than 3 feet away and tell the subject to speak loudly toward the built-in microphone in the camcorder. You can assure the quality of your audio by monitoring it using standard headphones connected to the camcorder's headphone jack.

Prep the Camera.   Make sure you have a fresh DV cartridge, cued to a blank place on the tape. If you won't be using a wall plug for power, be sure the battery is charged. Mount the camera on a tripod and connect the microphone and headphones you will use for monitoring the sound quality. Set the camcorder to the Camera setting (rather than Play), and remove the lens cover.

Set Up the Scene.   Assemble the props identified in the storyboard step. Set up the scene and instruct the actors on what will be happening. Do a final lighting check.

Phase 2: Gathering

Now you are ready to create the video clips for your project.

Shoot the Video

1. Before you begin to record, focus and properly frame the subject or action in the center of the frame. Get as close as possible, to fill the frame. This eliminates unwanted or distracting background movement.
2. Press the record button to start recording, but wait five seconds before beginning the action.
3. Zooming in and out tires your audience. Experts suggest holding the camera on your subject at least 10 seconds before you change angles, zoom, or switch to another subject. The overall quality of your clip will be improved, and you can cut out extra footage later, if necessary.
4. Let the camera run for 5 seconds after the end of the shot. Press the record button to stop the recording.
5. Now it is time to check the quality of the shot. Switch the camera to the VTR setting, and rewind the tape.
6. Press the Play button and review what you shot. Also, listen to the audio.
7. If you are happy with the results, stop the tape at the end of the clip and set up your next scene. If the clip is not 100 percent what you want, shoot it again. It's OK to shoot the same scene several times and pick up the best clip later. In fact, you might try shooting from a different angle, with different lighting, or with a new form of composition, so you have some choices when it comes time to edit the video.

Follow these simple guidelines, and you'll be surprised at how good your video can be.

Phase 3: Build

Next, learn how to build the finished product. Macintosh users are addressed first. Windows users should skip to the next section of this chapter

GETTING STARTED WITH iMOVIE (MACINTOSH)

iMovie is a Macintosh-only application that allows you to edit and share digital video. It is one of the iLife suite of tools found on all new Macintosh computers. All you need to get started is a digital video camera, its FireWire cable, and iMovie. You begin by importing the video clips from the camera into your computer.

Import Your Clips

To import your clips into iMovie, do the following:

1. Open the iMovie application
2. Connect the DV Camera to your iMac using your FireWire cable.

3. Turn the Camera on to Playback/VCR mode.
4. Switch to DV mode in iMovie.

iMovie provides remote camera controls for capturing, recording, playing, rewinding, fast-forwarding and pausing. That is, iMovie and your computer will control the camera from here on out—you need not touch the controls on the camera. Once you click Import, iMovie's automatic scene detection creates individual clips of each scene you've shot. The clips are placed automatically onto the *shelf* of the iMovie work area.

iMovie Work Area

Monitor window. See the controls at the bottom of the monitor window? Use them to preview your movie or to control your digital camcorder directly.

Shelf area. Think of the shelf as a virtual warehouse. Use it to store video clips you may want to use in your movie. To use a clip, simply drag it to the Clip Viewer.

Effects palette. The items in the effects palette allow you to jazz up your movie with titles, transitions, music and sound effects.

Viewer. Click the Clip Viewer tab to edit and place your clips, and click the Audio Viewer tab to position your music and sound effects.

Mode buttons. Choose between Camera Mode (for transferring video from a camcorder) and Edit Mode (for building your movie). Use Full Screen Mode to show your movie full screen.

1. Use the controls to play the clip. Play each clip. While a clip is in the monitor window, you can shorten it by holding down the shift key and dragging the play head to select the part of the clip you don't want. Press the delete key on your keyboard.
2. Drag edited clips to the Clip Viewer (the timeline at the bottom of the screen).
3. Move the clips around on the viewer by dragging and dropping them.

Adding Titles

1. Click Titles on the editing effects bar.
2. Experiment with title types, clicking Preview to see how they look.
3. When you're ready, drag the title effect to the viewer by grabbing the little T and dragging to the spot in the viewer where you want the title to appear.

Adding and Editing Sound

You can import three types of sound files to play along with your iMovie:

- Music from your iTunes Library
- iMovie Sound effects
- Recorded voice clips that you record while you are using iMovie

To add audio, open the audio viewer by clicking the small clock:

- Click the Audio button in the Effects bar. A drop-down list of your iTunes Library opens automatically. You can drag a song directly into the audio viewer.
- At the end of the iTunes Library list, you'll find the iMovie Sound Effects. To add a sound effect, simply drag it to where you want it to play in your movie.
- To record your own narration for your iMovie, click the Record button to begin and end your narration. The audio will be placed at the playhead in the audio track.
- For all three types of audio, once they are in the audio track, you can drag the sound to where you want it to begin, make it louder or softer, or have it fade in and out.

Adding Transitions

Add transitions between some of your video clips to make one fade into the next, cross dissolve, and so on. Add your transitions last. iMovie comes with a set of transitions, and you can download more from the Apple web site at www.apple.com/imovie/transitions.html.

Here's how to place a transition between clips:

1. Click the Transitions button in the Effects palette.

2. Choose a transition, and then click Preview to see how it looks. When you've decided on a transition, drag it to the viewer and place it between two clips.
3. Notice that there's a little red line growing between the clips as iMovie renders the transition. Some transitions require two clips, while others can be placed before or after video clips. You can add several transitions and they will all render at the same time.

Preview Your iMovie

Preview your movie as you build it. Use the controls under the Monitor window to play your movie. From left to right, these rewind the movie to play from the beginning; play the movie in the monitor window; and play the movie full screen.

Share Your iMovie

As you create your iMovie project you should be saving the project every once in a while. Then, when the iMovie is complete, you'll export the finished project. You have two main choices:

- Exporting back to your DV camera
- Exporting your iMovie to a QuickTime file

Exporting to Your Camera

1. Connect your computer to your DV camera using FireWire.
2. Make sure your camera is in VTR mode and that the tape is rewound to a place where you're not erasing important video!
3. Under the File menu, choose Export Movie.
4. Click Export.
5. You can now plug your DV camera into a TV monitor and watch your movie, if you wish.

Exporting to QuickTime: Choices

To use your iMovie in multimedia projects and web pages, you'll want to export it in Quick-Time format. Here, you'll have several choices, each of which has a major impact on how large your movie appears on the screen and how much memory it takes.

- *Email* gives you the highest compression, the smallest movie that takes up the least amount of disk space. However, these movies are tiny on the screen.
- *Web* and *Web Streaming* movies are the next largest movies, suitable for inclusion in a web site.
- *CD-ROM* movie will give you a decent sized movie, good for inclusion in a slide show.
- *Full Quality DV* is the easiest to watch but takes up a huge amount of disk space.
- The *Expert* controls allow you to set image and audio compressions manually.

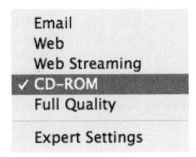

GETTING STARTED WITH MOVIE MAKER (WINDOWS XP)

Movie Maker is the video editing and publishing software for Windows XP. Most new Windows XP computers come with Movie Maker. If you don't have it already, it's a free download from Microsoft (www.microsoft.com). Your computer will need a FireWire connector, also called an IEEE 1394 connection. This section will help you get started creating a Movie Maker project, gathering its elements, and publishing it.

Plan

As in any multimedia project, it's a good idea to follow the Plan, Gather, Build sequence as described earlier. Choose a topic, make a rough plan, shoot all the video clips, gather any still images into your library, then build your movie. If you don't follow this sequence, you may find yourself having to stop and start many times, and the results will not be satisfactory. The following steps will help you take advantage of the unique features of Movie Maker.

Gather

Gather audio and still photographs. Audio in MP3 format and images import easily into Movie Maker. (Import from Collections in the Tasks menu). Still pictures can be dragged directly into the storyboard (a series of boxes all set up for you to drag and drop).

Build

Once you've created all the video clips you need for your project, open the Movie Maker application (located in the Programs folder) Then, follow the steps outlined in the Movie Tasks pane to construct your movie. If the Tasks pane is not open, click its button in the button bar (it's labeled *Tasks*).

Capture Video

Connect the digital video camera to a FireWire card (known as IEEE 1394). Turn the camera on to VCR/playback mode. In the Movie Maker Tasks pane, click *Capture from video device*. If everything is connected properly, the camera will show up as an option as an Available Device. Click the camera. You'll be asked to name the video, choose where it will be saved, and a video setting. Then, you'll have some choices:

> **Capture the entire tape.** The camera will rewind and Movie Maker will capture the entire video tape. You can click *Stop Capture* at any time to save just the beginning of the tape.
>
> **Create clips when wizard finishes.** Allows you to capture short clips.
>
> **Capture clips manually.** In this mode, you'll be able to start and stop your capture as the tape plays. Using either the controls on your camera or the DV camera controls in the wizard. Click *Start Capture* to begin capturing, then click *Stop Capture* to end your clip.
>
> **Finish.** Click *Finish* when you have completed capturing and return to the Tasks pane to begin editing and enhancing your movie.

Trim Clips

In the timeline view, select the clip you want to edit. It will appear in the preview window. Here, you can drag the scroll bar across and choose exactly where you want the clip to begin. Choose *Set Start Trim Point* from the Clip menu. If you want to trim the end of your video clip, drag the scroll bar to the point where you want the clip to end. This time, choose *Set End Trim Point* from the Clip menu.

Adding Titles

In the Tasks pane, under the Edit section, choose *Make titles or credits*. You'll need to decide where to add the title by clicking your choice (at the beginning of the movie, before a selected clip, on the selected clip, and so on). Type your title and click *Change the title animation* to choose how you want the title animated. Click *Change the text font and color* to adjust these items. When you are happy with your title, click *Done, add title to movie.*

Sound

In the Capture Video section of the Tasks pane, choose *Import audio or music.* Automatically, your music folder will open. Select the music you want, and click *Import.* Note that your music will be copied into a Collections folder, ready for you to drag it to the timeline. Once in the timeline, you can drag the music to where you want it to begin playing.

Transitions

In the Edit section of the Tasks pane, choose *View video transitions.* Make sure you are in storyboard view. Then drag a transition between two video clips in the storyboard.

Video Effects

In the Edit Movie section of the Tasks pane, choose *View video effects.* Make sure you are in storyboard view. The effects are applied directly to the film clips when you drag them to the starred square on the clip.

View Your Movie

Click the *Rewind Timeline* button, then click the forward arrow to play your movie.

Finish Your Movie

Under the File menu, choose Save Movie File. The Save Movie wizard will walk you through the steps of saving your movie, beginning with deciding where you want to save your movie to:

My Computer. Saves the movie for playback on your computer. It will be in WMV (Windows Media Video) format.

Recordable CD. This format works only if you have a recordable CD drive.

E-Mail. This works for very short movies. You will get a warning if the file size exceeds 1 MB. If your Internet Service Provider allows you to send larger files, you can go ahead and save it for email, then attach it as you would any other file.

Send to the Web. The wizard will ask you what kind of connection you have and adjust the compression of the movie accordingly (see the last section of this chapter for an explanation of compression).

Send to DV Camera. If your digital video camera is attached properly (with an IEE 1394 cable) and turned on, you'll be able to record the completed movie back onto a video tape.

VIDEO ON THE WEB

Many teachers have asked how they can post videos on the Web. Many of their students have produced short videos that show the results of an experiment or the dramatization of a story or a performance of music, that they would like to share with others on the Web. In fact, we have seen a boom in the production of video by students and teachers, due in large measure to three factors:

- The easy availability of digital video (DV) cameras. These now cost less than $300 for a small, sturdy, and easy to use brand-name camera.
- The development of video editing software. Most new computers arrive with video editing software built-in, such as Apple's iMovie or Windows Move Maker, and with a FireWire connector for the DV camera.
- The growth of broadband connections in homes, schools, and offices, that enable more and more people to send and receive video files over the Internet.

But even with the latest DV compression and broadband connection, it is not easy to get these video projects to work well online. The video files themselves are huge. For instance, we recently produced a one-minute clip of a professor to be used in an online course. The folder of video footage on the computer amounts to 203 megabytes, too much for even the fastest connections to handle.

Compressing and Saving

Before it is usable on the Web, the video needs to be compressed and saved in a format that will work well online. Here is how to do this:

- In iMovie, choose File, then Share from the menubar. Click the QuickTime icon, then choose Web from the popup menu. For more details, consult iMovie Support at http://docs.info.apple.com/article.html?artnum=150073.
- In Windows Movie Maker, click *Save to my computer* in the Task pane. Choose a place to save the video, then from the list of settings choose Video for Web. For more details, consult Windows Movie Maker 2: How-To for Beginners at www.microsoft .com/windowsxp/moviemaker/getstarted/default.asp.

If you are using another video editing program, the saving commands will be similar. Save your movie with a filename that will work on the Web. That means no spaces, no punctuation, and no special characters. The resulting movie will be small and a bit grainy, but it will travel well on the Web.

Publishing

You may post the compressed video directly to the Web, by simply copying it to your web server. The URL of the movie will be the URL of your web site, plus the filename of the movie, such as www.lengel.net/mymovie.mov. When viewers connect to this URL, your movie will download and begin to play in their browser.

But this movie will play in a window all by itself, with no explanation, no text around it, no title. If you'd like all of these things to appear around the movie, then you can *embed* the movie into a web page, and copy that page to your web server. You can find detailed instructions on how to use Dreamweaver to accomplish this in Chapter 8. Be sure to copy to your web server both the HTML page created by Dreamweaver as well as the movie file.

In most cases, the video will need to download itself completely to your viewer's computer before it begins playing. But if you have Macromedia Flash on your computer, you can use it to create a video that begins playing right away. Here's how:

HOW TO . . . PUBLISH A STREAMING VIDEO WITH FLASH

You need: A digital video file, edited and prepared as described above; and a copy of Macromedia Flash.

You get: A highly compressed video that streams to the user and begins playing immediately.

1. Create and save your movie as described in the sections for Macintosh and Windows users.
2. Launch Flash, and use Modify, then Document, then Dimensions to set the size of the Flash stage to what you want. If all you want to display is the movie, then make the Flash stage the same size as your movie, such as 240 pixels wide and 180 pixels high. If you want to display a title and explanation along with the movie, set the dimensions of the Flash stage large enough to accommodate this additional information.
3. In Flash, choose File, then Import, then navigate to the video that you saved.
4. In the Import Options dialog box, choose Embed movie.
5. In the Import Video Settings dialog box, set the Quality to 90%, the Keyframe interval to 24, and the Scale to 100%. Also check the Synchronize video and Import audio boxes, and make sure the frame correspondence is set to 1:1.
6. Click OK to import the movie. This will take some time.
7. When the file has imported, check Yes to expand your Flash movie with enough frames to accommodate the video.
8. You may drag the video wherever you wish on the stage. And you may use the Flash tools to create titles and other information on the stage as well.
9. Save your Flash file with a filename that will work on the Web.
10. When you are done, choose Control, then Test movie from the menubar. It will take some time for Flash to recompress your video, but when it's done you will see it play.
11. Find the .swf file that Flash created when you tested the movie. It is this file that you will copy to your web server. The contents of the video are embedded into this .swf file. (SWF stands for Shock Wave Flash.)
12. Copy the .swf file to your Web server.

The URL of the movie will be the URL of your web site, plus the filename of the Flash file, such as *www.lengel.net/mymovie.swf.* When viewers connect to this URL, your movie will begin playing almost immediately in their browser. They'll need the Flash Player, which most people already have. If they don't have it, they can download it for free (www. macromedia.com).

■ ■ ■ ■ ■ ■ ■ ■ ■ ■

VIDEO CONFERENCING FOR TEACHING AND LEARNING

The arrival of broadband access in more and more schools and homes, and the invention of new technologies for compressing and streaming video over the Internet, have combined to make it easier than ever to use video for teaching and learning. The last section of this chapter looks at video conferencing in particular—the use of live video to enhance learning. We'll look at its history, its technologies, and its applications to the work of a teacher. But first, a glimpse into some classrooms:

Picture this.

The third seal from the left (the students had named him Oscar) was about to move across the rock and challenge the authority of the old bull. The students in this Iowa classroom were observing first-hand, in real time, the activities of aquatic mammals off the coast of California, thanks to a live video feed from a science observation post over the Internet and into their classroom.

Rosa's treatments put her in the hospital for a long stay this time—two months. But she kept in close contact with her teacher and fellow students through instant messenger. From her hospital bed, she could type her responses to the teacher's questions; she could hear the discussion in the classroom and speak up when it was her turn; she could also, if she chose, see the class and let them see her, all by using a simple laptop computer with a tiny camera.

He was the world's expert on King Lear, *but he was in England and the class of eleventh graders was in Florida. As soon as school opened, they fired up the classroom computer and navigated to the site where the lecture would appear. There he was, live and in real time. The video cut back and forth from the lecturer to the players who were acting out the scenes he analyzed. The students typed in questions now and then, and heard the lecturer respond to them.*

The debate was in full swing. The students in Saskatchewan took the affirmative. Though they were animated and seemed eloquent and convincing, nonetheless the students in Arizona found their logic to be suspect and took notes during the presentation. In their rebuttal, the Arizonans one by one came forward to the camera, refuted the Canadians' arguments, and watched them furiously taking notes. This debate was held live between the schools, using Internet video.

Not Your Father's Videoconferencing

These are not futuristic scenarios—these activities are happening right now in schools around the world. They all use some form of videoconferencing to enhance teaching and learning, and do it simply and cheaply using classroom computers and the Internet. Videoconferencing has been available since the 1960s, but has always been too expensive and too unwieldy to be used in classrooms. In the beginning, you needed two television studios, two transmitters, and two receivers to conduct a videoconference like the ones described above—impossible to fit in a classroom, and hundreds of thousands of dollars to set up. One-way transmissions were possible, using satellite networks through which many classrooms could view a single event, but these were neither interactive nor everyday events, and cost thousands to produce.

In the 1980s came interactive point-to-point videoconferencing using a special camera plus TV combination at each site, connected over specially configured telephone lines. This brought the equipment costs down to under $100,000 and the transmission costs to under $500 per hour, and allowed direct interaction between the parties. But videoconferencing was still far beyond the capabilities of everyday teachers.

Then in the 1990s came the Internet into schools and homes. We quickly figured out how to send text to anyone at any time over the Web, and later pictures and MP3 music. For the first time, we had a multimedia network that could connect us directly with any other classroom or computer, at very low cost. But video and voice were beyond its capabilities.

The millennium brought video software into the mainstream of computing: all of the new computers came equipped to show video and sound as well as text and pictures. The new century also brought broadband to more and more homes and schools, and spurred the invention of new compression and streaming technologies that let that digital video travel through the Internet in real time. There has been an explosion of video conferencing over the Web, based on these new capabilities.

How It Works

If you and I want to videoconference, we each attach a video camera to our computers, make a connection between us over the Internet, and begin to watch and listen. It's that simple from a user's perspective. (While I was on sabbatical in France, my daughters remained behind in Boston. We videoconferenced every other day, with one click at either end.)

When you and I connect, the video signal from the camera and its audio (any digital video camera can be used), are compressed by my computer, and then immediately, frame by frame, sent over the Internet directly to your computer, which decompresses them and displays them in a window on your screen. With a solid broadband connection, the video is clear and the transmission delay is imperceptible.

Some video transmissions, like the seals on the rocks, are accessed through a web site—go to the site, click a button, and watch the video. Try www.racerocks.com. Conferences between individuals are most often arranged through a directory service such as AOL Instant Messenger (AIM) or Microsoft NetMeeting: find your correspondent in the buddy list, click on them, and begin conferencing. It's that simple.

Compressing Video

The secret to making all this work is video compression. Your computer needs to very quickly take a video signal from the camera that contains many megabytes of high-quality information each second, and compress it so it will fit through the bandwidth you actually have available (a cable modem will provide about 500 kb, or half a megabit, per second). It does this by making the video window smaller, removing some of the information, and reducing the rest to a bare minimum. The more it compresses, the lower the quality of the video. Between France and Boston, with a cable modem at both ends, we get quarter-screen video with enough quality to see facial expressions and enjoy natural voices.

The development of video compression software has advanced significantly since the turn of the century, with many companies competing to fit better quality into less bandwidth. At the same time, the processing power and speed of even the low-end computers enables them to accomplish this compression (and decompression at the receiving end) in real time. And most computers now include a FireWire connector that can take digital video directly from the camera. So what was once a technical experiment with lots of special equipment and a flock of engineers is now a point-and-click operation.

What You Can Do

To experience the reality of live video, connect to a site such as Race Rocks and watch the live video. You won't be able to talk back to the seals, but you will see the possibilities. For a list of similar virtual video field trips, see the information at http://ali.apple.com/ali_sites/ali/vft.html.

To get started with interactive, point-to-point videoconferencing, follow these steps:

1. Make sure that your next computer has a FireWire connector and videoconferencing software. Computers so equipped are available for less than $1,000 today. The software is free for downloading from the vendors, whose sites are listed at the end of this article.
2. Connect a digital video camera to your computer. A home camcorder works fine. So do the little $100 clip-on cameras such as the Pyro Webcam or the Apple iSight.
3. Fire up the software. The most popular are Apple's iChat AV and Microsoft's Net-Meeting. (The Apple iChat is much easier to set up and configure.)
4. Connect to a correspondent. With iChat, you can use your AIM screen name (free from AOL) and get your correspondent to do the same. Use the AIM buddy list to connect to each other. With NetMeeting, you'll need to know the IP address of your correspondent, and vice versa.
5. Watch and talk. With a good broadband connection, you should be able to achieve a 3-inch video window and good quality sound.

Once you've got it working, think of ways to apply this new capability to teaching and learning in your classroom. Find live Internet video events in your subject area. Conduct joint investigations between your students and students in other schools around the world. Bring homebound students, or experts from afar, as guests into your classroom. Produce a news program and broadcast it to the kindergarten classroom. The possibilities are endless.

HOW COMPRESSION WORKS

They're all compressed—the pictures, the songs, the videos. Just about all the media that you see on the Web and on your computer have been trimmed down from their original full-blown bulk so they will travel better. Every time you see a .jpg or .gif or listen to an .mp3 or watch a .mov, you are witnessing a file that has been shrunk before it was sent, and then reconstituted upon viewing. To use the proper terms, the data has been compressed at the source, and later decompressed at the viewer. Without compression, images, sound, and video would be impossible on the Web as we know it.

How does this compression work? Why do we need it? This section provides a primer on the process of data compression as it affects the work of teachers and students.

Why Compress?

Pictures, sounds, and video contain lots of information. On a computer, they are *digitized.* A picture, for instance, is broken up into thousands of tiny squares less than 1/70th of an inch across. The color and brightness of each square—called a *pixel,* or picture element— is recorded as a number, one number for each pixel. A passport-size picture, for instance, consists of about 40,000 pixels, and so in its natural state would require 40,000 numbers in its file. So to display this uncompressed image on your computer, you would have to wait for all 40,000 numbers to flow from the server, over the Internet, into your computer's memory, and onto the screen. That would take some time—perhaps 15 seconds on a 56k modem. And that's just for a little picture. (For more information on how photos are digitized and compressed, see Chapter 11.)

A digital video consists of 15 pictures like this displayed in rapid succession each second, so a 1-minute uncompressed video the size of my photo would consume 15 (pictures) × 40,000 (numbers per picture) × 60 (seconds). This amounts to 36,000,000 numbers. The file containing all these numbers would be very large and take a long time—hours—to get to you.

To solve this problem, mathematicians and engineers combined forces to reduce the amount of data necessary to convey the information in the media. They invented ways to find patterns and repetitions in the long string of numbers, and they discovered that they could leave out certain numbers that made little difference in what people saw or heard. These methods of reducing the necessary numbers are called *algorithms.* An example is the JPEG algorithm, invented by a group of engineers and photographers (the Joint Photographer Expert Group is what they called themselves). The JPEG algorithm is used to compress the data in photographic image files. It's used for the photos on most web sites.

The Compression Flow

Data compression is best thought of as a process that begins with the author of a web page or other computer presentation, and ends with the viewer. Here are the steps in the process:

1. The author digitizes the original media item, and saves it as a file on her computer.
2. The author compresses the original media file, using software designed for this purpose.

3. The author links to or embeds the compressed copy of the item in the web page.
4. The user downloads the web page over the Internet, and with it comes the compressed media file.
5. The user's browser decompresses the media file and displays it on the computer's monitor or through its speakers.
6. The user sees or hears the decompressed media item.

In most cases, what the viewer sees or hears is not exactly the same as the original item. The process of digitization, compression and decompression slightly degrades the image, sound, or video. The more a file is compressed, the smaller it gets, the faster it travels over the Web, but the lower its quality. There is a tradeoff between compression and quality.

Instant Coffee

The process of compression and decompression of media files is like instant coffee. To make instant coffee crystals, the coffee company brews several gallons of real coffee, then freeze-dries it to remove all the water. The result is dry brown powdery crystals, shipped to the user in a small jar. The coffee company has in effect compressed the coffee, so it can travel much smaller and much lighter. The drinker decompresses the coffee by adding hot water and mixing. The drinker replaces exactly what the manufacturer removed, the water. If all works well, the instant coffee tastes something like the original brew. And one little jar can recreate gallons of coffee. There is some loss of aroma and flavor in this process, but for many people, the reduction in quality is worth the convenience.

Media compression is not accomplished by removing water from a file. But in a similar way to coffee, in most cases it involves taking things out of the file that are later replaced at the user's end. Many different techniques can be used to compress a file, and new methods are invented regularly.

Codecs

The mathematical algorithms that are applied to the numbers in the media files in order to compress them are called codecs, which is short for compressor-decompressor. Codecs are software routines that use the math to compress the file. In most cases, these routines are included the programs that the author and receiver use to make and view the file. The author applies the compression part of the codec as she saves the file from her media-editing program; the viewer's computer applies the decompression part of the codec (automatically) as he views the media.

Viewing Compressed Media

When you view a compressed image, sound, or video in your browser, it will decompress and display the file for you without your being aware of it. The codecs for JPEG and GIF compression are built into the browser, but audio and video codecs are not included in the browser. Instead, they are provided in a plug-in or player, such as QuickTime. You need the plug-in in order to view certain compressed media files. The plug-in contains the codec necessary to recreate the original media from the compressed file. So in most cases, if you have an up-to-date browser and have installed the standard media plug-ins (QuickTime, Flash, Windows Media Player, and RealPlayer), you will not have to worry about the details of decompression.

Creating Compressed Media

If you or your students create media for their web pages, you'll need to be a bit more aware of the compression you need—it's not automatic. If you are editing images in Photoshop, for instance, you will most likely use the Save for Web command when you are ready to store the file. This command causes Photoshop to apply one of the image codecs, such as JPEG or GIF, to the data in the file. Photoshop lets you adjust how much compression to apply to the image. If you apply too much, you get a smaller and faster file, but it will seem dull and grainy. If you apply too little, the file will look better, but will take a longer time to reach the viewer through the Web. Photoshop contains the tools for the author to apply the appropriate amount of compression to an image file.

The same holds true for sound and video. The standard editing programs for these media allow you to choose the amount of compression, and even the specific codec, that will work best for your project. To compress all their files, many professional developers use a single program, such as Media Cleaner, which provides minute control over every aspect of the process. But most teachers and students will find that the compression controls that are integrated into Photoshop, iMovie, and QuickTime Pro are sufficient for their needs.

As you create media files for your projects, don't be afraid to try various compression levels and codecs, and see how they work. Sometimes the only way to arrive at a satisfactory result is through trial and error.

Made from Concentrate

Not every compressed media file that you see or hear on the Web carries a warning label, but you can be sure that most of them are indeed reconstituted. To learn more about the details of how compression works, you might look at *The Web Wizard's Guide to Multimedia,* by James G. Lengel, published by Addison Wesley.

LEARN MORE . . .

About Shooting Good Video

http://desktopvideo.about.com/od/editing/ht/goodvideo_ro.htm
This site provides some more basic rules that will help you create better video in the first place, making the editing process easier.

About Using Digital Video in the Classroom

http://scnc.misd.k12.mi.us/technology/dig-video.html
Technology 4 the Classroom provides a rich collection of lesson ideas using video in the classroom from around the country.

About iMovie

www.apple.com/imovie
At the Apple Computer web site you can explore tutorials for every function of iMovie.

www.apple.com/imovie/freestuff
This web site features free resources from Apple including sounds, images, and so on.

www.apple.com/imovie/edit.html
Here Apple also provides free Visual Effects, like mirroring and trails.

www.apple.com/imovie/compatibility.html
Look at this site for considerations when choosing a compatible digital video camera.

www.apple.com/imovie/enhance.html
Use this website to enhance your iMovie with cool titles, transitions, and special effects.

www.apple.com/imovie/share.html
Tips on sharing your iMovie with audiences can be found here.

About Third-Party Resources for Digital Video

www.disistotech.com
Look at Disisto Tech's web site for information on handheld recording microscopes. These small devices serve as a video camera, allowing you to import video directly from a small microscope to iMovie.

www.ezedia.ca
This site features cool effects including backgrounds, frames, etc.

About Movie Maker

www.microsoft.com/windowsxp/downloads/updates/moviemaker2.mspx
You can download MovieMaker from this site. It's free.

www.microsoft.com/windowsxp/using/moviemaker/default.mspx
This section of the Microsoft site offers lots of resources for those beginning to use MovieMaker. Included are tutorials, sample projects, and articles on every phase of creating, editing, and sharing movies.

About Videoconferencing

www.ali.apple.com
Apple presents the Apple Learning Interchange, which provides ideas for Internet video in the classroom.

www.sasinschool.com/resource/pages/ethread_videoconf.shtml
Here SAS inSchool provides lesson plans and ideas for using videoconferencing in the classroom.

www.apple.com/ichat
Here you can learn more about Apple iChat AV. This product comes with Mac OS X. You need a digital video camera to send the video—the iSight camera works seamlessly as does any digital video camera equipped with firewire.

www.microsoft.com/windows/netmeeting

Look here for information on Microsoft NetMeeting, a videoconferencing product.

www.meetings.sunet.se/clients/marratech.html

This web site features information on Marratech, a web-based software that allows many people to meet in the same virtual space with audio, video, chat, and shared whiteboard space.

About Compression

www.aw-bc.com/catalog/academic/product/0,1144,0201745615-VP,00.html

This links to the *Web Wizard's Guide to Multimedia* by James G. Lengel. In it, you'll find much more detail about how compression works.

www.aw-bc.com/catalog/academic/product/0,1144,0201745615-VP,00.html

Here you can access the How Stuff Works web site article on how compression works.

■ ■ ■ ■ ■

CHAPTER THIRTEEN

MEDIA IN THE CLASSROOM

IN THIS CHAPTER

- **Getting Started with Graphic Organizers**
- **Evaluating Multimedia Assignments**
- **Learn More . . .**

In Chapter 1, we introduced the current crop of students as the *wired* or *connected* generation. They might also be characterized as the *multimedia* generation, having grown up in a world full of images, sounds, motion, and media. From the dozen films available at the local Cineplex, to the hundred channels on the cable, to the thousands of songs on the iPod, to the full-color illustrations in their textbooks and the scientific animations on the Internet, the media are with them and in them. They are both consumers of the new media, and creators of multimedia projects.

As these media become more and more a part of classroom work, we need to consider how they are best applied in our own setting. You've read in Chapters 9 through 12 about using computer text, numbers, images, and video in teaching and learning; this chapter helps to conclude that discussion with a look at the simple but effective medium of the graphic organizer, which has dozens of applications in a variety of subjects and levels. This is followed by some guidelines for evaluating the quality of multimedia projects that can help you judge the worth of the digital works produced by students.

GETTING STARTED WITH GRAPHIC ORGANIZERS

The term *graphic organizer* is used to describe a number of different software applications that allow students and teachers to develop ideas and present them in a pictorial or symbolic format. This section introduces two common graphic organizers, *Inspiration* and *TimeLiner.* Inspiration is a common tool for developing writing and project assignments. TimeLiner is, as you may suspect, used to develop and understand a variety of timelines.

Inspiration

The most common organizer is Inspiration, used in classrooms across the country. Teachers use Inspiration for their own planning, as a brainstorming tool with students, and as a way to help students organize themselves, express their ideas in a nonlinear format, and deepen their understanding of classroom topics. The junior version of Inspiration is Kidspiration, found in many primary classrooms. Learn more about Kidspiration on its website (www.kidspiration.com).

Picture this:

> *Mr. Dewey's third-graders watched the big screen as the teacher asked again, "What's the most devastating weather event in the world?" "Hurricanes," said Annie. "No, floods." "Floods are not weather." "Drought." For each response, Mr. Dewey created another topic on the screen. After a dozen kinds of bad weather were posted, the class brainstormed a list of questions they could ask about each one: What does it look like? What causes it? Where does it happen? When does it happen? What kind of damage does it do?*

Mr. Dewey is using Inspiration software to build and display a web of brainstormed ideas, with links between them and an ability to change from graphic symbols to a text outline. Here's an example:

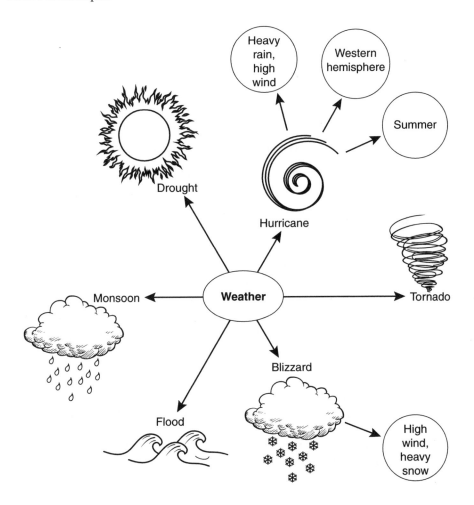

Weather
   Drought
   Hurricane
      Western hemisphere
      Summer
      Heavy rain, high wind

Flood

Blizzard
   High wind, heavy snow

Tornado

Monsoon

Inspiration is a tool with multiple purposes, usable at all grade levels. Here's how to get started using Inspiration.

HOW TO . . . BUILD A CONCEPT WEB WITH INSPIRATION

You need: Inspiration installed on your computer; a topic from the curriculum.

You get: An exciting classroom process and a versatile learning product.

1. **Open the program** by double-clicking on the icon.
2. **Watch a new web appear** with Main Idea highlighted. Type the title of your project here.
3. **Add subtopics** to your idea symbols by clicking the bubble, and then click the Create button in the direction you want your new idea to appear. A new bubble will appear off your topic.
4. **Brainstorm your ideas.** To quickly add subtopics to an idea, select the idea, then click the Rapid Fire icon. A lightning bolt will appear after your text. Type in your first subtopic and press return. The subtopic appears as a new bubble. Continue to type subtopics and press return until you have thought of as many subtopics as you can.
5. **Add notes to your topics.** Click the topic. Handles will appear around the topic. Double-click the handle in the upper left corner. A note pad will appear. Type your notes here. Continue to add notes to each of your topics.
6. **See your web as an outline.** Click the outline icon at the far left of the menu bar. Your web will appear as an outline. You can go back to web view by clicking its icon. Or, you can copy the outline and paste it into a word processing document and begin writing your paper.
7. **Moving your ideas** around the screen is easy. Click the bubble and drag it where you want it to go.

8. **Rearrange your ideas.** Click the Arrange button to see your options.

9. **Spell check.** Click Spell Check and decide for each unrecognized word whether to substitute the suggestion, ignore it, or retype the word.

10. **Change how your diagram symbols look.** Inspiration has an extensive library of clip art that can be used to illustrate your symbols. To see the libraries, click the arrows at the top of the symbol palette; slide down to the category, then across to the library. To change a symbol, select it (click it), then choose a new symbol from the symbol palette.

11. **Add Hyperlinks.** Type the web site URL and it immediately becomes a link to the Internet.

The Inspiration application includes many lesson ideas and templates for teachers K–12 in all subject areas. These include author studies for language arts, science lessons with cause and effect webs, social studies webs, and so on. Teachers wishing to try Inspiration for 30 days can download it free from the Internet (www.inspiration.com).

■ ■ ■ ■ ■ ■ ■ ■ ■ ■

TimeLiner

You can create many types of timelines for a variety of purposes using TimeLiner. In this section, you'll learn the fundamentals of creating your own timeline.

Types of Timelines.   Timeliner lets you create six different types of timelines:

- **Standard.** Standard timelines are typical chronological timelines that list events by date.
- **Yearly/Monthly.** Yearly/monthly timelines keep track of events that occur in the span of a single year or month, such as students' birthdays.
- **Weekly.** Weekly timelines mark weekly events, such as band practice.
- **Daily.** Daily timelines track events that occur at the same time every day, such as when school starts.
- **Geologic.** Geologic timelines illustrate events that occur over millions of years.
- **Custom.** Custom timelines display non-time-based data (such as temperature, distances, or percentages) in timeline form.

Viewing Timeline Data.   TimeLiner offers five different ways to view your timeline data:

- **Data.** Data view contains your unformatted timeline information. It allows you to edit dates and events directly.
- **Banner.** Banner view displays events on a horizontal timeline. This visually conveys the passage of time.
- **Compact.** Compact view condenses event data in your timeline into a graph format that can usually fit on a single page. This is helpful for handouts.
- **List.** List view events are listed vertically. Use this view for easy editing.
- **Slideshow.** Slideshow view displays each event as a slide in a multimedia presentation. Each slide includes the sound, video, and pictures you've attached to its event.

HOW TO . . . CREATE A STANDARD TIMELINE OF YOUR LIFE

You need: TimeLiner software installed on your computer; information about the events of your life.

You get: A sample timeline.

1. Open the TimeLiner application.
2. Click the New button on the opening screen.
3. Make sure Standard is selected, and then click OK. A new timeline opens in Data View.
4. Click New Event on the clock toolbar to create an event for your timeline.
5. Type your birth date, including the year, in the When box.
6. Type "I was born" in the What box, then click OK. Your entry appears in Data View.
7. Click New Event on the clock toolbar to create another event.
8. Type the year when you began elementary school in the When box.
9. Click the To box and type the year you graduated from elementary school.
10. Type "Attended elementary school" in the What box. Click OK. You've just created an event with a starting and ending date.
11. Repeat these steps to add two more events from your life.
12. Click the Show Banner View icon to see the events displayed as a horizontal timeline. Click the Show Compact and Show List View icons to see how your timeline data appears in these views.

Add a Title to a Timeline

In Banner, Compact, or List View, click Label on the clock toolbar. Tip: You can add a title in all views except Data and Slideshow. However, the title you add will be visible only in the view in which you add it.

1. Type "My Life," then click OK.
2. Select Choose Label Font from the Edit menu.
3. Choose a font, size, color, and style for the title, and then click OK.
4. Drag the title where you want it to appear

Edit an Event

1. In any view, click an event.
2. Click Edit on the clock toolbar.
3. Modify the event description (What) or date (When) and click OK.
4. Tip: You can also add pictures, movies, sounds, and Web links in the Edit Event dialog box using the tabs at the bottom of the dialog box.

Delete an Event

1. Select the event and click Delete on the clock toolbar.
2. Choose OK in the dialog box that appears.

Add a Graphic to a Timeline

1. In Banner, Compact, or List View, click Graphic on the clock toolbar.
   Tip: You can add a graphic in all views except Data and Slideshow. However, the graphic will be visible only in the view in which you add it.
2. Choose a category from the scrolling list and then select a graphic. Click OK. (To use your own graphic, click Browse in the New Graphic dialog box and locate and select the graphic on your hard disk. Click Open.)
3. Drag the graphic where you want it to appear on the timeline.

Print a Timeline

1. In Banner, Compact, or List View, click the Print button on the clock toolbar. The Print Preview dialog box appears, giving a thumbnail sketch of how the timeline will look when printed. (In Data and Slideshow views, there is no Print Preview box.)
2. Tip: Change the page orientation by clicking Page Setup in the Print Preview dialog box and then select either landscape or portrait. You can also change the scale. This will reduce or enlarge the timeline to fit better on the page.
3. Click Print.

TimeLiner is appropriate for all students K–12. More information and demonstrations can be found at www.tomsnyder.com.

■ ■ ■ ■ ■ ■ ■ ■ ■ ■

EVALUATING MULTIMEDIA ASSIGNMENTS

A Tale of Two Teachers

Molly's sixth-grade teacher assigned the class a research project: Greek and Roman Art. This was in the early days of computing in schools, and Molly was among the few whose home computer contained all the latest multimedia programs. She quickly found on the British Museum CD-ROM enough pictures of classical sculpture to fill several slide shows, along with explanatory text. She was good at copying and pasting. It didn't take her long to produce a slide show with dramatic views of statues and facades, which she delivered to the class on a big projection screen in the computer lab. Nobody, including her teacher, had seen anything like this multimedia report. By a 12-year-old, no less. Her peers, who worked much harder (and probably learned much more) were relegated to standing in front of the class and reading from their note cards. Molly got an A, no questions asked.

The assignment: Choose a battle from the American Revolution, research it, and present it. Next week, turn in a complete outline of your research plan in the form of a graphic organizer. Week two, bring in at least five original sources. Week three, make your presentation to the class. Week four, respond in writing to fellow students' questions on your battle. *Molly, as usual, found quickly on the Internet enough original sources to overwhelm even the rustiest Redcoat—but not her teacher. "What does this cartoon of the Boston Massacre," he asked, "have to do with the Battle of Lexington and Concord?" Molly went back to the drawing board. In the end, her project had more multimedia than the others—including a live rendition of a historical fife tune—but earned only a B, not because it wasn't the flashiest in the class, but because not all the examples related directly to the battle she had chosen.*

If It's Multimedia, It Must Be Good

In the early days of computers in school, it was enough to assemble a series of seemingly related images and sounds, with funky fonts and dithering dissolves, to make a report that impressed the teacher. But now we have learned to see beyond the pretty pixels and can apply the same rigorous rubrics to multimedia projects as we do to their traditional precursors. What do those rubrics look like? This section proposes a method for grading a multimedia project that focuses on content as well as creativity, on ideas as well as images. The rubric consists of four areas for evaluation: the *ideas* behind the project; the extent of the *evidence* for each idea; the quality of the *presentation* of each piece of evidence; the *logic* of the narrative; and the student's ability to *defend* the ideas and evidence through questioning.

Ideas (30 points).   The first step in grading a multimedia project is to identify the ideas that the project presents. Not the pictures, not the words, but the ideas that are behind them. In a good report, an idea or three will come through clearly. For the Revolutionary War project mentioned above, the ideas might be:

- The British were outnumbered at Concord
- The Americans used guerilla tactics in the battle
- The British lost more men on the march back to Boston than on the battlefield

If you can't easily identify the main ideas that the project is getting at, it probably does not deserve a good grade. Make a note of the main ideas of the project. Then evaluate these ideas in terms of:

- How many ideas are presented? (10 possible points)
- How well do those ideas match the assigned curriculum? (10 points)
- How deeply do those ideas delve into the subject? (10 points)

A grading sheet may help you here. In a simple table, jot down the main ideas in the first column, and in the second award the points. At the end of this section, you will find a sample grading sheet for your information. Because the strength of the ideas is the most important aspect of a multimedia project, ideas are worth 30 points on our 100-point scale.

Evidence (20 points).   For each idea, the project should present evidence that supports or explains the idea. Evidence can come in may forms, from images to text to voice to music to diagrams, and each idea must be accompanied by adequate evidence. Points should be awarded on the strength of the evidence at this point:

- How well does the evidence support the particular idea? (5 points)
- How much evidence is provided for this idea? (5 points)
- How interesting is this evidence? (5 points)
- How much of it is in the form of original or unexpected source material? (5 points)

You are looking here not for how well the evidence is presented—that comes in the next section. Here you are evaluating the quality and extent of the evidence presented for each main idea.

Presentation (20 points).   For each piece of evidence, you should evaluate how well it is presented. Judge its format, its technical quality, and its visibility (or audibility) to the audience. Here you can also evaluate the design of the project in terms of its readability and consistency. A good way to evaluate is to examine the work with these questions in mind:

> **Format.** How well does the format of the evidence serve to support the main idea? Is it the best medium to get the message across? Might another format have worked better? (5 points)
>
> **Technical Quality.** How well did the evidence survive the process of digitization and presentation? Was its original quality preserved? Is it free of rough edges and unclear aspects? Are the words spelled correctly? (5 points)
>
> **Readability.** How well did the evidence come across to the target audience? Was it the right size or the right volume? Did the audience immediately perceive its meaning? (5 points)
>
> **Design.** Did the color scheme, font, and placement of objects facilitate the audience's understanding of the ideas? Did the evidence and the idea maintain center stage in spite of the design and decoration? (5 points)

You are not evaluating here how flashy the project appears, but how well the evidence is presented so as to achieve its objectives. In fact, unnecessary decorative elements that distract the audience from the main ideas should be discounted as you compute this score.

Logic (20 points).   A good presentation is more than a collection of ideas and evidence. A good presentation tells a story through a series of related facts that build on each other and takes the audience through a thought process that increases their understanding. Sometimes this logic is embedded in the presentation itself, but often it's provided by the presenter orally as the project is shown to the audience. Sometimes referred to as the narrative or flow of the work, this logic serves as the manifestation of the student's ability to think through the ideas and to understand their meaning in a larger context. Some questions to help evaluate this aspect of the project might be:

- How well does the presentation place the issue in a larger context? (5 points)
- How strong is the link or transition from one piece of evidence to the next? (5 points)
- How well are the individual pieces of evidence tied to the main idea? (5 points)
- How well did the audience follow the flow of the argument? (5 points)

This is a bit harder to evaluate than the other aspects of the project—there's more subjective judgment involved. But it's important, and often distinguishes the thoughtful multimedia project from the slapdash collection of pictures.

Defense (10 points).   A student may assemble a great collection of evidence around a set of key ideas, present them well, and tell a nice story, but not understand the topic in any depth. Sometimes the only way to find out if students truly understand their ideas is to ask them questions and challenge their pronouncements. Often both the teacher and fellow students participate in this process. After the presentation, they ask questions that test the student's knowledge of the subject. Some points to consider here include:

- Can the student explain the relationship of each piece of evidence to the main idea? (5 points)
- Can the student defend their conclusions in the face of contradictory evidence? (5 points)

If students can do this well and use the items in their presentation to explain their answers, the chances are good that they have a deep understanding of the subject.

Multimedia Grading Table

Many teachers develop a system for evaluating multimedia projects that centers on a grade sheet on which they record their evaluations. A sample sheet that follows the method described above might look like this:

IDEAS	POINTS	EVIDENCE	PRESENTATION	LOGIC	DEFENSE
The British were outnumbered at Concord.	7/10	6—good image of battle scene	4—image is blurry at edges	8—good numerical analysis	answered questions well
The Americans used guerilla tactics in the battle.	8/10	4—picture needs some explanation in text	7—image is clear and crisp	2—no explanation of effects of tactics	N/A—no questions
The British lost more men on the march back to Boston than on the battlefield.	8/10	7—good use of data and graph	4—numbers are too small to see	6—conclusion supported by data	need some work on geography
Totals	23/30	17/20	15/20	16/20	7/10

This project scored 78 on a 100-point scale.

Communicating with Students

All of these standards and rubrics serve little purpose unless the students are aware of them. Explain in advance to your students how you will evaluate their multimedia projects. Develop a list of questions that you will use as you evaluate their projects (feel free to copy those listed in this chapter) and distribute it to students. Encourage them to apply these questions to their own projects before they turn them in. Provide a time for them to apply the rubric to each others' work. In this way, you can raise the expectations for the work they do on their computers.

LEARN MORE . . .

About Multimedia Assessment Tools

http://www.ncsu.edu/midlink/rub.mmproj.htm
> This multimedia project rubric was produced by a classroom teacher and is downloadable and useable by classroom teachers.

www.ncsu.edu/midlink/rub.mmproj.htm
> This set of multimedia project rubrics comes from the North Central Regional Educational Laboratory (NCREL).

http://rubistar.4teachers.org/index.php
> The Rubistar site helps you develop your own rubrics for a range of topics including multimedia and subject area reports.

About Graphic Organizers

www.inspiration.com
> The Inspiration home page includes a rich set of sample diagrams for both Inspiration and Kidspiration (the K–3 version of Inspiration). From the home page, click What is Visual Learning? Use the Quick Jump menu to visit great examples of Kidspiration diagrams.

www.tomsnyder.com
> At Tom Snyder productions, you will find many examples of different timelines. From the home page, click TimeLiner 5.0. Scroll down to see the TimeLiner Resources.

www.sdcoe.k12.ca.us/score/actbank/torganiz.htm
> The California Online Resources for Teachers is a fine set of graphic organizer ideas produced by both teachers and students.

www.teachervision.com
> The Teacher Vision site has a range of teacher resources, including graphic organizers. From the home page, use the search engine with the keywords *graphic organizers*. This site is commercial but has good ideas for teachers.

www.graphic.org/goindex.html
> This index of graphic organizers has a number of good examples that show the range of organizers.

About Sources for Clip Art and Data

www.loc.gov

The Library of Congress is the place to find images, as well as original documents, sound recordings, and motion pictures from American History. The Library's American Memory site archives thousands of images, many of which are copyright-free.

www.nasa.gov

The National Aeronautics and Space Administration has a huge database of images, movies, statistical data, news, events, history, and it can all be used for free.

www.kodak.com

The Eastman Kodak Company offers a few images of famous cities and landmarks on its site that can be used for non-commercial purposes. Please read the copyright notice for information.

www.google.com

Google is one of several "safe" search engines that allow you to search just for images. Click the Image tab, then type in your search words.

CHAPTER FOURTEEN

PRESENTING IDEAS

IN THIS CHAPTER

- **PowerPoint Presentations**
- **PowerPoint: More Hints and Tips**
- **Animation with PowerPoint**
- **Flash: An Introduction**
- **Learn More . . .**

In school, we present ideas all the time. Teachers give lectures and explain things on the board. Students write reports and give speeches and create projects. The presentation of what you have learned serves often as the ultimate expression of knowledge. The oral presentation and the written paper have been the staples of presentation in schools for hundreds of years. But the new technologies have enabled a form of presentation that combines text, images, and speech that has transformed business and academic communication over the last decade. This chapter provides practical assistance in preparing these kinds of presentations.

We begin with the most popular form of new media presentation, the illustrated slide show, and its ubiquitous software tool, PowerPoint. We show you (and your students) how to get started building a presentation with PowerPoint, and then go on to explain some advanced topics such as animation. The chapter closes with an introduction to the newest, and most web-savvy presentation tool, Macromedia Flash.

POWERPOINT PRESENTATIONS

In Chapter 11 on creating digital images, you learned how to capture and edit pictures from a variety of sources. But once they are edited, how do you publish them? This chapter teaches you how to arrange your images into a slide show with PowerPoint. PowerPoint is one of the programs in the Microsoft Office package, so most people already have it on their computer, and it's easy to use, even for beginners. And because almost everybody has PowerPoint, you can send your slide show to them and they'll be able to watch it.

A slide show can present an event in history, or explain a geometric proof in math. It can illustrate an oral book report, or report the results of a science experiment. Teachers use slide shows as backdrops to their lectures, students use them to deliver reports, and schools use them to show the community what they are doing. A slide show can be a valuable tool for teaching and learning.

The best way to use this section of the chapter is to construct your own slide show as you read it. To do this, you'll need a collection of images that can be arranged to tell a story. If you need help getting those images ready, refer to Chapter 11, *Media: Images.* Once you have the images you need, save them in a folder and get ready to construct your slide show. Make sure all of your images have been saved in the right size and resolution for the screen. This means that all images should be saved at 72 pixels per inch, and none should be larger than 800×600 pixels.

Open PowerPoint

1. When you launch the PowerPoint program, it may ask you what kind of document you want to create. Choose to create a blank PowerPoint presentation.
2. PowerPoint will then present you with a New Slide dialog box, where you can choose what kind of layout you want for your first slide. Choose the Blank slide layout, the one in the lower right corner.
3. Now you are in PowerPoint's editing mode. It's here that you build your slide show, creating new slides, inserting your images, and accessing all of the tools that Power-Point provides. The viewers of your slide show will not see this editing display; they'll see only the slides themselves filling the screen.

In the editing display, you will see a white rectangle on the right. This represents your first slide. Onto this slide you can place images and text. Here's how.

Put a title on a slide. Select Text Box from the Insert menu. Click and drag a text box across the blank slide. Type the title. Use a large font size to ensure the audience can read it at a distance. You can change font and size by selecting the text, and then choosing Font from the Format menu.

Add a new slide. Choose New Slide from the Insert menu.

Bring in a picture. Choose Picture from the Insert menu, then choose From File. Locate your image file, click the Insert button, and watch the picture appear in the document.

Draw on a slide. Open the Drawing toolbar by choosing View, then Toolbars, then Drawing from the menubar. Then select a shape or a line from the Drawing toolbar at the left of the screen. Click and drag across the slide to draw the shape.

View the slide show. Select View Show from the Slide Show menu. Click the mouse to go on to the next slide. Press escape on the keyboard to exit the slide show.

Change the background color of the slide show. Choose Slide color scheme under the Format menu. Then choose the Custom tab, and click on the color you want.

Make a slide open with a dissolve or a wipe. Choose Slide Transition...under the Slide Show menu. Squeeze the pop-up button under the picture to assign a transition to this slide.

Create forward and back arrows. Use the Slide Master under the View menu to view the master elements: those that appear on every slide. Use AutoShapes from the

Drawing toolbar to select a right-facing arrow. Click and drag to place it in the corner where you want it to appear. Select it, then use Action Settings from the Slide Show menu and assign this item to jump to the next slide. Repeat this process to create a left-facing arrow to jump to the previous slide.

Put a shadow under a picture. Use the drawing tools to make a box just a little bigger than the image. Select the color for this box. With the box selected, use Send Backward under the Arrange section of the Draw button at the bottom of the screen to place this box just under your picture but above the background.

Use PowerPoint clip art. Under the Insert menu, use Picture . . . Clip Art. There you will find lots of pictures to choose from. They will appear on the slide, where they can be repositioned and resized to fit your purposes.

Make several images appear on a slide one after another. First place all the images on the slide where you want them to appear. Choose Animations, then Custom from the Slide Show menu. Choose the Effects tab. Select the image you want to animate from the list (not from the picture). Then select an Entry Effect from the drop-down menu. Click OK to close this window. When you run the slide show, the images will appear one after the other as they mouse is clicked. Don't forget to save your slide show as you are building it.

Publishing Your Slide Show

Once built and saved, what's the best way to distribute your slide show to the audience? Here are some of the possibilities.

On the computer screen. Simply gather your audience around the computer, and view the slide show. This works well for groups under ten, and calls for full-screen, close-up images as well as large plain text titles.

On a projector. Connect the computer to a projector, and present to the whole class, or to the whole school in the auditorium. This method of distribution demands the same big images and large text as the first one.

On a disk. Save the PowerPoint file to a floppy disk, and distribute it to the audience. You will find this method adequate for short slide shows, of up to about twelve large images. Beyond this, the size of the file will be too big to fit on a floppy disk, so you may want to use a Zip disk or CD-ROM for longer shows.

On a CD-ROM. If your computer has a CD-ROM burner, you can simply copy your PowerPoint slide show, no matter how large, to the CD-R and burn a CD. When members of your audience get the CD, and double-click your slide show file, it will open in PowerPoint.

On the Web. You have two choices for publishing on the Web: you can copy the PowerPoint file to a web server in its original format and link to it, or you can save the slide show in HTML format, as described below.

Linked to original file. Copy your PowerPoint file to a web server (the school webmaster can help you with this.) Then link to the file with a standard URL, such as www.myserver.net/myfolder/myslideshow.ppt. When members of your audience link to this URL, their browsers will download the PowerPoint file and play it on their computers.

Converted to HTML. In PowerPoint, choose Save As Web Page from the File menu, then follow the instructions. This will convert your slide show to web pages. It will create a folder full of HTML pages and JPEG images. Copy this entire folder to a web server. When your audience links to this folder, they will see your slides play in a browser window.

On the LAN. If your school has a Local Area Network, with file servers where people can store and share their work, you can copy your PowerPoint slide show file to a server on the LAN, whence the audience can view it on their own computers.

POWERPOINT: MORE HINTS AND TIPS

The instructions above can help you or your students to create simple slide show. To create a more complex presentation, you might find these hints and tips to be useful.

Put music or sounds under several slides. Choose Slide Transition . . . under the Slide Show menu. Squeeze the Sound pop-up button on the lower right to import a sound. When this slide appears the music will start; the music will continue under subsequent slides until the music is over. You may have to adjust the delay on the slides to match the duration of the music.

Jump to another slide. Select the text or picture or button you want the user to click to initiate the jump. Choose Action Settings from the Slide Show menu. Click the Hyperlink button, and then select the slide you want to jump to from the popup menu.

Put a movie on a slide. Get the slide you want up on the screen. Chose Movies & Sounds under the Insert menu, then find the movie you want. (It should be in the project folder on your desktop.) When the movie appears on the screen, you may drag it to the desired location. But don't stretch or shrink it; movies play better if they are left in their original size. As soon as this slide appears, the movie will play. For help preparing movies for your PowerPoint presentation, see Chapter 12, Video.

Put a sound on a slide. Get the slide you want up on the screen. Use Insert, then Movies & Sounds, then find the sound you want. (It should be in the project folder on your desktop.) The sound will appear on the screen as a little speaker icon, which will not show when the slide show is run. As soon as this slide appears, the sound will play.

Use text as an interactive menu. Use Insert, then Text Box to create each line of text as a separate text box. Drag each text box to its place on the slide. Select the textbox (not the text itself) you want to link from. Then use Action Settings from the Slide Show menu to select a slide for it to jump to. Do the same for the other text boxes. (Make sure the user can return to this main menu from wherever he jumps to.)

Add a hyperlink to a slide. If you want to open an Internet page while you run your PowerPoint presentation, you'll add a hot link. If the web address (URL) is a long one, it's a good idea to copy and paste from the address box in your browser. This will save you from misspellings. Here's how:

1. With your PowerPoint document open, go on the Web and locate the page to which you want to link.
2. Select and copy the URL from the Address box: select the address, choose Copy from the Edit menu.
3. On your PowerPoint slide, place your cursor where you want the link to appear and select Paste from the Edit menu. When you press the Return key, the link becomes live.

Link from a word or picture. If you want to link from a word (or picture) instead of pasting in the whole URL, select the word or phrase you wish to serve as the link. Choose Hyperlink from the Insert menu and paste the URL into the Link to box, then click OK. Test the link by viewing the individual slide. Click the Slide Show icon at the bottom left of the slide to view it and check your link.

Change the order of your slides. Choose View, then Slide Sorter from the menubar to see all your slides at once. Click and drag the slide sorter icons to change the order of the slides.

ANIMATION WITH POWERPOINT

Picture this:

Mr. Jackson, teacher of eleventh-grade U.S. History, wants to show the great westward movement of the population during the first half of the nineteenth century. He wants his students to develop in their minds a graphic image of the spread and sweep of people from the east coast settlements across the mountains to the midwest. He's got the census figures, and the maps, but he needs a way to make them appear dynamic and memorable.

Group #6 had completed its dissection, and faced the task of documenting their findings. The digital photos they took at various phases of the process were all ready, but these were quite general, showing the entire frog. The assignment called for the isolation and identification of certain very specific parts of the amphibian. How could they show this most accurately in their report?

Triangles, squares, circles: she had repeated this lesson with her second-graders over many years on the chalkboard, building each shape from its constituent lines. But once was not enough. Many of her students needed to see the construction over and over again, if they were to remember. How could she publish this process in such a way that students could access it whenever they wanted?

Three very different classrooms all faced a similar challenge: how to represent certain important curriculum concepts in a graphic and dynamic manner, to aid in students' understanding and effective presentation. In the last section of this chapter, you'll be introduced to using Macromedia Flash to build animations, but Flash is beyond the scope of these folks, takes a bit of time to learn, and is not available on their computers. But all three have

PowerPoint, and for them it might be just the tool they need to construct their simple animations.

Users of PowerPoint tend to focus on two kinds of presentations: bulleted text, and slide shows of images. But PowerPoint contains some simple drawing tools and animation capabilities that allow it to be pressed into service for projects like these. PowerPoint is part of the Microsoft Office suite of programs that is widely available in schools, on both Windows and Macintosh platforms. And its animation capabilities are easy to use. This section gets you started using PowerPoint to create and present a simple animation.

Plan Your Work

To create your storyboard, take a piece of blank paper. Orient it sideways, the same shape as the computer display. Sketch what you want to see on the screen: titles, images, graphics, and so forth.

> *Mr. Jackson drew a big map of the U.S. covering most of the paper, with the title Westward Expansion in big letters at the top. Then he sketched a growing blob of population, with lines showing where the frontier moved every ten years.*

> *Group #6 sketched the photo of the frog on the right, taking up about half the paper, with the labels of the various organs appearing on the left, and then arrows leading from the labels to the organs in the photo. Their plan was to have these labels and arrows appear one by one as they presented their oral report.*

> *The second-grade teacher sketched the triangle on the left third of the paper, the square in the middle, and the circle on the right, each with their label on top in big letters.*

When you plan, you need to consider two things: *placement* and *order.* The placement shows where the various items will appear, in such a way so they all fit and the meaning is clear. The order of appearance determines when they appear, so that they tell a story. Planning on a paper that's about the same size and shape of the computer display lets you see also how big each element needs to be. (For example, a 2-inch frog would not show enough detail, but a 12-inch frog would not fit on the screen.)

Prepare the Raw Materials

From your sketch, it should be clear what you need to create your animation. Mr. Jackson needs an outline map of the US, about 8 inches wide. The dissectors need to crop and shrink their digital photo to be about 6 inches high and 4 inches wide. The second-grade teacher will build her shapes using PowerPoint's drawing tools, and so needs no raw materials from outside—though some photos of these three shapes in nature (beach balls, pyramids, and windows, for instance) might make an interesting introductory slide for the lesson.

Mr. Jackson might find his map (and the second-grade teacher her pictures) in a clip art collection, on the Web, or scanned from a book. Group #6 needs to get the photo from the camera into the computer. Once graphics have been located and saved, they need to be sized properly to fit the plan. In many cases the scanning or camera software allows you to save the image at various sizes, choosing one that best fits your plan. You may save the raw materials as files on your disk (which you will later import into PowerPoint), or you may keep them in view on the screen ready to be copied (and then pasted into PowerPoint.)

Build in Order

Launch PowerPoint. Create a blank slide, with nothing on it. You'll build the animation on this slide, one piece at a time. Avoid fancy backgrounds and decorations—in most cases these distract from the educational content. Insert your items on the slide one at a time, in the order that you want them to appear in the animation. This is important.

> *The frog students first imported their photo, using Insert, then Picture, then From file from the menubar. Then they moved the photo to the right, as they had planned. Mr. Jackson copied his outline map from his Web browser, and then pasted it onto the PowerPoint slide.*

All three of our cases then added a title to their slide, using Insert followed by Text Box from the menubar. They dragged out a box, and then typed *Frog Dissection, Group 6,* or *Westward Expansion,* or *Shapes* into the box. By selecting the text in the box, and using Format, then Font from the menubar, they adjusted the title text to fit their plans.

Now comes the second-step element, the item that will appear next in order. For the dissectors, it's the first label, *heart,* which they type into a text box, adjust the size, and position on the slide. For Mr. Jackson, it's the first wave of settlement, which he draws with the PowerPoint freeform tool. And for the second-grade teacher, it's the baseline of the triangle, drawn with the PowerPoint line tool.

Drawing Tools

Can't find these drawing tools on your PowerPoint? Choose View, then Toolbars, then Drawing from the menubar. On the Drawing toolbar, the arrow is the tool that lets you select an item on the slide. The capital A is the tool that lets you create a text box and type into it. You will also find a line tool, a rectangle tool, a tool full of shapes, and a box full of special tools including arrows and freeform shapes.

Before constructing your graphic item, play around with these tools. Create a new blank slide and draw something with each tool, so you can see how it works. For most of the tools, you select the tool, then click and drag on the slide to draw using it. Once an item has been drawn, you can change its size and color with the size and color tools on the drawing toolbar.

Add the elements you need, in the order you want them to appear. When you are done, the slide should appear as it will when the animation is complete. Mr. Jackson drew five separate shapes with the freeform tool, one on top of the next, representing the spread of population in each of the census periods 1800–1840. The students in group #6 entered six labels and six arrows. And the second-grade teacher created seven lines, one autoshape circle, and three labels.

Animate

If you show this slide, using Slide Show, then View Show from the menubar, you will see all the elements at once. What you need to do is animate them so they appear one at a time. Here's how:

1. Select the item you want to appear first. In most cases, this is the title, or the background item. Use the arrow tool from the drawing toolbar to make this selection.
2. Choose Slide Show, then Animations from the menubar.
3. From the drop-down menu, select how you want the item to appear. It can fly in, crawl in, wipe across, dissolve in, or simply appear.

Repeat steps 1–3 for the rest of the elements. Make sure you follow the desired order. When all the items have been animated, test the slide by choosing Slide Show, then View Show from the menubar. Click the mouse to move from step to step.

Present Your Slide Show

Your animation can be presented at the front of the class as a demonstration, or left available on a learning station for the students to work through. The PowerPoint file can be emailed to someone else, copied onto a CD-ROM or memory stick, and even placed on a Web server and linked to a web page. Because so many people have PowerPoint on their computers, your work can be made widely available.

FLASH: AN INTRODUCTION

Animation is a powerful tool for communication and education. It can illustrate a complex process, entertain an audience, or introduce a new idea. With the arrival of Macromedia Flash, animation has appeared more and more on the Web and in a variety of programs for teaching and learning.

Animation need not be of the Disney variety, with lifelike characters, or of the television variety with spinning logos and shiny surfaces. In fact these flashy animations often contain little content of importance. More useful animation might show the formation of a thunderstorm in a weather front over time, or the growth of U.S. territory in the 19th century, or a schematic of the plot of a novel. These kinds of animation are more useful in school, and easier to create for the student or teacher who is not an artist.

This section gets you started creating a simple animation with Flash. If you don't have a copy of the program, you can download a trial version at Macromedia's web site.

Creating Animation with Flash

Flash provides tools for creating text and graphics for your animation, and for moving these around. You can also import JPEG, GIF, or PICT images into Flash, and animate them as well.

Set Up the Stage

Open Flash. Set your Flash project to a size appropriate to the animation you want to build. Do this by choosing Modify, then Movie from the menubar, and enter the appropriate numbers in the boxes. If your animation needs a background color, choose it now. You will see the stage change size, with the color you have chosen.

Create your Objects. You must import any photographic or bitmap images that you need for your animation. Before you import them, set them to the proper size and resolution with Photoshop. Use a resolution of 72 pixels per inch, and keep the images within the size limits of your stage. To import a bitmap image, choose File, then Import . . . from the Flash menubar, and you will see your images appear on the Stage.

You should create within Flash any text or graphic elements you need for your animation. Choose a tool from Flash's tool palette, choose line and fill colors, then draw (or type, if it's text) the object you need onto the Stage.

Animate the Objects. You can animate several aspects of an object:

Location: Move the object from one place on the Stage to another.

Transparency: Make the object fade in and out of the scene.

Rotation: Make the object spin.

Size: Make the object get bigger and smaller.

. . . and you can combine any and all of these. Text, images, and graphics can all be animated in these ways.

Animating location. When you imported or created the object, it went into frame 1 in the Timeline. This will be the first frame, the beginning point of the animation. To make the object animate, you need to create several more frames and a last keyframe, move the object in the keyframe to the ending location of the animation, then create the in-between frames. Follow these steps:

1. Create or place the object on the stage, where you want its animation to start. It should show up in frame 1 on the timeline.
2. Choose Insert, then Convert to Symbol from the menubar, and convert the object to a Graphic symbol.
3. Create a keyframe in frame 15 by selecting frame 15 in the timeline and choosing Insert, then Keyframe from the menubar.
4. With the keyframe (frame 15) selected in the timeline, choose the black arrow tool, then move the object to where you want it to end its animation.
5. In the timeline, select frame 1.
6. Choose Insert, then Motion Tween from the menubar.
7. Use the Control menu to rewind, and then play the animation.
8. Watch the object move across the Stage.

Animating Transparency

In Flash, the transparency of an object is called its *Alpha* value. An Alpha of zero is invisible; and Alpha of 100 is fully opaque, and an Alpha of 50 is halfway there—you can see through it. To gradually change the transparency from opaque to transparent, follow these steps:

1. Create or place the object on the stage. It should show up in frame 1 on the timeline.
2. Choose Insert, then Convert to Symbol from the menubar, and convert the object to a Graphic symbol.

3. Create a keyframe in frame 15 by selecting frame 15 in the timeline and choosing Insert, then Keyframe from the menubar.
4. With the keyframe (frame 15) selected in the timeline, select the object.
5. In the Properties window, locate the Color popup menu.
6. From the popup menu, choose Alpha.
7. Use the slider to set the Alpha to the ending value (for example, 5%).
8. In the timeline, select frame 1.
9. Choose Insert, then Motion Tween from the menubar.
10. Use the Control menu to rewind, then play the animation.
11. Watch as the object disappears.

Animating Rotation

Any object can be rotated, and rotation is expressed in degrees. Three hundred and sixty degrees makes a complete circle. Animating the rotation of an object is very much like animating its transparency. Follow these steps:

1. Create or place the object on the stage. It should show up in frame 1 on the timeline.
2. Choose Insert, then Convert to Symbol from the menubar, and convert the object to a Graphic symbol.
3. Create a keyframe in frame 15 by selecting frame 15 in the timeline and choosing Insert, then Keyframe from the menubar.
4. With the keyframe (frame 15) selected in the timeline, select the object.
5. Open the Transform window by choosing Window, then Transform.
6. In the transform window, enter a new number for the rotation (for example, 45 degrees).
7. In the timeline, select frame 1.
8. Choose Insert, then Motion Tween from the menubar.
9. Use the Control menu to rewind, and then play the animation.
10. You should see the object rotate smoothly as the frames play.

Animating Size

You can shrink or stretch an object over time to create a size animation. It's very much the same as creating a rotation animation. Follow these steps:

1. Create or place the object on the stage. It should show up in frame 1 on the timeline.
2. Choose Insert, then Convert to Symbol from the menubar, and convert the object to a Graphic symbol.
3. Create a keyframe in frame 15 by selecting frame 15 in the timeline and choosing Insert, then Keyframe from the menubar.
4. With the keyframe (frame 15) selected in the timeline, select the object.
5. Open the Transform window by choosing Window, then Transform.
6. In the transform window, enter a new number for the horizontal and vertical size (150% to make it larger, 50% to make it smaller.)

7. In the timeline, select frame 1.
8. Choose Insert, then Motion Tween from the menubar.
9. Use the Control menu to rewind, and then play the animation.
10. You should see the object shrink or stretch smoothly as the frames play.

Combined Effects

By the same method, you can create an object that moves across the screen as it disappears, or performs all four types of animation at once—just apply all the settings to the last frame, one after the other, and then create the Motion Tween.

Multiple Objects

You can animate several objects at the same time, in different directions, by adding them to the Stage and then animating them. Just make sure that you select only the object that you want to animate as you set the transformation parameters. It's easier to keep track of these if you put each object in its own layer.

Multiple Scenes

To create a new Scene, choose Insert, then Scene from the menubar. Create the second scene as you created the first. This second scene will play as soon as the first one is finished. To test the entire movie, choose Control, then Test Movie from the menubar.

Animating Along a Path

To move an object along a path that is not a straight line, you simply draw the path with the pencil tool in a special invisible layer called a *Motion Guide*. Open the location animation that you created earlier, and follow these steps:

1. Select the layer with the animated object in it.
2. Choose Insert, then Motion Guide from the menubar.
3. Select the pencil tool, and draw the animation path. Make sure you start the path at the exact center of the object. (The pencil tool has options for different types of lines—try them and see the results.)
4. Use the Control menu to rewind and see the animation.

Publishing Your Animation

When you have created and tested your animation and it's ready to be published, choose Publish from the file menu. This will create a web page with the Flash animation embedded in it. When you open the web page with your browser, you will see the animation play. The animation file will have a filename extension of .swf (that stands for Shockwave Flash.) If this animation is to be part of a web site, it can be copied to a web server and be accessible to the public from there. If the animation is to be distributed on disk or CD-ROM, it can be copied to one of those formats.

No matter which way you publish it, viewers will need the Flash Player installed on their computers in order to see your animation. They can download this player for free at www.macromedia.com.

LEARN MORE . . .

About PowerPoint

www.electricteacher.com/tutorial3.htm
Electric Teacher presents tutorials and ideas for using PowerPoint in the classroom.

www.actden.com/pp
Act 360 Media is a site co-sponsored by Microsoft with more tutorials for producing Power-Point in the classroom.

www.spa3.k12.sc.us/PowerPoint.htm
This site, produced by teachers in Spartanburg, Virginia, features sample student and teacher products using PowerPoint.

http://208.183.128.3/tutorials/pptr/resources.html
Jefferson County Schools has a fine list of links for clip art, sounds, multimedia, and tutorials focused on PowerPoint.

About Flash Examples in School

www.tygh.co.uk/students/
This British site offers many examples of student projects that use Flash animation.

www.macromedia.com/resources/education/whitepapers/
Here, you'll find white papers describing ways that educators are using Flash, including electronic portfolios.

CHAPTER FIFTEEN

ONLINE LEARNING

IN THIS CHAPTER

- **Supply and Demand**
- **Distance Learning**
- **Online Education**
- **Learning Objects**
- **Synchronous Online Seminar**
- **Learn More . . .**

Five seemingly unrelated facts arrived at my desk this morning:

- The state of Maine has purchased 40,000 laptop computers for its middle school students, and is about to do the same for its high-schoolers. Soon every student from grades 7–12 will sport a laptop, wirelessly connected to the Internet, at school and at home.
- The two largest textbook publishers, Pearson and Harcourt, are in the midst of a long-term plan to publish all of their learning materials online, and to sell them to schools and students by subscription.
- A committee of the French Ministry of Education has proposed the development of a system whereby teaching and learning materials would be *numerisé* (digitized) and organized on the Web for all of the country's teachers and students to use.
- The faculty of the University of Nantes, where I am working, is demanding the ability for each teacher to publish all of his or her course materials online and accessible to students over an intranet.
- The Blackboard company that developed the CourseInfo system for organizing teachers' instructional documents online is preparing its initial public offering and its expected to raise hundreds of millions of dollars.

These facts, taken together, portend a sea-change in the way we organize and access the materials we use for teaching and learning. This chapter looks at the nature of online learning, and its implications for the classroom teacher. We begin with an examination of the trend away from textbooks and toward online resources for students, and then go on to describe how online distance learning is changing the face of higher education. The last part of the chapter introduces the new concept of *online learning objects,* and describes how live discussions can be conducted using the Internet.

SUPPLY AND DEMAND

The laws of supply and demand are acting in their natural and inevitable manner to shift the 500-year tradition of textbooks toward an online future.

Demand

On the demand side, we have teachers who are clamoring for a more efficient way to provide materials to their students. They do not wish to saddle their students with a five-kilogram textbook that costs more than $50. But neither do they want to turn to the copy machine, the course packet, and the reserve shelf, which are more work for them and much less useful to students. They demand from the school authorities a system that makes it easy for them to identify and publish their learning materials, and for their students to use them. And to update them quickly and efficiently.

Many schools have met this demand by providing easy-to-use systems for teachers to develop and acquire rights to the documents they need for teaching, and to post them in a protected environment accessible only to their own students. These systems are often run jointly by the librarians and the information technology people at the school, and respond well to the demand. As a result, the quality of teaching improves.

Also creating a demand are the students, armed with their laptops and a lifetime of Internet use. They would rather read from the computer screen than from the printed page. They are looking for the latest research that has not yet arrived in print. They expect to be able to browse a wider range of ideas and facts than is contained in the school's library. These expectations come no longer just from a privileged minority but from the vast majority of students.

When the people demand something in a free marketplace, the suppliers are eager to provide it. This principle of economics applies as well to the supply of learning materials.

Supply

Books are expensive to develop, print, ship, keep in stock, and update. And they are heavy and consume natural resources. Textbook publishing is therefore a tough business. And the people who run these businesses see the same facts that we do: a new generation that is more comfortable getting its information online, a burgeoning of connected laptops in homes and schools, and a growing unwillingness to shell out half a hundred for a history of Hungary. They are actively preparing for a very different future, and making major investments in online publishing. They foresee the day when the school (or the student himself, at the college level) will buy not a textbook but a subscription to the subject accessible online in a variety of forms. They are already realizing a substantial portion of their income from online publishing, and you can see this trend for yourself by visiting Pearson's

MyMathLab (www.mymathlab.com) or Harcourt's Holt Online Learning (http://my.hrw.com/hrw/login_all.jsp).

A publisher can make more profit selling an online subscription at $10 per student than from a $40 textbook. As more and more schools and students demand their materials digitally, the more the publishers will supply them in that form. The law of supply and demand will drive the change.

Also on the supply side are the purveyors of learning management systems, software that organizes and facilitates the libraries of educational content that one resided in books and paper journals and photocopies. The two biggest, Blackboard and WebCT, work closely with the textbook publishers to make sure the new online content works through their systems. They want to ensure a good supply of educational resources. More and more schools and colleges are licensing the systems, indicating that what they are supplying is meeting a real demand.

Lament

Shall we bemoan the death of the book? Will people stop reading as they spend more and more time in front of the computer screen? It's not that simple.

We are considering here the school textbook—the wide and unwieldy tome used for presentation and reference in school subjects. Not the kind of object you can curl up with in a comfortable chair. The laws of supply and demand that we have been discussing apply to this kind of book, and not to all books. The new technologies seem to be better at providing reference information and learning materials, and the marketplace is changing to reflect this.

Will I still take my copy of *The Old Man and the Sea* off on the boat with me every summer, and read the story from the printed page as I slouch in the stern sheets? You bet I will. The paper book is the best way to interact with this story, and I suspect it will be for my great-grandchildren as well. The novel and the newsmagazine are less apt to be converted to the online context. There's little demand for it.

When all the textbooks are gone and the reference libraries closed and the students all staring at their screens, will we become a nation of nonreaders? Hardly. Most of what our students do with their computers today is read and write. Email and instant messenger are their two most popular technologies. It's the television and the video game, not the computer, that steal time from reading and writing. There's plenty of demand for reading and writing, but not necessarily on paper.

The laws of economics will dictate the speed and extent of this shift. Rather than lamenting a natural progression, we might be well to look for opportunities to capitalize on the capabilities of the new supply of online educational materials, and to create a demand for high-quality digital documents.

DISTANCE LEARNING

Distance learning is in the news these days, and in the discussions of many educators. Colleges look to distance learning to find new sources of students, businesses are replacing on-site training courses with online learning programs, and thousands of students and teachers use the Virtual High School every day to do their lessons. And like me, you may receive in your email spam each week an offer to earn an advanced degree by distance learning, with no admissions hurdles, no tests, and guaranteed diplomas. The Internet seems to have given birth to a rapidly growing educational pathway. But distance learning is not new . . .

First Aid

Many years before the Internet was even thought of, I took a distance learning course in first aid. In order to be the manager of my high-school football team, I had to be qualified in first aid. But there were no courses offered in my town that would prepare me for the upcoming fall season, so I signed up for a correspondence course. They sent me materials to read, tests, essays to write, situations to analyze, and pictures and diagrams to study. Once a week, I mailed my work to an unseen teacher, who corrected and commented by return mail. I did well on the written part of the course, but this was not enough. I needed to display my competence at tourniquets and bandages to a live expert at the local Red Cross. Just in time for the first football practice, I received my certification.

Sociology

He was a strange teacher. He'd come into class (often late), pose a question, then wander around the room waiting for us to answer it. This was not what we were led to expect from our college experience. On many days his wanderings would lead him to the window, where he would gaze and daydream, and on several occasions he found himself behind the curtains, invisible to his students. He was quite distant from us, in many ways. He assigned excellent, provocative readings that I recall to this day, and with his questions sent us off on provocative discussions among ourselves. He made us write more papers than most, and was insightful and careful with his commentaries—just the opposite of his behavior in the classroom. We learned, not from his presentations in the classroom, but from the readings, papers, comments, and discussions that he had set up for us but that we essentially carried out independently.

Blended Learning

Both of these successful examples of distance learning took place more than 30 years ago. And if you look back, you may recall many topics and concepts that you learned by a combination of independent reading, discussions with peers, and commentary from an expert. In fact, most learning, even in the best universities and schools, is in actuality a blend of reading, listening to the teacher, discussion, homework, and independent reflection. In very few courses or programs does most of the learning occur in the classroom with the teacher. The blend varies from course to course, depending on the subject matter, and the way the teacher has structured the learning, but all of them contain a significant measure of distance learning, learning that occurs not in the presence of the teacher in the classroom. Learning is most often a blend of . . .

- Face-to-face interaction with the teacher: lecture, class discussion, office hours
- Distant interaction with the teacher: readings, papers written and corrected
- Independent study: readings, homework, problems to solve, reflection, writing

- Interaction with peers: discussion, argument, group projects
- Hands-on application: experiments, lab work, projects

Of all these, only the first one takes place in the classroom with the teacher. The majority take place at a distance. We deceive ourselves as teachers when we think that our students are only learning when they are with us in the classroom. Good teachers realize that their job is to define a set of assignments and set up a learning environment of which the class meeting is only a small part. Good students know that to rely simply on what happens in class is not a path to success in most courses.

Designing a Distance Learning Course

To design a good distance learning course is very similar to designing any course. In designing a course, the teacher must:

- Clearly define the objectives of the course, in terms of what the student is expected to learn
- Set forth a list of assignments for the students to do, which include readings, problems, experiments, and other activities appropriate to the content
- Provide opportunities for discussion with other students and with the teacher
- Require students to turn in evidence that they have learned, through tests, projects, writings or other work
- Evaluate and comment on the work turned in by students

If you look carefully at this list, you will see very little that requires all the students to be present in the classroom with the teacher at the same time. Of course, the blend works best when the face-to-face experience is part of the mix, but when classroom presence is impossible, a good course can be constructed nonetheless.

Suppose a group of students somewhere in Asia wanted to learn from you, and a personal visit was out of the question. How would you structure the course for them? How would you ensure that the five elements listed above were covered? How would you use the new features of the Internet, such as instant messaging, audio chat, video, and multiple document types, to construct a rich learning experience for these students? My teachers in first aid and sociology succeeded 30 years ago to construct an effective distance learning experience. Think of how much better we should be able to do it today.

ONLINE EDUCATION

Some say it will take the place of schools and colleges. Others suggest we are in the midst of a revolution as far-reaching as the invention of the printing press. But the critics suggest that online education will never duplicate the intimacy of the classroom or the central role of the teacher. Many consider the attention being paid to learning over the Internet to be a fad with lots of hype but few concrete results. This section looks at the current state of web-based schooling, and offers some suggestions for the future.

The National Center for Educational Statistics, a part of the U.S. Department of Education, released recently a report entitled *Distance Education at Degree-Granting Post-secondary Institutions: 2000–2001*. At about an inch thick, this is probably the most comprehensive study to date of how U.S. colleges and universities are providing education over the Internet, outside of the traditional classroom. It's not a set of opinions or commentaries on the subject, rather it's a collection of dry facts and figures drawn from a scientific survey of about 1,600 schools. (The response rate to the survey was 94%, an amazingly large proportion, which makes this study perhaps more believable than most.) We'll base our discussion in this section on the findings of the survey. Remember that this survey represents reports from the 2000–2001 academic year, so it's a bit behind the times—we may predict that any trends in the survey have continued and increased by today.

What's Going On?

Not surprisingly, most of the schools in the U.S. are providing online courses for students—56% provide at least a few courses taught at a distance, without a classroom. Interestingly, public colleges are ahead in this trend, with 89% of them online, versus 40% of private colleges. And this seems to be more than just an experiment or a pilot project: about 3 million students are enrolled in 120,000 different online courses. Most of the colleges that offer these courses are fully accredited, traditional bricks-and-mortar institutions that offer hundreds of courses in the classroom, along with a few dozen online.

But it's not just a few courses here and there: one in five colleges allow students to earn a degree through online courses only, never setting foot in a classroom. Only a few degrees are offered in this manner, mostly in subjects that lend themselves to distance learning. And the proportion of online courses and degrees seems to be higher in graduate professional programs than in the traditional undergraduate liberal arts.

What Technologies Are Used?

Distance education has long been available by correspondence and through television, but the technology of choice today is the Internet. Ninety percent of the distance courses are delivered over the Web. Video conferencing and CD-ROM are also used for some of these courses, but their percentage is small, and I suspect shrinking.

On the Web, the methods used most for online instruction are email and asynchronous text discussions—forums or bulletin board where students and teachers post messages and comments about the course topics. Fewer than half the online courses use video, synchronous discussion, or multimedia presentations. That's probably due to the higher cost of developing the richer media, and the difficulties in receiving them over a slow Internet connection.

In fact, the University of Phoenix, which advertises itself as the world's largest online university, uses none of the fancy media technologies—its courses are conducted solely by email correspondence. One might conclude that much of the online education going on today is similar in form to the correspondence courses that have been offered by colleges since the 19th century. The federal study did not address whether or not students enjoyed their online courses, or how many dropped out, but other studies suggest that online courses suffer a much higher dropout rate than classroom courses.

Why Are They Doing This?

The study asked colleges why they were offering online education. In order of importance, they reported that they wanted to:

- Make courses available at locations more convenient to the student
- Make courses available at times more convenient to the student
- Make courses more affordable for students

And while more than 60% of the colleges see online education as a way to reach new and underserved audiences, and to increase enrollments, only 15% reported that online education was aimed at lowering costs. Community colleges seem to take this outreach mission seriously, and are first in line to offer online courses to reach students who can't come to campus—about half of the enrollment in online courses is in two-year colleges.

So we might conclude that colleges are not using online education to replace the traditional four-year, classroom-based bachelor's degree program. Rather they are using it to reach new audiences for whom the campus and the classroom may not be the best way to learn.

Why Isn't Everyone Doing This?

Almost half of the schools in the United States are not offering online courses. When asked why, they report these reasons:

- Online education does not fit with our basic mission (44%)
- Program development costs are too high (33%)
- Course quality is not as good as in the classroom (26%)
- Our technical infrastructure is not up to the task (24%)
- We don't perceive a need for online courses (22%)

So, while online education is thriving and growing at the college level, it's far from universal, and a long way from replacing the campus and the classroom. Since many colleges see their mission as providing a comprehensive four-year education in a campus setting, many with a residential component *in loco parentis,* it is not surprising that they find little need to offer courses online.

Though the NCES report did not survey K–12 schools, we might extrapolate the findings to suggest that the K–12 educational mission is most like the traditional college setting, where the classroom and the campus and the presence of a teacher is the most important part of the experience, and the most difficult to duplicate online. However, the growth of virtual high schools in many states, and the offering of online high-school courses by many publishers, suggest that K–12 education is not immune from the online trends in college education.

What Does It Mean to Me?

If you are a teacher in college, you should consider making your course materials available online, so that your students can access them right now, and so that you can be ready to offer your course to students at a distance when the time comes. As a teacher in the K–12 schools, you need not worry about online education replacing your role in the classroom, but you should be aware of your students' increasing use of the Web to find educational information and to learn new things. And you may find that many of the materials, techniques, and software tools developed for online education may be put to profitable use in your own classroom.

LEARNING OBJECTS

Heavy Metal

Thirty-some years ago, at the beginning of my teaching career, long before the arrival of computers, I borrowed a MOVE Kit from the local college museum. MOVE stood for Museum Objects for Valley Educators, and these kits contained artifacts that could be used for teaching. My favorite was the whaling kit. I took an object from the kit, a heavy bronze metal casting with a point at one end and a hole in the middle. With no introduction, I passed it around the class, with the question, "Describe this object." A good lesson on adjectives for these fourth-graders: cold, heavy, metal, yellow, brown, golden, pointed, rusty, tarnished, green, solid, shiny, warm. (Warm because by now it had passed among many hot hands.) "What might it be used for?" Paperweight, part of a car, part of a loom, holds railroad ties, part of a big clock mechanism. By now they were curious. I refused to tell them what it was, or to let them see the name of the kit.

The next day, we watched a short video clip taken from *Down to the Sea in Ships,* an early film of the last Nantucket whaling ship, produced in 1922. "Tell me when you see something familiar in this film." About five minutes into the video, there it was. The harpooner moved to the front of the whaleboat and raised his weapon as the camera zoomed in for a closer shot. Attached to the end of a long iron rod we all saw the brass harpoon tip that we had hefted and described the day before.

A Learning Object

The harpoon, according to the museum, was a learning object. The teacher's guide in the kit explained how to use this object to provoke curiosity, learning, and understanding. The kit provided complementary learning objects such as the documentary film that helped make sense out of the first. Also in the kit was a facsimile of a diary of a whale fisherman, complete with salt-stained pages and misspelled words. Another learning object. The lessons we experienced with these kits were brief, concrete, powerful, and memorable. When I was finished with the kit, it went back to the collection and was soon borrowed by another teacher. It was listed in the card catalog under Social Studies, Whaling, and Technology, so that it might be found by teachers (or students) searching the collection for a variety of purposes.

The museum educators dreamed of the day that their collection would contain hundreds of learning objects, well-cataloged, each with a lesson plan, able to be combined into extended units of study.

The Learning Objects Movement

Thirty years later, Learning Objects are back in the headlines, this time capitalized. Online educators today dream of a collection of Learning Objects available online to anyone, anytime, from anywhere, fully indexed by a variety of criteria so that a student or a teacher can find exactly what he needs just when he needs to learn it. Such a library of Learning Objects promises to schools a ready and rich store of lessons from which to build a curriculum. It promises to teachers a wealth of ideas tailored to various levels, learning styles, and subject specialties. It promises to individual students a virtual online teaching factory that they can use to chart their own course through the sea of education. It promises to publishers a way to reorganize and resell all the content that they have been printing in textbooks in a more profitable manner.

We are witnessing today the development of an L.O.M. (Learning Objects Movement) led by C.B.E.'s (Computer Based Educators) who dream of L.M.S.'s (Learning Management Systems) with a worldwide set of I.M.S.'s (Instructional Management Standards). These folks have joined together in groups such as the I.E.E.E. (International Electrical and Electronics Engineers) to agree on standards for L.O.M. (Learning Objects Metadata) that you can see online (http://ltsc.ieee.org/wg12). Their most recent document is titled *XML Schema Definitions* (XSD) that accompanies the current draft of the XML binding for L.O.M. Sounds like an enjoyable bedtime reading selection. In their zeal to quantify and classify and index these objects, the engineers have cooked up quite an alphabet soup of acronyms.

From the IEEE documents we learn in Section 3, Definitions, what a learning object is: 3.6 Learning Object: For this Standard, a learning object is defined as any entity, digital or nondigital, that may be used for learning, education or training.

It would seem that the harpoon I showed my fourth-grade students would qualify as a learning object. So might my worn-out copy of *Charlotte's Web* that I used in that same classroom, or the Flash-based simulation of signal speed and spectrum that the hTech project just published as part of the Fourier transform module in our online engineering master's degree program. And the MIT Open Courseware Initiative, in which professors voluntarily make available to the world free and online the documents they provide for their students in the classroom, would also qualify as a set of Learning Objects.

Many of us teachers have developed our own learning objects that work well with students, provide an interesting experience that we use over and over from year to year. Imagine that thousands of resources like this, provocative, structured, interesting, and valuable for learning, were available online. That's the dream of the Learning Objects Movement.

What Makes a Good Learning Object?

Solid content. A good learning object helps students understand a worthwhile concept, accurately, concretely, and well-presented. Many go beyond text explanations to include physical items and appropriate images, sounds, and animation.

Effective method. A good learning object takes students through a structured experience that draws on creative pedagogy. Like the harpoon lesson, it provides not only the object but instructions on how to present the object in such a way as to capitalize on curiosity and surprise.

Right-sized. The educational experience offered by the object is neither too brief, nor too lengthy, to be easily accomplished by a class or by a student in the time periods most often available for study. The size of the educational morsel is appropriate to the intake capabilities of the student. The most valuable learning objects tend to be aimed at a 30- to 60-minute experience.

Re-useable. The format of the object is open, so that most people can use it without a special system or a proprietary interface. And and the nature of its presentation is self-contained so that it can be used in a variety of situations—it makes sense by itself, even outside of its original context.

Indexed and accessible. The teacher or student who needs the learning object can find it and use it because it is well-indexed and made available easily. Not necessarily for free, but easy to find, and, if necessary, easy to buy.

Where Can I Find Learning Objects?

They are all around you: in the library, at the museum, in the field behind the school. And on the Internet, which is what most people are talking about these days. Some of the best online learning objects, that meet the criteria listed just above, are WebQuests designed by teachers (see Chapter 7, Building a Web Assignment). The Apple Learning Interchange has an indexed collection at http://ali.apple.com. The Shodor organization has organized and indexed many learning objects on the Web (www.shodor.org/curriculum).

How Can I Learn More?

Refer to All About Learning Objects at www.eduworks.com/LOTT/tutorial/learning objects.html, or Learning Objects and Standards at www.learnativity.com/standresources.html. You will find, unfortunately, that many of the experts who write and talk and propose various standards for Learning Objects spend more time on the methods for indexing the objects, than on developing them. So we have hundreds of pages describing the SCORM and IMS systems for indexing Learning Objects, but very few actual objects to be indexed. The building of useful learning objects can better be found among the voluntary collections built by teachers, such as those at http://webquest.org.

SYNCHRONOUS ONLINE SEMINAR

Elections are in the news these days—students can't help but encounter the worldwide concern for the democratic process. Wouldn't it be great if the students in my classroom could discuss issues face to face with students in Iraq, France, Haiti, Afghanistan, and California? Is there any way that technology can help students interact directly with people facing the same problems but in a very different setting, across the world or across the country?

This section reports on a recent experience conducting a Synchronous Online Seminar with correspondents widely separated by distance, using hardware, software, and networks widely available to classrooms. And then goes on to discuss how this technique might enhance instruction in our classrooms.

The SOS

We were separated by distance and time zones, but all working on the same issue. David was in Boston, at the School of Education at Boston University. Kathi was at the Massachusetts Elementary School Principal's Association. Mathieu and Pascal worked at UVPL: Université Virtuelle des Pays de la Loire in France. Stephane taught at the Université de Technologie de Compiègne (UTC), while Christian and Martin worked at the École des Mines de Nantes (EMN), also in France. Joe worked for a software company somewhere in California. We were a diverse group, unlikely to be considered a community, except for our shared interest. A few of us had met one of the others in person, but for the most part we were strangers. And yet we all faced similar struggles in our work, and wanted to discuss them.

We had exchanged ideas via email, but this proved impersonal and required a slow delay for interactivity. We wanted to meet at the same time (synchronously), and in the same place (a seminar room, perhaps), where we could see and hear each other and exchange papers and sketch things out in diagrams as we talked. But none of us had the money or the time to travel to a single meeting point. Why not meet virtually (online)? So was born the idea of a Synchronous Online Seminar, hereinafter referred to as an SOS.

Online Meeting Software

Many of us had tried to use this form of discussion. We had used the PictureTel videoconferencing system at Boston University to work with a group of teachers in Illinois. The folks at the School of Mines had used Microsoft NetMeeting and Meeting One to work with students in Morocco. David and Jim often conversed one-to-one with audio and video using iChat. These experiences encouraged us, but none of the systems was capable of conducting the seminar we desired.

- The Picture Tel system required each correspondent to be in a special room outfitted with a PictureTel TV and special cameras and a dedicated ISDN line. None of us had such a room available to us, and to build one would cost upwards of $20,000. And it would allow only one location on the screen at a time, not the six simultaneous faces we wanted to see.
- According to the folks at the School of Mines, Net Meeting is "not the best tool and it works only on Windows . . . but it works and we only buy an Exchange server to hold the conferences. We don't use the voice capabilities of Netmeeting. It's not reliable and our students from Morocco don't have a good Internet connection for using voice."
- iChat AV worked very well for a one-to-one session, but was not designed to handle six simultaneous conversations, and worked only on Macintosh.

- The EMN team reported that "Meeting One tools, like the Centra One, can easily be used to make such a presentation using PowerPoint slides and voice. It's reliable and it works fine with Asia or America. The main drawback is the cost. We must rent some server time. We cannot use it on a regular basis."

Our research toward a better tool for SOS led us to Marratech eMeeting, which worked on Windows, Macintosh, and Linux. The client software could be downloaded for free, it worked well with all the standard microphones and video cameras, and allowed us to all see each other at the same time, to talk, to write, and to place documents on a whiteboard. The Internet2 consortium in Boston had installed the Marratech server on a computer (donated by Apple Computer) at Harvard University, which we were able to use.

In our first tests of this system, it worked right out of the box, across the Atlantic and across town. So we scheduled a six-way meeting for February 17 at 7:30 A.M. PST, 10:30 A.M. EST, and 4:30 P.M. in Europe.

Our First SOS

To join the meeting, we each simply entered the URL of the server into the Marratech software. Of course we had plugged our cameras and microphones into our computers beforehand, using the standard USB and FireWire ports that are present on most modern computers. (The video cameras we used cost between $50 and $150, nothing fancy.) We began to see faces appear on the Marratech screen as each person connected. Each person showed as an icon about an inch square. We could hear each other talk. If you clicked on someone's face, they appeared in live video in a larger window. You could set the software so the one talking was automatically featured in the larger video window.

As someone was talking, another would enter a question or comment into the text chat. We listed our names on the whiteboard. We sent clickable URL references in the chat window. We pasted illustrations on the whiteboard. We posed questions and listened to the answers of the others. We endured awkward silences and confusing times when three of us tried to talk at once. We laughed. We almost got to the point where the computer and the software became transparent to us, and we were conversing as if we were in the same room, around a seminar table. We talked for an hour. We each remained at our desks, in our offices the whole time. After the hour, we disconnected and went back to our work.

This first SOS was not a complete success. The folks at the EMN and UTC were unable to get through the firewalls that the network administrators had set up in their schools to block the UDP* packets that transmit the video and audio material over the Internet. My little camera shut itself off about three-quarters of the way through, but I was able to carry on with voice and text. Someone used loudspeakers that caused audio feedback at the outset, but switching to headphones quickly cleared that up.

We should have done a little more preparation beforehand, not only to iron out the technical wrinkles, but to read up more on each other's projects before the meeting, so we

---

*UDP = User-Defined Protocol, a method used to send continuous streams of information like audio and video over the Internet. Text is sent with the Hyper Text Transport Protocol, which you know as HTTP.

spent less time at the SOS introducing our work and more time tackling the common issues. But the SOS worked. It cost us little or nothing. We used the existing computers on our desks.

The Possibilities

Imagine this capability in your classroom. "How does it feel," asks an American student of the Iraqi student, "to get ready for the first election in decades? Do the people know how to vote?" His correspondent replies with an explanation of the traditional tribal voting system that, though only open to men, served as an underground democratic force all along. Imagine your students exchanging photos and opinions on environmental regulation with their peers in quickly growing countries like China or Brazil, where the green movement takes a back set to economic growth. Imagine a joint data-collection project, with six widely dispersed classrooms reporting their findings with charts and graphs, in their own SOS.

What You Need

A modern computer. We all used off-the-shelf computers, half of us on desktop computers, half with laptops. Some were on Windows, others on Macintosh, one on Linux. Some of us used USB video cameras, while others used FireWire (DV) cameras.

A broadband connection. You can't do an SOS with a modem. You need a direct connection such as the Ethernet drop in your classroom, or a cable modem, or a DSL telephone line. Our correspondents used all three in this first SOS.

Camera and microphone. Some us used simple little webcams, others connected their home video camera, and at least one of us used the Apple iSight camera with microphone. Some of us used the built-in microphone on our computer, some used an external or headset mike.

The software. We used the Marratech client and a Marratech server.

A good topic. You need a good reason to conduct the seminar, a strong topic that you're all interested in. The more preparation beforehand, the more valuable the live experience will be. You can learn more about the Marratech software at www.marratech.com. And you can find some great lesson plans on elections—not requiring SOS—for kindergarten through high school at the web site of the U.S. Secretary of State, at www.vote.wa.gov/outreach/index.tpl.

LEARN MORE . . .

About Online Publishing

www.mymathlab.com
  Pearson's math lab online
http://my.hrw.com/hrw/login_all.jsp
  Harcourt's Holt Online Learning

About Distance Education

http://nces.ed.gov

Search the web site of the National Center for Educational Statistics, a part of the U.S. Department of Education, for a report entitled Distance Education at Degree-Granting Post-secondary Institutions: 2000–2001.

About Learning Objects

http://ltsc.ieee.org/wg12

This site provides IEEE's (International Electronics Engineers) standards for LOM (Learning Objects Metadata).

http://ali.apple.com

The Apple Learning Interchange has an indexed collection of Learning Objects.

www.shodor.org/curriculum

The Shodor organization has organized and indexed many learning objects on the Web.

http://webquest.org

Bernie Dodge has produced a large collection of learning objects as well as tutorials for building your own.

www.eduworks.com/LOTT/tutorial/learningobjects.html

All About Learning Objects—tutorials on creating and using Learning Objects.

www.learnativity.com/standresources.html

Here Learnativity.com presents resources for Learning Objects and Standards.

About Synchronous Online Seminars

www.marratech.com

Check out this site for information on Marratech software.

www.vote.wa.gov/outreach/index.tpl

Need a topic for a synchronous online seminar on the election process? Check out the lesson plans on elections—not requiring SOS—for kindergarten through high school at the web site of the U.S. Secretary of State.

INDEX